Journeys
TO *Justice*

Journeys
TO Justice

PHILIP HUNT

WORLD VISION AUSTRALIA
Vision for a better world

HarperCollins*Religious*
HarperCollins*Australia* Pty.Ltd

Published by HarperCollins*Religious*
HarpersCollins*Publishers* (Australia) Pty Limited Group
17–19 Terracotta Drive
Blackburn, Victoria 3130
ACN 008 431 730

© Copyright World Vision Australia, 1996
All rights reserved. Except as provided by Australian copyright law, no part of this book may be reproduced or transmitted by any form or by any means, electronic or mechanical, including photocopying, recording, or by information storage or retrieval system, without permission in writing from the publishers.

First published 1996
Text designed by David Constable
Cover designed by David Constable
Cover photograph courtesy of the author

Typeset in 12/14 Bembo by David Constable
Printed in Australia by Griffin Press Pty. Ltd.

The National Library of Australia
Cataloguing-in-Publication data:

Hunt, Philip J., 1948-
  Journeys to justice.

  ISBN 1 86371 677 7.

  1. Hunt, Philip J., 1948--Journeys. 2. World Vision of Australia - Bibliography. I. Title.

361.763092

The author and publishers would like to thank the following for kind permission to reproduce copyright material: Paul Wilson, *Black Death, White Hands*, George Allen & Unwin, Australia, 1982, p37; Napranum Aboriginal Corporation (NAC).

Every effort has been made to trace the original source material contained in this book. Where the attempt has been unsuccessful, the publishers would be pleased to hear from the author/publisher to rectify any omission.

To Judy
who has always been ahead of me on the journey to justice

Contents

1 The Madras–Hyderabad Express   1
India 1977

2 The Road to the Airport   15

3 Discovering the World   20
Travels 1978–1987

4 Looking Out   33
South Africa 1985

5 Going Downhill   37
Sri Lanka 1987

6 A Day Dealing With Death   45
Sudan 1989

7 A Clash of Cultures   53
The USA 1990

8 Would You Like Fries With Your Security Check?   56
Israel and the Occupied Territories 1990

9 A Look into the Future   82
Guatemala 1990

10 Selamawit   86
Ethiopia 1991

11 Flying a Kite   91
China 1991

12 If You Were Here, Would You Be Different?   95
South Africa 1991

13 Interludes 101
London and Assisi

14 A Country on the Mend 111
Vietnam 1992

15 Drinking From Ancient Wells 121
Israel and the Occupied Territories 1992

16 Happy Birthday in Cambodia 138
Cambodia 1992

17 The Reporter was a Prime Minister 146
Somalia 1992

18 A Crack in the Door 164
Mozambique 1993

19 After the Fighting's Over ... 174
Somalia 1993

20 Australia's Occupied Territories 185
April 1993

21 Final Thoughts 208

1 | The Madras–Hyderabad Express

India 1977

The Chinese have a name for it: *Yahn-hey*. Human air.

The aroma of people is the most enduring memory of the first time I arrived in Bombay. It would be wrong to call it merely a *smell*; it was not the coarse, acrid unpleasantness of body odour. It was the sweet, fetid, warm, thick smell of people. Many people. Very many people.

Bombay was my first overseas experience. In the thirty years of my life before that day I had always responded with a wise crack if asked about overseas travel.

'Been overseas?'

'Sure.'

'Oh, really? Where?'

'Bribie.' Bribie Island is a large sand hill off the coast of Queensland, an hour's drive north from Brisbane. It is separated from the mainland by a passage across which most young Australians could swim.

The first whiff of Bombay touched my nose as the plane's air conditioning took its first gulp of local air. Like Hong Kong, where one's arrival by air was marked by the sucked-in smell of an open sewer, Bombay too had its own arrival smell.

But it was at the top of the stairs leading down to the rattly bus that the aroma struck me. The hot, humid night air seemed to combine with the perspiration of ten million people. It was redolent of sweat, incense and human endeavour. The very air seemed full of life. I could feel it sucking the energy right out of me.

We are all 'innocents abroad' when we make our first overseas trip. I was attempting to obscure my fear under a veneer of inscrutable confidence. I had already discovered that the less one says the more confident one appears.

It was 30 November 1977. A few days before I did not have a passport. Now I had No. K855340 in my pocket with twenty-four blank pages and one Indian visa.

A week before, a cyclone and tidal wave had swamped part of the east coast of India. World Vision of India had decided to help the victims. As part of the international network of World Vision organisations, World Vision Australia, for which I worked, needed to raise money for the relief effort.

We waited vainly for the story to be picked up by the Australian media. It rated merely a few paragraphs in the World News pages of the serious newspapers. Nothing elsewhere. Television images were not available quite so easily then, so Australian television news did not mention the fact that perhaps 20,000 had died in one night. A few radio stations picked up the story, but it rated no mention after the longer 7.45 a.m. bulletin on the ABC. If World Vision were to raise any money to help, we would need the story to be better told.

I rang Mike Willesee, who was fronting 'Willesee at Seven' on the Seven network. We did not know if he was aware of the disaster, or even if he was aware of World Vision. In those days, we were not quite the household name we became later. I had never spoken to Willesee before.

To my surprise he came on the line immediately. He was very friendly. I explained about the cyclone and tidal wave in India and proposed my idea of taking a film crew to cover it.

He had heard about it but was not enthusiastic at first. 'I have to say, Philip, it's not our usual story', he explained.

'I realise that. But no-one else on TV has given it a mention. And', I added, 'we could help with the airfares'.

'Well, that would certainly make the story more accessible for us', replied Willesee, 'but I can't see how it's an economic proposition for you people.'

'Last year when "Four Corners" ran our documentary on Ethiopia ... '

'The one Anne Deveson did? I remember it.'

'That's the one. It showed one night. We raised a million dollars.'

'Phew', whistled Willesee. The power of television is in its reach. We knew that if we could get a few million Australians to see what was happening in India, we could follow up with advertising and direct mail. We could raise some of the money that would be needed.

'Leave it with me', he said and hung up.

An hour or so later, Phil Davis, Willesee's executive producer, called back.

'I don't want to do this story', Davis said up front, 'but you've managed to convince Mike. He's very excited about it. That's good enough for me.'

Within a couple of days I found myself on my first overseas trip, and my first trip as coordinator for a film team. A young Howard Gipps was the reporter. John Bowring, who I heard later made a killing by investing in Paul Hogan's *Crocodile Dundee*, was the cameraman. And making up the team was a sound technician named Ian, whose long hair was, and still is, *de rigueur* for his profession.

India was then a tricky place for film crews to visit. There was a risk that we would not be permitted to bring our equipment in at all. There was a risk that we would not be permitted to film where we needed to. There was a risk that we would not be allowed to bring out the film we shot, or, at least, be required to submit it for local processing and inspection. Any of these risks would scuttle a current affairs story.

Our plan was to be in and out in four days. That was about the fastest one could cover such a story in the late '70s. Fifteen years later you could do it all on videotape, edit on location, transmit the result via satellite and have the story in the local newsroom that night. But in 1977 video technology was bulkier than film, and although video was as reliable, it was always theoretically possible to repair a broken film camera. When a video camera broke, it usually needed a replacement part. Sony doesn't have spare parts in Lalibella, Ethiopia, or Vijayawada, India.

I was a worried man, although I was sure I looked calm enough.

'You are Mr Hunt?' The voice came from an Indian man on the bus that was to take us from the plane to the terminal. 'Mr Sojwal rang me and asked me to help you through customs and immigration.' Bhaskar Sojwal was our India director.

I shook his hand with unintentional vigour. As I look back I can see how remarkable his presence was. It is rare, anywhere in the world, for fixers and helpers to be allowed into the secure airport area – more rare in those places where there is paranoia about film crews. Of the many countries I have visited, this experience of being welcomed *before* the immigration counter has only happened in a few places: India, China, Cambodia. And in Lebanon, where Jean Bouchebl, our local director, arranged for a huge Chevrolet to pick me up at the foot of the gangway.

The next half an hour was a blur of heat, aroma, confusion, and the constant noisy press of people. John produced his long list of equipment. It was inspected and stamped under the watchful eye of our fixer, a man who worked for the Bible Society in Bombay. He organised three tiny taxis and argued angrily with the 300 boys who laid hands on our luggage, each claiming a right to porterage. Without his local knowledge our total budget might have disappeared into the hands of Bombay porters.

The fixer arrived at nine the next morning to take me to a Bombay bank. A friend who had left India a year or two before had left some money behind. 'I cannot bring it out', he had advised. 'You should use it while you are there.'

With justified but naive faith I allowed the fixer to handle all the arrangements. Although there was no particular difficulty, it nevertheless took almost two hours to withdraw a few tens of thousands of rupees.

Meanwhile, back at our hotel, the camera crew was already at work shooting local colour, including the obligatory snake charmer in the hotel forecourt. There was no opportunity to see the rushes and these shots never ended up in the report.

Our fixer got us back to the airport for a domestic flight to Madras, where World Vision's main office was situated. In Madras we were met and welcomed by Bhaskar Sojwal and some of his senior staff.

I was amazed by the city's cars. Motor cars have always had a fascination for me. Before I was twelve I could name every make and model on the roads. In India it was like a journey back to the '50s. The vehicles had different names, but really they were Morris Minors and Austin Cambridges. I suppose some State-run industry had bought the moulds from Austin-Morris and was stamping out these venerable machines in a market protected from imports. We were to discover that these vehicles had inherited all the unreliability of their forebears.

The other traffic phenomenon that I became aware of was that the horn is an essential element of normal driving in India. 'If you have an accident', said our driver seriously, as if explaining something logical to a small boy, 'and you haven't sounded your horn, you are in the wrong'.

There is a branch of sociology called 'ethnomethodology' in which sociologists describe the taken-for-granted rules of a society. Traffic is one place to see these rules and how they vary from place to place. In Australia, when there is a traffic jam, people stay in their assigned lanes. In most parts of Asia, the road markings become incidental in such circumstances. People just crowd their cars into any available space. A two-lane road can hold six cars abreast if you try hard enough.

One Indian traffic ethnomethodology is to drive right up to a problem, then wait for someone to reverse out. In Australia, drivers will hang back and leave some space if there is no clear way forward, or if someone in front obviously needs to move first. And in India, of course, you blow your horn always.

We horned off to the office in a brand new 1962 model Austin Cambridge. World Vision was housed in a couple of buildings that, like most buildings in India, seemed to me to have seen better days. *Why don't they paint them?* I found myself wondering. What I hadn't worked out at this stage was that an Indian visiting my country wonder why we did paint our houses.

Inside, young ladies in saris were crowded together in hot rooms. *These people need more space*, I thought. *They need air-conditioning. They need a Coke machine.* Some years later, while living and working in Hong Kong, I generously arranged for each of my staff members to have a desk of their own. To my surprise I soon found desks left vacant while two people sat together at another desk, and two desks pushed together where before each had a private space. 'We work better this way', my Chinese staff taught me.

Sojwal gave us tea in his office and we discussed our plan. We would fit into two cars, the brand new Austin Cambridge and another older car that looked like an Austin A40. We would drive to Vijayawada, a port city in the state of Andhra Pradesh, north of the area devastated by the cyclone and tidal wave. It was over 200 miles, but if we left early in the morning we could make it in a day.

Before light we set off from Madras. As the first flickers of morning sun made the sky red I noticed that we were passing a long line of squatting men attending to their early morning call of nature. Somehow (I can't believe I actually asked) I discovered that the women went into the fields. I made a mental note to be careful where I walked.

We stopped for lunch at a hospital run by an English missionary couple named Scott. Assuming they would serve up fish and chips, I was rather unprepared for my first taste of serious Indian curry. It seemed my whole face had been hit with buckshot. My nose went numb, and all my teeth seemed to have separated from the jaw. Taking pity on my distress, they offered a banana, the perfect cure for curry. I remember thinking that it must have been a practical joke. No-one ate this for real, did they?

Into the afternoon the A40 expired. We sat in the hot sun for half an hour while people wagged their heads and muttered together. The Indians were enjoying the discussion; it was a chance to add spice to their relationships. But for the visitors, talking about a problem did not rate as highly as actually fixing it. That doesn't mean we were right, of course, but it was a relief when John climbed under the A40, worked out the problem and helped repair it. I guess if you can fix a Bolex film camera, a motor car's differential seems pretty simple.

It was well into the night when we arrived at Vijayawada. We were accommodated on camp beds in a house next to a clinic. Whole families were living on the verandahs and in the run-down garden, refugees from villages destroyed by the tidal wave.

Thirsty from the long, hot day, I took a sip of water from a large pot provided for washing. It seemed to me that the water went straight through me. No sooner had I swallowed than it came out the other end. That night I endured my first experience of *Montezuma's Revenge*, although I had always thought this to be a Latin American affliction. Over the next few years I discovered Montezuma has visited many countries – even Europe and North America.

The necessary pills paralysed my bowels, and I prepared for the next day by screwing up the muscles of my sphincter so tight that my thighs ached. It took me a few years, and a few more bad experiences, but eventually I adopted the time-honoured practice of never drinking the local water anywhere. And never eating uncooked food, or fruit I had not peeled myself. Sometimes, the generous hospitality of hosts has made such precautions impossible. Then prayer has been a reliable option.

The devastation caused by the cyclone and tidal wave was immense. Huge trees were lying on their sides all over the place, their leaves completely torn off by the winds. Some landscapes looked bomb-blasted. Power poles were bent over near the ground, like Muslims at prayer.

Most people had simple houses. They were blown away. But if that had been all that had happened, we would not have been here. Cyclones are regular visitors to this part of India. Normally the people literally pick up the pieces of their houses and rebuild.

But this time, a wave of water had hit the coast with such power that most of the villages in a strip fifty kilometres long were obliterated. Thousands of people were drowned instantly. The wave inundated villages five to ten kilometres inland.

This much we knew as we set out for our first proper day of reporting. Before we had gone a few kilometres, Howard asked for the convoy to stop.

'I need that field', he said pointing to a field of half-grown maize. The heads of many stalks were stripped and damaged. The field was waterlogged with salt water and the remaining crop would certainly die soon.

Howard, John and Ian set up quickly and Howard did a walk through the field.

'I'm standing here in Andhra Pradesh', he said into the camera lens, then went on to speak authoritatively about the situation. I was surprised, because we hadn't seen the situation. It dawned on me that Howard already had the story written in his head. He knew what to say and what shots he needed. He didn't need to come here to find out the facts. He only needed to come here to get the pictures, quotes and stand-ups to make his story.

At that moment I saw the strengths and dangers of current affairs television. 'Reporting' and 'going to get the facts' are luxuries not available under the time constraints of current affairs.

The reporter has to make rapid assessments and judgments, then get on with the job of finding the pictures.

A good reporter, of course, will get it mostly right, as Howard did then. But the danger remains that if a reporter begins with wrong assumptions, the product can be a grave distortion of the truth. Yet it will appear true on television. Television can be a very credible medium – even when it is telling lies.

The stories were heart-breaking. People who had lost their families. A woman who had lost her husband and children. Another who had saved her baby by clinging to him in a tree as the waters rushed around them, only to discover that somehow he had drowned in her arms. But there were stories of joy too. People reunited after the night of terror. The one saved, when all others were lost.

In one place a whole village had rushed into a stone church building for shelter. Over a hundred people were crowded in when the wind pushed the walls over. A man and a young girl were the only survivors. They happened to be standing by the door as the building fell, Mack Sennett-like, around them. When the winds died down, these two pushed the door up and found their families quiet and still under the rubble.

It sounds trite, but to me the whole thing was like living in a disaster movie. I found myself in something so far beyond my experience that it had no meaning. The cultural difference and the remoteness of a cyclone from my own world served to keep the whole tragedy at a distance from my emotions. I reported it. I wrote things down. I took many photographs. But it failed to touch my heart, or my soul.

The wailing of one woman came spearing towards me, but I managed to deflect the potential pain by suggesting we capture her story on film. When in emotional danger, become technical.

Within two days the story was in the can. At this stage, Sojwal and the other senior people left us in the hands of George, a junior colleague. They went to host the international president of World Vision, Dr Stan Mooneyham, who was arriving by helicopter.

George took us to a leper colony for tea.

I knew about leprosy which, given its bad reputation, was trying to rehabilitate itself under a new name, Hansen's disease. I knew it was not very contagious and that it was quite safe to visit with lepers. Naturally, as everywhere else in India, our arrival was a matter of curiosity. In most places, crowds quickly gathered to stare quietly. At the leper colony, there was rather more enthusiasm as we seemed happy to shake people's hands.

'The people are very impressed that you show no fear', said the English Salvation Army officer who was the administrator here.

'I understand that leprosy is not as contagious as people used to think.'

'That's true. But most people around here don't know it, or don't believe it yet. So the people here feel very affirmed by your openness towards them.'

Inside, our hosts treated us to the first familiar meal of the visit: English-style roast chicken and vegetables. Our dinner was interrupted by a small bat which came searching for the light and did tight circuits of the dining room until knocked down with a broom.

The plan was to go to Bapatla station and wait for the train – the Madras–Hyderabad express. We had reserved seats. Just to make sure, George had left before dinner to catch the train further up the line. He would then watch out for us when the train reached our station.

At around nine o'clock we piled into a series of pedicabs, a kind of bicycle rickshaw, and formed ourselves into a pile of luggage and bodies on the station platform.

Time passed.

Our host family consisted of the Salvation Army missionary couple, their bored, doe-eyed fifteen-year-old daughter visiting from England, and two adopted Indian boys. They waited a polite time, then begged their leave owing to the late hour. They reassured us that the train was no doubt late owing to the cyclone, but that we only had to wait and it would come.

We passed the time playing cards on a suitcase lid, and the crew shot some promotional pieces for Channel 7 – groups of people making 7-finger signs to the camera.

Soon after midnight the train arrived. I made myself responsible for finding George. I expected to see him hanging from a window, calling 'Here it is', so I walked along the carriages searching for a familiar face. The others trailed behind with a few score of porters each carrying a kilogram of baggage. The train was crammed to the gunwales with people. Hundreds of faces peered out into the light of the platform, but none was familiar to me.

Before I was half way along, the train pulled out, and we were left on the platform, dumb struck in surprise.

We were lost in India. Somewhere called Bapatla. Tomorrow we were scheduled to leave Madras for Singapore and home.

'Let's get a taxi', suggested Howard, full of enthusiasm. Howard was used to making things happen.

'OK', I said without betraying my doubts and turned to one of the many locals standing around staring. 'Where do we get a taxi to Madras?'

The locals were dumbfounded. It wasn't just that my accent was funny. The problem was that what I had asked was quite beyond their conception. *A taxi to Madras? That's 200 miles! No-one takes a taxi that far.*

Finally we managed to get a couple of pedicab wallahs to humour us sufficiently to take us to find and rouse the sole local taxi driver. Howard and I sped off in separate pedicabs into the dark of Bapatla. As we left the light of the railway station I felt vulnerable. I wondered how wise it was to be placing our lives in the hands of these people. If we went missing now, who would know where to look?

The taxi driver was not in a good humour and asked Howard for an amount of money that, in his terms, was exorbitant. Naively, it seemed to us a fair price. But a moment's consideration of the state of the taxi convinced us that we would be better to wait for the next train. There seemed to us a high chance that we would find ourselves repairing more than the differential of this vehicle, and a moderate chance that we might fall among thieves en route.

'Let's go back to the leper colony and ask for their help', I suggested.

Sometime around two in the morning, we all arrived at the front door of the darkened house of the colony administrator and his family. He came in response to our knocking and, not having much choice in the matter, invited us in. I'm ashamed to recall the way we forced our way back into their home. We were dead tired and lost. We would have been quite happy to sleep on the floor, but they somehow found beds for us all.

In the morning, Howard said he would like to film the youngest of the adopted boys. This was a little Indian fellow about one year old. He was wearing nappies, thus marking him as the child of foreigners. John set up the camera facing a broken-down wall by the house looking across empty fields towards a distant village. Howard asked the girl to bring her young brother over by the wall. John filmed as the boy stood forlornly alone by this picture of apparent devastation.

Then he suggested to the girl that she go inside. The little fellow by the wall suddenly realised that he was surrounded by strangers, and as the cameras rolled, he cried loudly and sadly.

That wall had tumbled down long before the cyclone, but the picture fitted the cyclone story. It provided the concluding scene for the report when it was shown on television, communicating the loneliness of a child who had lost his family and his home. That wasn't his story, mind you, but that was the story we were telling. It was a true story; it just wasn't *his* story. Do you still believe everything you see on television?

At around 8.30 we pedicabed to Chirala station which was nearer to the leper colony than Bapatla. We wondered why we hadn't come here the night before. I went to the station master and asked him about the train.

'Can you tell me what time the Madras–Hyderabad express is coming through?'

'Oh, Sir', he replied deferentially, 'we are not knowing. But if you are waiting on the station, it is coming'.

Presuming this meant we should wait here for the train, we piled up our gear and prepared to pass the time of day. We played cards, listened to the daughter talk about life for a missionary kid at an English boarding school, and the crushing boredom of being a foreign teenager in Chirala.

The previous night's experience had made me anxious about Indian trains, so I decided to check regularly on progress. At 9.30 I again asked the station master, 'Can you tell me what time the Madras–Hyderabad express is coming through?'

'Oh, Sir', he repeated deferentially, 'we are not knowing. But if you are waiting on the station, it is coming'.

I was to have this conversation about a dozen times over the next few hours. Each time the same question. Each time the same answer.

The day passed slowly. A few trains came through and John filmed them. None was going our way. Finally, at 5.00 I asked the station master again. This time, for some reason, I asked the question differently.

'Can you tell me what time the Madras–Hyderabad express stops here?'

'Oh, Sir', replied the station master with surprise, 'it does not stop here.'

I was still processing this amazing fact when a few minutes later a British woman arrived in a Land Rover. 'I heard there were some foreigners here waiting for the train to Madras', she said, addressing me. 'You can't catch it here, you know.'

'Err, yes', I replied like a schoolboy trying to explain missing homework. 'I just found that out.'

'Come with me', she said and bundled us all into her Land Rover. It carried Oxfam decals on the doors; she was their local representative. She spoke with the tired confidence of someone who had been in India a long while and had seen precious little for it.

Within minutes we had returned to the scene of the previous night's crimes – Bapatla station.

'The train comes in each night at around 9.00', she explained carefully, 'although it might be a bit later. Let's go and meet the station master.' We all followed like a line of goslings after Mother Goose.

The station master stood to attention and the lady from Oxfam gave a Joyce Grenfell-ish speech. 'Very important Australian journalists ... extremely valuable photographic equipment ... Need your very special service ... Making a film for international television (really?) ... friends of the Indian people ... Need your very special service.' This went on for about five minutes while the station master stood at attention and nodded his understanding. She was magnificent. I almost started humming 'Land of Hope and Glory'.

'This man', she went on, pointing in my direction, 'will be most grateful to you for your very special service. He would like to take your photograph and send you a copy in appreciation of your fine service.' I said that this was definitely what I had in mind. The station master smiled broadly and shyly, anticipating the honour of having his photo taken by this Internationally Important Photographer. He took a huge ring of keys and we followed while his porters carried all our luggage to the First Class waiting room. I took out my Nikon and took a series of photos of him at his desk. When I later sent him copies, he sent me a nice thank you letter and asked if I could get a job in Australia for his nephew.

The Oxfam lady disappeared in her Land Rover into the night. God had sent an angel. I doubt she found us entertaining.

When the train approached at around 9.30, the station master was true to his word. He carried a lamp with a red filter over the light. He positioned us on the platform at the place he wanted us to board. When the train arrived, he sent two men on board to clear out a cabin for us. I had no energy to consider the injustice of this, but then I had little frame of reference to do so. It seemed to me that we had a right to a sleeping berth, perhaps because we always slept on beds, unlike so many locals. Such arrogance is painful to recall.

Not until all our bags were on board, and we were all settled in place, did the station master withdraw the red filter and replace it with a green one. As the train pulled out, he stood to attention and saluted.

I slept the sleep of relief for the ten hours it took to trundle into Madras. We found our way back to our original hotel and were permitted to check in a day late. I called the Madras World Vision office. 'Praise God', the operations director said. 'We thought you were lost altogether. George arrived back yesterday without you, and he has been worried sick. He could not find you on the train at Bapatla.'

He didn't have a station master with a red light. That was his problem.

In the afternoon I went by the office to sort out what to do with the money I had left over from my friend's account. We discussed the matter in the lounge room of the director's house. While waiting for the others to arrive I looked around the modest room. It lacked decoration, save for a couple of black figurines each about the size of my hand.

As Mrs Sojwal brought my tea, I attempted conversation. 'What are those figurines?' I asked.

She told me where they were from. 'There are many dancers there. My husband and I visited there once.'

'They are very lovely', I said. Actually they were quite plain and clearly had more value to her as reminders of a visit than any intrinsic value.

Today these figurines are in my own lounge room. Since I had expressed interest in them, Mrs Sojwal felt duty bound to give them to me. As I left after our meeting, she met me at the door with a small parcel wrapped in a sheet of newspaper. 'This is for you', she said quietly, 'and your wife'.

I thanked her not knowing what she was giving me. These days, the figurines remind me of my own carelessness, and of an important lesson in cross-cultural communications.

Getting flights out proved not too troublesome, and getting through customs with our film even less so. Again, careful work by our Indian colleagues smoothed the way in advance.

The report went to air in December 1977. Willesee tagged it with an appeal for funds through World Vision. *The Australian* ran one of my pictures and a few paragraphs under my by-line. We raised $100,000 for the relief program that provided clothing, medicines, shelter and agricultural rehabilitation.

2 | *The Road to the Airport*

I had come to World Vision from radio. I was a disk jockey. The station I worked for, 4BK Brisbane, was on the third floor of Newspaper House, Queen Street, Brisbane. In the heart of the city.

Today, only the facade of the building remains. A huge arcade has been built behind the preserved faces.

The same can be said of 4BK. Owned by Queensland Newspapers, the publishers of *The Courier-Mail,* Queensland's most popular newspaper, it was sold and converted to FM. No traces of my old haunts remain.

I left school at the end of 1966. My first job was with the National Bank. I started on my birthday, 16 January 1967. I was nineteen, having sat the Senior examination twice owing to lack of diligence.

My trouble as a student was that I was interested in too much else. I was organising and playing piano at Methodist youth rallies. I was involved in youth camps. I was compering at church discos and coffee shops. With two other guys, Ron Goward and Paul Mills, I sang in a folk group called 'The New Road Trio'. We tried to sing like the Kingston Trio and compensated for lack of musical ability with pure enthusiasm.

From childhood I had been interested in radio, playing with my Dad's AWA *Magictape* tape recorder. I recorded John Laws and Bob Rogers and could imitate their contrasting styles in my early teens.

George Lovejoy, best known as a flamboyant football commentator, was manager of 4BH in Brisbane in 1967. He knew me casually from my involvement in Temperance League shows that he had organised. I called him and asked about getting into radio. Within a few weeks I had an 'audition tape' in my hand, produced with the skill of the 4BH audio engineer. It purported to show I had not only radio talent but experience.

Pat Maher, at 4NA Nambour, was not fooled by the production values, but he knew enthusiasm when he heard it. On 22 April 1968, my future wife's birthday, I started working in radio on the Sunshine Coast.

Later that year Judy Beeston and I were married and in 1969 we moved to Cairns, where I worked at 4CA and she worked for a local firm of solicitor. We found a substitute family at the Cairns Methodist Church, where we led in the Sunday school with the older youth and formed enduring friendships with some families.

In late 1970 we returned to Brisbane and settled in Ferny Hills. Jamie and Melanie came along in the early '70s, and I became settled in the afternoon shift, playing modern country music. I decided to go back to university and study journalism, and I found that I had matured as a student. By 1976 I had completed an Arts degree and a year's post-graduate work in screenplay writing. By that time I was working my radio shift, doing voice-overs at Channel Seven, and tutoring journalism students.

One day I saw an advertisement in the Positions Vacant pages of *B&T*, the trade weekly. World Vision (I had never heard of them) wanted a 'Communicator'. The position was for someone with a grab-bag of communications skills and experience – someone who could write for all media, who could take photos, who knew television, radio and print media, who knew music and art – the creative side of the media as well as the production side.

It had never occurred to me that my background was genuinely useful to someone. I had felt that being a jack of all trades and master of none was a disadvantage. There was always someone who was better at me in anything. But there were few who could turn their hands to so much.

A little disenchanted by recent changes at the radio station which had moved me into the (admittedly more prestigious) drive-time shift, I applied. World Vision flew me from Brisbane to Melbourne and I met the communications director, David Longe, and the executive director, Harold Henderson.

I was impressed. They were business-like and professional. And they were Christians. Sadly, the combination was, and is, rare. Too much that passed for Christian work lacked the discipline of good management. Not so at World Vision.

Admittedly, I had learned the value of good management in the church itself. Lew Born, the most significant mentor figure in my life after my own parents, had taught this to me (and many others). Lew was head of the Methodist Department of Christian Education. He was dynamic, creative and organised. More than that, he knew how to empower others. He took the enthusiasm and raw talent of young people and let them loose. It was high risk leadership that invariably paid off.

Under Lew's leadership, a series of Gold Coast New Year discos became an annual Pop Festival. One year it was televised live and pop groups from all around the country were flown in to perform. I compered. Similarly, camps for secondary school students were held. Lasting a week, they would attract more than 500 campers. The whole organisation was handled by a tiny group of paid staff and a huge group of volunteers, who committed themselves to pre-camp training, daily in-camp evaluation and post-camp de-briefings.

At World Vision, I found this same commitment to taking the job seriously. I flew back to Brisbane and told Judy that I wanted the job. David Longe must have posted the letter the next day. We were in Melbourne in time to see Hawthorn win the premiership, which began another love.

The India trip described in the previous chapter came a year later.

Soon, I was travelling once or twice a year for World Vision. Mostly my task was to go with a photographer to get stories and pictures about what World Vision was doing. One series of trips to Korea was to organise a visit to Australia of the Korean Children's Choir. Three times I produced documentaries, in Uganda, in Somalia and with the Vietnamese boat people in Thailand. In the two latter cases, programs were produced that were shown on national television. Anne Deveson was the reporter for all three visits.

In 1978, David Longe went to the United Kingdom to work for World Vision there. I was invited to become communications director.

Four years later, the whole family was in Hong Kong where I had been appointed executive director of World Vision of Hong Kong.

World Vision had been providing assistance there since the early 1960s, but by 1982 the colonial government was taking its social welfare responsibilities more seriously and the need for World Vision had diminished. Simultaneously, however, the Hong Kong community was becoming richer and many people wanted to share their wealth. A local Christian magazine, *Breakthrough*, ran a story about World Vision and almost a thousand people became child sponsors. I was despatched to Hong Kong to set up an office to build on this wave of support.

After establishing a foundation that local people could build on, I moved back to World Vision Australia in mid-1985. I was appointed director of planning and later director of donor services. In 1988, Harold Henderson moved to Geneva with World Vision International and on 1 January 1989 I took over as chief executive.

It is not my intention to be autobiographical. I'm not old enough, nor significant enough, to warrant a biography. Rather, I want to show how I have journeyed towards justice. Much of that journey has been the consequence of the cross-cultural encounters I have had with the poor and the oppressed. In other words, as I have travelled with World Vision, I have grown in insight, understanding and compassion.

There are other factors too, of course. It seems cruelly unfair to merely mention in passing the impact of people like Harold Henderson. He was my boss, friend, mentor, father-figure and confidant for almost a decade. He shaped World Vision Australia so effectively that, when I took over, I made no significant changes. Of course, time makes ancient good uncouth, so there have been many changes since. Yet all have been built on the strong foundations Harold laid. These included foundations of structure and knowledge. He taught us a great deal. Some of it we only discovered years later. *So that's what Harold meant!* has been a common experience of my leadership.

But my main purpose is to bring you on my travels with me. As I have travelled in a physical sense to scores of places around the world, I have been on an ethical and philosophical journey as well. Travel has reshaped the way I think and experience the world – it has literally transformed me. It is both the inner and outer journey I want to try to share in these pages. In the beginning there is much innocence and naivete. Towards the end (the end of this book, not of my journeying) I have discovered much about justice and compassion in myself and in my own country.

So let me continue ...

3 Discovering the World

Travels 1978–1987

My first encounters with the world, as the following stories from Korea, Kenya, Uganda and Somalia show, concentrated on my discovery of just how different the world was from home.

I discovered that there is such a thing as a 'world view' – a way of looking at the world.

Sometimes, as in Korea, I discovered that this world view is part of cultural difference. It touches matters such as how one negotiates and how one deals with conflict and criticism.

In Kenya I discovered that people have different priorities. They give value to things, events and experiences in ways that I found different and unexpected. Finding myself again in India, I discovered that words mean different things in different places.

My journey plumbed new depths of discovery in Uganda where I ran up against new and disturbing realities. By that I mean that what was considered the real world by Idi Amin and his government was quite different from how I experienced it. It seemed to me that they had constructed a world of macabre and unreal rules, values and beliefs. Yet it seemed not at all unreal to them. This was hard to understand.

In Somalia I found that I carried stereotypes in my head about Africa and Africans. Looking back, much of these recollections reveal my gaucheness and naiveté. In my diaries I find I concentrated on differences, treating these differences as bizarre and amusing.

In Somalia, too, I first began to flesh out the complex reality of the aid business I had joined. I had intellectual theories about it; now I discovered that the real world of aid was even more complex and chaotic.

Seoul, Korea in early 1978 was cold and bleak. It was not snowing, but snow piled up icily all around

The World Vision Music Institute was near the airport and it was warm and welcoming. Mr Yoon was the choir conductor. Peter Lee, our director in Korea, explained that David Longe and I would meet with Mr Yoon to discuss the program for the visit to Australia of the Korean Children's Choir. But first, we were taken to the Music Institute for a welcome.

The children were waiting and said, in heavily accented English, 'Good evening, Mr Longe. Good evening, Mr Hunt.'

I said, 'G'day', and the children tittered.

We sat and the children sang a bracket of songs. What showmanship. What thoughtfulness. At first, something forgettable from a musical to warm us up. Next, a beautiful Korean folk song, mournful, gentle, soulful. Then, the stab in the heart, 'Waltzing Matilda', sung slowly, *a capella*, in beautiful high harmonies. I wanted to go home: I wanted to stay here forever. Finally, 'The Lord's Prayer'.

It was impossible to say thanks properly. We had been drawn in, knocked down and possessed by the enchantment of this choir.

I heard them sing often after this, but to me they never sang as well.

Buoyed up, we prepared for our discussions next day with Mr Yoon. These took place at a new hotel high on a hill above Seoul. Peter was our interpreter and adviser.

David began by hoping that we might reach a wide audience for the upcoming Year of the Child tour. Peter translated. Mr Yoon responded in gentle tones and his body relaxed. Peter said, 'Ah, Mr Yoon have same opinion.'

'Perhaps we could discuss some of the classical repertoire?' suggested David. So we discussed and agreed to five or six numbers from the classics.

'I was wondering if we might have some Australian folk songs', ventured David next.

Peter translated and Mr Yoon sat forward, his voice still gentle and agreeable.

Peter said, 'Ah, Mr Yoon have different opinion.'

This seemed reasonable, but it soon became clear that Mr Yoon really only wanted to perform *serious* music. Perhaps one bracket of three folk songs, but the rest should be serious.

David and I saw people falling asleep in the stalls. Or worse, not turning up at all.

David tried. He suggested light classics. Then show tunes. Then pop songs. Each time Peter translated, and Mr Yoon became more agitated. His voice descended into a guttural growl. His head shook. And his right fist started pounding the arm of his chair.

Each time Peter would listen carefully, then turn towards us, a deep, calm pool of serenity, and say slowly, 'Ah, Mr Yoon have different opinion'.

When David mentioned Abba, who were big at the time, Mr Yoon did not wait for the translation. He launched into a venomous tirade that needed no interpretation. Peter waited for this to subside, then said, 'Ah, Mr Yoon have different opinion'.

I had visions of Mr Yoon throwing the lounge chair through the twelfth-storey window, and himself after it. And Peter, watching the body descend, would turn and say calmly, 'Ah, Mr Yoon have different opinion'.

I learned from David and Peter my first lesson in Asian negotiation. Australians tend to go to the heart of the matter. Our tendency is to get the big issues out of the way first, then the little issues are swept away in good humour. This does not work in Asia. Indeed, it is usually thought to be very rude and barbaric. Civilised people, in Asian terms, skirt around the edges of difficulties. Deal with all the easy bits first. Gently probe the harder issues. Retreat often. Find small compromises. Little by little the problems are solved.

Neither approach is right nor wrong. They are simply different. And to complicate things further, I have also found some of the rudest and most direct people in Asia, and the most obtuse and gentle negotiators in Sydney.

Soon after the Korean visit, I was on my way to Kenya. My companion was Ossie Emery, a Sydney film-maker and photographer very experienced in Third World travel. He was an ideal teacher for the new boy. Much of what I learned about how to behave, what to expect and how to cope, I learned in those first few trips with Ossie.

Ossie was also a marvellous but unstoppable raconteur. If interrupted in the middle of a story, he could pick it up again mid-sentence a day later.

In Kenya I saw the Mathare Valley and the Eastleigh community in Nairobi. We travelled into the countryside, including a visit to a Maasai community in the Rift Valley. These are all worthwhile stories in their own right, but I mention only two incidents.

The first happened one day while walking through a village. I looked up at the clouds and commented, 'Looks like rain, eh?'

The farmer walking beside me looked up at the same clouds, appeared to analyse what he saw, and said, 'Yes, it will rain at four o'clock'.

I was impressed with such forecasting. 'At four o'clock, eh? How do you know?'

'It rains every day at four o'clock.' He didn't need to look into the sky to know.

Similar logic was applied by this farmer to World Vision's reporting requirements. Our office in Nairobi had been pressuring him for quarterly reports on the progress of a dam he was building and we were financing. He took us out of the village and showed us an impressive circle of earth containing many millions of litres of water. 'I don't know why you people want a piece of paper that says I have built the dam', he said. 'There's the dam.'

I couldn't argue with his logic. Seeing was believing.

The second incident occurred when we flew in a single-engined Cessna low under Lake Victoria clouds. It was a bumpy and uncomfortable ride, although there was little danger. Nevertheless, when we landed I put my hand on a propeller blade, took a firm hold, shook it and said, 'Well done,' to the aeroplane.

To my surprise, the blade rattled under my grip. I had assumed it would be rock solid.

'That blade is loose', I said to the pilot. 'Is that right?'

The look of alarm on the pilot's face confirmed that it was most definitely not right. It was late in the day, so the pilot decided to leave the problem overnight.

Next morning, he called base in Nairobi and they asked him to check certain things. While he did this, another pilot came over. He was a white Kenyan with a colonial swagger, a thick moustache and an accent more British than British.

'I say', he said, 'trouble, what?'

'The propeller is loose.'

'What-ho. Propeller loose, eh? Wouldn't fly in that one. Had a friend once with a propeller loose. Vibration so bad, engine fell out.' He paused for effect. 'Damn hard to fly without the engine.'

We flew with him. Later a replacement propeller was flown up and fitted. The mechanic who repaired the plane flew back in the plane he had repaired. I was told this was a common practice that helped to keep mechanics' minds on the job.

On this trip I was also planning to retrace some of my Indian steps, to report on the progress made since the cyclone. But one small matter had been overlooked – a yellow fever vaccination.

Fortunately I discovered the oversight when I arrived in Nairobi, and at the airport a doctor gave me the jab and stamped my yellow vaccination book. Now I only had one problem. According to the book, the vaccination took ten days to be effective. I was due to leave for India in seven days.

'Don't worry', said the Kenyan doctor. 'Everyone knows that this vaccination is effective in seven days. The extra three days are just a safety factor. If you don't have yellow fever in seven days, you are not going to get it.'

Thus, on the seventh day, Ossie and I flew into Bombay.

The man at the health counter inspected my book and said, 'You do not have a valid yellow fever certificate'.

'I know that', I said confidently, 'but, as everyone knows, the yellow fever vaccination is effective after seven days'.

'You want to see my book?' the man asked me. I didn't understand. 'My book', he said, producing a book the size of a pulpit Bible, 'says ten days'. Then he added, 'Perhaps we can come to some understanding'.

Naive in matters of negotiation, I took my papers and went off to the side to discuss things with Ossie. 'He wants you to offer him a bribe', he said.

'Should I?'

'Well, I wouldn't. But it's up to you.'

I felt distinctly uncomfortable about adding to the corruption of the Third World, so I decided not to offer him a bribe. And I have never offered, nor paid, a bribe since. It is possible, of course, that someone else has paid a bribe for me without telling me. I went back to the counter and asked the man what my options were.

'You can take the next plane out. Or you can go to the Yellow

Fever Quarantine Hospital for three days.' Naturally, he was not going to add, 'or you can offer me a bribe'.

Ossie and I discussed these choices and decided to take the next plane out.

'Unfortunately, there is no plane out until the morning. You will have to go to the Quarantine Hospital and make later arrangements.'

'Is there a phone there?'

'Oh yes, there is a phone there. You will be well looked after.'

'Can my friend come and visit me there?'

'Of course. He can come and go as he pleases.'

I joined a young Indian man in a van and we disappeared into the night. His story was a misery. Studying in Kenya, he had ten days leave to visit his family on the other side of India. He would spend the entire time in the Quarantine Hospital.

It was not a hospital but a jail.

The windows and doors were barred, although one could move about inside quite freely. Purpose-built many years before, it had individual rooms, each containing a wooden bed, a chest of drawers and a chair. Shuttered, windows without glass opened onto an overgrown garden, visible through the bars.

Lonely and disorientated, I fell into bed, resolving to call Ossie the next day and get on our way.

Meanwhile Ossie found his way to our hotel. Next morning he tried to get things moving. He rang the phone number he had been given for the Quarantine Hospital. It rang and rang. No-one answered.

Back at the hospital I had discovered that, yes, there was a phone there, but, no, it was not working.

Undaunted, Ossie asked the information desk where the Quarantine Hospital was. Nobody knew. He called the Department of Health, the airport authorities and anyone else he could think of. Only the airport authorities showed any recognition.

'Yes. The Quarantine Hospital. What do you want to know?'

'Well, I have this number, but it just keeps ringing.'

'I'll get the number for you.'

'OK.'

The man gave Ossie the number he already had.

'Yes, but no-one is answering at that number.'

'Oh yes, sir. The phone is not working.'

Outside on the taxi rank, Ossie finally found a taxi driver who claimed to know where the hospital was. Ossie said that he would hire him for the entire day if he first would take him there.

About mid-afternoon Ossie turned up. I told him about the snake on the floor of the bathroom. I told him about the curry I had tasted at lunch. I told him about my decision to go on a hunger strike until he got me out. He told me that the phone didn't work.

'Oh, really?'

He agreed to get me a typewriter so I could work while he tried to get me out. He accomplished this by asking for a typewriter to be put in his room back in the hotel. In 1977 ordinary typewriters were not very portable. This one was a metal-framed Olympia. Ossie put it under his arm and marched out through the lobby.

I stayed in the hospital for three days. It took so long to move the bureaucracy that, in the end, a flight out became available at the time I was due to be released anyway.

Two other journeys during this period are especially relevant in my journeys towards justice: Uganda and Somalia.

The international president of World Vision was Dr Stan Mooneyham. Stan was a charismatic figure, tall, articulate, good-looking. He was also an American who carried his culture with unconscious comfort. When I started with World Vision, he had recently put a blue rinse in his greying hair. This may have been kosher in California, but it was strange in Sydney, and eccentric in Ethiopia.

Nevertheless, just as you cannot judge books by covers, so neither can you assess people by the colour of their hair. Stan was a beautiful man, a gifted communicator, even if, at least then, flawed by an apparent belief in his own image. I did not know him well, so what I report can only be my impressions.

I travelled with him a few times, once in Australia, once in Uganda and once in China, his last official business for World Vision at the end of his presidency in 1982.

In Uganda, in May 1979, Idi Amin was on the run. The Tanzanians had 'liberated' Uganda from Amin's oppression (only, as time would reveal, to subject it to a greater oppression). World Vision had been poised on the border to follow in Amin's wake with relief supplies to the victims of the fighting. As Amin left Kampala our trucks crossed the border.

Two days later I was in Kampala with TV presenter Anne Deveson. We joined a team led by David Toycen, then World Vision's international communications director, who was making a documentary for American television starring Stan. We were among the first arrivals in many months, and the Kampala airport was total chaos.

We found rooms at the Inter-Continental. It sounded grand, and it might have been, but now little in the hotel was working. The chef, however, was an artist: supplied only with bananas in quantity he managed to provide a different menu every day. Pizza base made with banana rather than flour was, I thought, a significant culinary achievement.

There were many memorable moments on this visit. One involved a young American woman who inveigled herself into our convoy. She was the archetypal gauche reporter. She made Norman Gunston seem aware.

A Ugandan woman, daughter of a murdered judge, was describing the horror of the murder. The reporter took notes and kept asking breathlessly, 'And then what happened?'

'They took him outside.'

'And then what happened?'

'They took a machete and chopped off his arms.'

'Yes, yes. And then what happened?'

'They chopped his head off.'

'Yes, yes. And then what happened?'

'Well, he died, obviously.'

'Oh, yes. I see ... And then what happened?'

We thought it divine justice when her passport was stolen with her purse. Later her purse was retrieved from a pit latrine, but her passport was gone. To our shame, when we arrived back at Wilson airport in Kenya, we all deserted her at immigration while she was trying to explain how her passport was lost in a toilet. The last words I heard were from the immigration official: 'Yes. And then what happened?'

Such macabre lighter moments were necessary to balance the horror of Uganda at the time. It was my first encounter with systematic, paranoid violence. I had not seen Yad Veshem then. I had not seen the extermination camps of the Nazis. I had not visited the killing fields in Cambodia, nor the sites where Aboriginal people in my own country were slaughtered to make way for the conquerors. This was my first encounter with a killing place.

It was called 'The State Research Centre'. Its innocent face, a U-shaped three-storey office block, obscured a horrid interior.

Two days before, Amin's troops had made a fast exit. Within hours, Tanzanian troops liberated hundreds of people imprisoned inside. The foyer was a jumble of broken furniture and scattered books. A pile of smashed glass and pamphlets advertising sophisticated weapons lay against one wall. In the middle of this pile was a shattered portrait of Idi Amin, defaced by the inmates in futile but brutal revenge.

A priest from the Church of Uganda (Anglican) had come to show us around. He was one of the hundreds who had been liberated from the Centre. For thirty days he had been kept with up to thirty other men in a single cell about three metres square. It had a boarded up window and a door that was permanently locked. The guards did not attempt to care for their prisoners. Occasionally, a bucket of water would be provided, but sometimes days would pass and the men would start drinking their urine in desperation.

There was no toilet, so the men lived with their own waste.

There were many similar rooms for both women and men. The priest did not know how many people were there altogether.

Most people in his room had died, either starved or dehydrated. Twice during the thirty days of the priest's incarceration, soldiers came and took away the dead bodies. Meanwhile, the living piled the dead on one side and lived with the stench.

Quite regularly, two or three times a day, sometimes more often, soldiers came and took someone away. 'We didn't know why some were chosen and some were not', said the priest. 'Actually, we wanted to believe it meant that there was hope, that they were setting us free. But we knew deep down it was just another way to die. Still, it would have been a blessed release from this living hell.'

He took us to a door off the foyer. As he opened it, a sickly, musty smell came from the room below. We went down. It was dark, and I put my hand out to balance myself against the wall. The wall was sticky.

The priest turned on a light. We were standing in an abattoir. The walls and floor were caked with dried blood. A large wooden block in the centre of the room was the only furniture. The priest put his neck on the line, to show where the prisoners had been brought for their execution.

It was a place of unspeakable evil and horror. For many years I pushed the memory of it away.

But how did people come to be in this place? Were they convicted of crimes? Were they spies? Saboteurs? Political activists?

Hardly. Whatever the original motivation, the ultimate reality was that Idi Amin was systematically killing off all supposed opposition. The priest's own case showed the lunacy of Amin's last days.

One night the priest drove his car to a suburban hotel for a meeting with some members of his congregation. In the car park he found a parking place beside a grey Mercedes-Benz. He should have been alert to the fact that this car was parked with spaces either side of it, but nothing registered.

It was Idi Amin's car. Such was the paranoia that anyone who parked their car next to Amin's was suspected of treachery.

Later that evening, the priest was woken from sleep. His internment began immediately. Nobody knew where he had gone until he turned up at home thirty days later.

Ahuma Adodoadji, from Ghana, accompanied us into Somalia. His companionship unwittingly revealed a stereotype in my thinking. Often I hear people talk about Africa as if it is monolithic. They say 'Australia, France and Africa', as if Africa were a single country. It is, of course, enormously varied, politically, geographically, culturally, musically. I too was guilty of accepting this stereotype. I assumed, because Ahuma was an African, that he would be at home in Somalia. I found that he was even more out of place there than I was.

We discovered this on arrival at Mogadishu. I was travelling with Ossie Emery, Anne Deveson and Stuart Mudge (our sound recordist). We were to make a documentary about the refugees who were crossing the border in northern Somalia to escape fighting between Ethiopia and Somalia. Called *On the Margin of Life*, it was to be highly commended in the United Nations Media Peace Prizes that year.

One problem about the arrival of aid workers is that it distorts local prices. Sometimes aid workers are a little too quick to pay the asking price because it seems so cheap by international standards. We miss the fact that the price being asked is ten or twenty times normal. Worse, if we say 'yes', we set the price for the next person.

This must have happened with the taxi drivers in Mogadishu. A few days before, some United Nations people had come through. When I asked a taxi driver for the price to drive us from the airport to the hotel (about two miles) he said, 'Fifty dollars'.

To be honest, I didn't believe my ears. I don't mean metaphorically; I mean I literally thought my ears were not working. He could not have really said 'Fifty dollars'. But he had.

'Ahuma, this is outrageous', I said 'Can you negotiate with this fellow?'

It soon became clear that Ahuma could not. An able man who later directed an entire field operation for World Vision, Ahuma was out of his depth with Arab-style trading required in Mogadishu.

I weighed back in and negotiated a nine dollar fee. Even that must have been thirty times the real fare, but there was a matter of face involved for the driver, having started so high.

Our hotel in Mogadishu was built around a courtyard with a lovely poinciana tree spreading shade over an *alfresco* restaurant. It was old and run down. Built in the grand Italian colonial style, it was a modest, tranquil haven. The hotel was destroyed, along with much of Mogadishu, a decade later.

So too, I suppose, was the roof top restaurant we ate in one cloudless evening. We climbed stairs on which it was easy to confuse the banister with the loom of electric wires that connected everyone in the building to the electricity grid. A few old tables were scattered about upstairs. The restaurant lacked all pretension, but it possessed style and a good range of splendid pasta.

'Would you like wine?' asked the waiter.

'Yes', I said, 'bring the wine list.'

The waiter looked at me strangely and walked away. Moments later he returned with a bottle of red wine in each hand. 'There is claret and rose', he said, showing his left and right hands. This was the complete list.

In Hargeisa, in the north, World Vision had rented two houses as a base. Our medical team was one day ahead of us. When we arrived, they were preparing to visit the refugee camp to survey, so we joined them.

About an hour's drive away along sandy tracks, the camp had only one feature that commended it as a place to live: a river. A dry river, but water was available a metre below the surface. Otherwise, it was a barren place. Already 10,000 people were living there in huts made from branches and plastic sheets. No trees were visible for a kilometre circle. As more people came, the daily walk for firewood would push this circle out another five kilometres.

There was little food and it was being distributed without experienced or effective organisation. Our medical team, led by Sri Chandar from Singapore, knew what to do and set about it quickly. A feeding centre was set up for the children and assessments were rapidly made of the worst cases. A secure area was created for storing supplies. A medical centre was set up and began treating people. As supplies were needed, they were unpacked and put on shelves. Organising, by doing.

By the end of the first day, a minor miracle had been accomplished. But more needed to be done.

The Somalian army was trucking in people by the hundreds every day. Nomadic people, ethnic Somalis like the locals, they roamed in nearby Ethiopia, across a border drawn without regard to their ethnicity. When the war came, they were caught in the cross-fire. Their water holes were seen as strategic so the water was poisoned. When their cattle and goats died, the people followed a time-honoured response. They folded up their homes and walked.

When they hit the Somali border, they were picked up and brought here.

The trucks would stop, disgorging the people from the back. Confused and shocked, with nothing but the clothes they were wearing and sometimes a cooking pot or two, they would immediately begin to make a home. Their industry was amazing.

For many, rescue into this alternate misery came too late. Many children had diarrhoea, and within a few hours they were so dehydrated, they died. Weaker ones, older men and others, also died.

Into this hell I saw World Vision bring hope. We brought stability where there had been confusion and progress where there had been decay.

But all around other issues conspired against us and the people. The war was the biggest. Until it was solved every step forward was merely coping.

I realised there in northern Somalia that our work existed in a context which needed to be taken seriously. This was not a new insight. Many others had discovered it before me, and indeed, I had given it intellectual assent long before I had ever heard of World Vision. But here I experienced the practical implications of the idea. These people needed help right now. That was certain. But there was a sense of futility about that help while the war waged around us unabated.

Some people, usually far removed from the pain of refugee existence, argue that 'the real problems' have to be dealt with. By 'real problems', of course, they mean the underlying causes. They are right to say these must be dealt with; peace is a prerequisite for effective development. But they are wrong to imply that these are the only 'real problems'.

Nothing is so real as the death of a child. It blights a parent's life more deeply than anything so generalised as war, famine or epidemic.

There is no deeper, more painful sound than the sound of a mother who wakes in the morning to find one of her children has died in the night. Every morning in the refugee camp began that way. Holistic thinking, the thinking of God's kingdom, requires us to meet people *where they are* and to react to their context as well as their need. It is not a matter of either/or.

4 | *Looking Out*

South Africa 1985

Evil flourishes when good people do nothing. *This always seemed a reasonable proposition. However, my journey to South Africa began to teach me that it is not always easy for good people to recognise evil – especially good people who are born, grow up and live in a society which systematically shapes values and beliefs. This was the case in South Africa. For the first time I recognised the awesome power of social engineering. And also the insidious* invisibility *of the process for those being engineered. It takes impressive courage and insight to recognise what is being done to you and to stand against it. For many, it costs everything.*

'We used to salute the flag at school', said Elizabeth.

I did not understand immediately why she was telling me this. We used to salute the flag in Australian schools, although the habit seemed lately to have lapsed in favour of 'I ♥ Australia' T-shirts.

'The Afrikaner believes that this is his land', explained David. The fact that he did not say 'his or her' also told me something about Afrikaner society. 'Afrikaners trekked north to get away from the English in Cape Town. They reckon they made this society – and really they have. In just half a generation the Afrikaner has changed from a farmer to a business giant. There is deep pride and profound belief in their own place within South Africa.'

David was not an apologist for Afrikaner society; he was simply explaining it. Elizabeth did not explain it; she described it.

'What was your attitude toward the English?' I asked.

'I hated them', said Elizabeth venomously. It startled me. 'If a shopkeeper spoke to me in English I would call for the manager and tell him that I would refuse to be served by a person who could not speak Afrikaans. I could not speak English. And I would not learn it.'

For a moment my mind sailed off on another track. I asked David, 'Did you speak Afrikaans when you met Elizabeth?'

'No. Not a word.'

'Then how did you ... er ... get together?'

'It was the eye language', they responded cutely in perfect unison. Apparently I was not the first to ask.

As we talked it became clear that if Elizabeth had been brainwashed to hate the English, her animosity towards the blacks had been even greater. 'We believed that the blacks were dirty and diseased. If they came to the house for water, we would not give them a glass or a cup. A jam tin – that's what we gave them a drink from, a used jam tin. We didn't want any of the black rubbing off onto our crockery.

'And they must not come to the front door. They had to come round to the back door.

'I have two brothers. If either of them came to our house and found a black sitting there' – (she pointed where I was sitting) – 'he would turn around and walk right out. And I would never see him again.' I actually found myself shaking with emotion at the thought of a racial hatred that strangled even the love between a brother and a sister.

'I remember the first night that a black man stayed overnight in our house', she went on. 'He was a lovely young evangelist. We had had blacks in our house for meals before, but suddenly I realised that this man was going to have to sleep in one of our beds. I went into my bedroom and said to myself, "How can I let a black man sleep here? He'll get black all over the white sheets!"'

She was not saying this as a joke. There was an awful loathing in her words which came from deep inside a heart that had been trained from childhood to despise the blacks. Again I was shocked at her passion. The emotion showed in her voice and eyes as she honestly recalled the struggle in her heart between her society and her God. It was not that she still believed such a silly idea with her mind. It was that her heart still believed it from her childhood.

'What did you do?' I asked like a straight man in a drama.

'I just prayed. "Lord help me to do this." And I just went calmly into my daughter's bedroom and put fresh sheets on her bed and invited him to sleep the night. A black man. Sleeping under my own roof. In my own daughter's bed! I couldn't believe it.'

In my experience until then, the beliefs of upbringing were nowhere more powerful than in South Africa. But Elizabeth could testify to the power of Jesus to reshape even an Afrikaner's sense of reality. Her family still did not know that black people had slept in her house. 'If they did, they would refuse to see me again.'

Some years earlier, Elizabeth and David decided to go without black servants. 'Everyone still thinks we are very odd', Elizabeth said with a grin. 'The kids get teased at school. Other kids say to them "You make your own bed?" They don't believe it. Our kids just reply, "We have six nannies at our house – and they're all white!"'

I cast myself in the role of devil's advocate and asked carefully, 'Surely there will be some people who will say that you are depriving a black woman of a job by not having a nanny.'

David and Elizabeth both attacked with a force that shocked me.

'It would just be impossible for us to have blacks in the house as guests if there were servants here too. They would not take us seriously', said Elizabeth quickly and precisely.

'If we could pay a housekeeper a just wage it would be different', explained David. 'But the going rate for a housekeeper is seventy-five rand (A$115) a month. The poverty level in Johannesburg is 200 rand (A$300) a month. For us it is simple exploitation.'

It did not need to be explained how Elizabeth and David had thrown off the values of society with which they grew up. The redeeming and transforming power of a lively Christian faith was in their eyes and on their tongues.

But how much was yet to be transformed? Clearly a revolution had happened in Elizabeth's life to permit her to share her home with black guests. But such behaviour is commonplace in other parts of the world, even among people who do not know Christ. Was this all that God required of whites in South Africa?

Evidently not. Elizabeth and David told me how, after many years at a Methodist church, they felt that God was calling them to leave. David's father and grandfather were Methodist ministers. Leaving was not easy.

Although the conviction to leave was strong, the place to go was not so easy to find. One day, Noel Vose, a member of the World Vision Australia board, was a guest for Sunday lunch in their house.

'Do you know this church?' Noel asked showing an address on a slip of paper. 'I have to preach here tonight.'

'It was a Baptist church just down the road', recalled Elizabeth. 'We couldn't just drop him off. We had to go in. The pastor was new. He'd come from Nairobi Baptist and this was his first non-black church! We heard a message like we had not heard in years. So we had found a new spiritual home.'

Within five minutes drive of Elizabeth's middle class house, with its brick walls, modern kitchen, swimming pool and proudly kept garden, was a town of blacks and coloureds. They lived in shanties, without drainage, sewerage, electricity, refuse collection or sealed roads.

'For thirty years this church had run a Sunday school down in the shanty town under a big tree', David and Elizabeth explained. 'The new pastor cancelled it and laid on a bus to bring the kids up to the white church. The first week he filled a VW Kombi van. Now we have a big bus load every Sunday. A lot of white people left the church, but many remained. We really enjoy teaching in the Sunday school.'

After they had been at the church a little while David and Elizabeth volunteered to start a Bible study in the shanty town.

'People thought we were mad. That we'd get killed', said Elizabeth. 'Now, every Thursday night, we drive over there and meet in one of the houses. If David's away, I go by myself. We meet around a candle in a room about half as big as this.' *This* was about three metres square. 'We try to do a lot of listening. But we share our feelings honestly and so do the others. I think most people think we are pretty foolish', Elizabeth said with a self-mocking smile.

I recalled Paul's words: 'God's foolishness is wiser than human wisdom' (1 Corinthians 1:25). A small part of South Africa was being transformed by such foolishness.

5 | *Going Downhill*

Sri Lanka 1987

World Vision's business is development aid. I learned much about it on my journeys. In Sri Lanka I began to see more of the complexity of the development process, and the need to work, plan and implement holistically, aware of that full complexity. Questions such as 'Whose project is it anyway – World Vision's or the local community's?' started to have meaning for me. My awareness of cultural differences, especially in attitudes towards the poor, increased. Along the way I recognised, through the observation of international adoption, that good ideas sometimes have bad side-effects.

For many years, everyone at World Vision thought our project work in Sri Lanka was the model of good development. It was based on revolving loan programs. Small amounts of capital were given to a community which then made loans to its people for agricultural or income-producing schemes, with the idea that the people would pay back the loans from the product of their labour. The repaid funds went back into the community loan bank.

There was only one problem with this excellent approach: it was hard to explain and therefore hard to sell to supporters. (Of course, this might have said more about the creativity of our marketing strategies than about the creativity of our development work!)

Then Peter Berry became our director in Sri Lanka. He took a good, hard look at this 'model program' and decided it had deficiences. He described it as a 'good but narrow ministry'.

'The question we asked was "How has the community's life improved?"', he explained 'Certainly economic conditions had improved, but hope for the future and steps towards the kingdom ... ?' He paused, to imply he was thinking out the answer. 'Nothing', he concluded.

Revolving loan programs could be a component, but they were not themselves the ministry. Peter realised that a measurable, *holistic* community development approach was needed.

Peter had made other innovations as well. He felt it was essential to help the people in the project communities, as well as his own staff, understand who sponsors and donors were. He recognised the dangers of uninformed support – a mythology of donors is created. So with the advantage of an American upbringing he became the surrogate sponsor. When he visited staff in projects, he pretended to be the sponsor. He asked questions, the dumber the better. The staff learned about sponsors and began to see their project through the sponsor's eyes.

Peter had also forged partnership links with Rural Development Societies, linking World Vision closely with the government. This was positive, but it had its downsides too. Politicians wanted to influence us to work in certain areas and on politically attractive activities. But we were not in the government's business. Often they needed to be sternly reminded of this.

I liked Peter. He was quirky and individualistic, but he was really making things happen. That appealed to my Western ways even if I was slow to recognise why. He had clear vision. He was building people. His pushiness was tempered with obvious sincerity and love for village people. He laughed a lot, which is always a good sign.

We sat in Peter's office in an upstairs room of an old suburban house. Colombo life went on around. The noises and heat of the morning enveloped us as we listened to his introductory lecture. When the heat began to build, Peter moved around his desk to a small refrigerator. It was full of Coke.

'A small but essential vestige of my culture', he said, grinning. As the Coke refreshed us the lecture continued.

Peter was pioneering an approach to project workers that was later to become more commonplace. These workers go under various titles in different countries. In the Philippines they are called community development workers (inevitably abbreviated to CDW). Sometimes they are called facilitators, sometimes project managers.

Peter's innovation was to move project workers out of the office. Instead of being responsible for many projects, Peter's plan was to give each one only a few, then to ask them to go and live in, or near, the projects. Only by entering the community personally could project workers really understand a community. And only with this understanding could they be agents for positive change.

'Everyone on staff visits projects', said Peter. 'I mean *everyone*.' I found myself thinking it would be good if everyone at World Vision Australia visited sponsors. 'Project workers will know every child and every family in their projects. They will especially know if children are sick.' Peter's idea had also removed the need for area supervisors. He had saved a layer of management – and cost.

'We don't own projects in Sri Lanka', Peter continued. (I hoped we did not 'own' them anywhere.) 'We are friends to projects. The communities must own them themselves. And they do.'

One area that concerned Peter was evangelism. 'There is no real evangelism component in our projects', he explained. An evangelist was paid to make fortnightly visits, distributing tracts and preaching. This was very unreliable, and not measured.

I saw his point but I didn't like his phrase, and said so. We talked about it later. Evangelism is not a 'component'; it is part of everything that happens. You cannot have a 'management component'. Nor can you have a 'Sri Lankan component'. Nor can you have a 'development component'. These are not activities, methodologies or techniques. They are core values and fundamental philosophies which underpin and flavour every activity, method and technology. You can emphasise the evangelism *aspect* or the development *aspect*, but talking about an evangelism 'component' reduces the work of sharing the Good News of the kingdom to a mere method. Of course, proclaiming the Good News by preaching and teaching is an important evangelistic activity. But so is development work done by Christians.

From my boyhood, two images of Sri Lanka had prepared me for this visit. One was *tea*. This was where tea came from, or so I thought. And not just tea, but *Ceylon* tea.

The other image was Arthur C. Clarke. I had read all of his science fiction novels and many of his short stories. The idea that a science fiction writer would base himself in Colombo attacked my limited stereotypes of the Third World. It helped me realise that the Third World must be full of great variety – poverty and riches, technological sophistication and primitive mechanics.

The present-day truth about Sri Lanka showed that the Arthur C. Clarke image was true of only a small, and depressingly decreasing, minority.

Universities were closed, in a country which for years boasted the best education in Asia. Medical students had not had exams for two years.

Tourism was down. The Hilton Hotel was at thirty per cent occupancy, and this was one of the highest. It was also the most expensive at US$35 per day. Such prices seemed incredible bargains to us; the cheapest decent hotel in Melbourne was twice this price. But the hotel we stayed in, Mount Royal Beach Hotel, charged a mere US$7 per day. It was only ten per cent full.

Up in the north and north-east the fighting was disruptive and frightening. We didn't know how the projects were going up there. No project visits had been made in six months, but recently someone had come to Colombo from that area and that helped us to stay in touch.

Unemployment continued to rise. Terrorist action by Singhalese against Singhalese six to nine months before had seemed to be directed against the government's action in not holding elections. Instead they held a referendum asking 'Do you want the present government to continue or not?' The people, faced with Hobson's choice, voted *Yes*.

Staying at our hotel were Scandinavian couples with Sri Lankan children who spoke what sounded like Swedish. They had already adopted the children who were with them, and now they were coming back for more. This sounded lovely to me.

The problem was that 'baby farms' had become established. Women had babies specifically to supply the demand from childless European couples. Middle men charged 10,000 rupees (A$500) for the service. This sounded like a bargain. But the mothers got hardly anything, and such activities exploited them for commercial gain.

I admit I found this question a tough one. One could not blame the childless Europeans. They were good people. I watched them play with their brown kids by the swimming pool. They were very loving towards one other. These children would probably never have been born except for a system that commercialised pregnancy.

Soon it was time to go and visit a project. We piled into a van in the heat and sweated our way along. Peter's plan was for us to walk through the village for an hour, then share lunch with some local government officials.

At eleven, I was already peckish. Reading my mind, Peter produced coconuts as soon as the van stopped. The juice and soft flesh were delicious.

We walked along a narrow road lined with a living fence: hundreds of tapioca and frangipani trees planted centimetres apart. 'Every few months', Peter explained, 'someone comes along with a machete and trims them back. Very practical. Appropriate technology, eh?'

Obviously you needed such an appreciation of local culture to be effective here. So much Western-sponsored development imported Western ideas. This may be unintended; it may not. 'Take Western-trained doctors, for example', suggested Peter. 'They are not part of the cultural system. People go to hospital and get put on a bed up off the ground on clean white sheets. For a person who always sleeps on a mat on the floor, they think they are dead already.'

But culture was not all positive. The philosophy of *karma* (fate) was sometimes a problem. 'People say, "What hope do you have? None really. It's just my fate. I'm suffering like this because of something I did in a previous life."' Other aspects of culture were equally negative. 'The caste system is terrible, awful. There is an iniquitous dowry system too.'

Unfortunately, the history of aid agencies in this country was spotty. Some people in Sri Lanka had taken photos of people and used them to raise funds for something else. The people in the photos got no benefit. As a result there was a stigma attached to photography. 'We never show our cameras when we begin work in a village. Build up trust first', Peter said.

This raised the whole problem of 'selling poverty'. Advertising often seemed unethical to the Sri Lankans. (*And not only to Sri Lankans*, I thought.) Opposition politicians could use print advertisements against us unfairly: *Look how this government is allowing foreign organisations to sell your children overseas.* A flick through the Colombo Yellow Pages showed that 'selling children' was a phrase readily understood here. Paedophilia was advertised not too discreetly. German and Dutch child abusers were becoming commonplace visitors.

We talked about the communications process, noting the narrowness of supporters' vision at the time they become sponsors and how they develop through four stages:

1. *Bureaucracy:* When donors believe that problems should be solved by the action of governments or other bureaucracies.

2. *Reciprocity:* When donors respond out of a desire to share their good fortune.

3. *Beneficence:* When donors develop an ethic of sharing.

4. *Solidarity:* When donors realise that their wealth is intrinsically related to poverty and they need to stand in solidarity with the poor to find mutual solutions.

We lamented the elitism of some agencies who only talked to the 'Solidarity' people and failed to communicate to the other ninety-seven per cent of the population.

People from the village came to meet us. Peter thanked them for allowing World Vision to give the opportunity to donors to express their love and concern for the poor and needy. He said that it was the hope of the donors that the community would use their development to help others.

Our small party walked into an area behind more living fencing. The ground was swept clean. A single-roomed hut stood in the centre of the compound. There we met Mahini, who at twenty-six was the mother of four children. She shared her hut with six others, including her husband and his mother.

Her husband worked at the nearby brick kiln as a labourer. For this he earned R30–40 (A$1.50–2.00) per day and averaged ten days work per month. Two of the children were home, the others at school. They were malnourished and on a feeding program every day.

'Why don't you grow things on your land?' I asked.

'Because my husband would have to stop work to be a farmer', explained Mahini, 'and that would mean no income for that period. The children would starve. We would need bridging capital.'

One of Mahini's children had haemophilia. The child needed to go to hospital, but that would mean time off from work for a parent. The father could not afford to lose one day's work or all his family would not eat that day.

I remembered one definition of 'the poor': *those who work for their daily bread*.

'Why don't you become the farmer?' I asked, perhaps a little rudely. Mahini shrugged. Dias, the project worker, explained.

'It's *karma*. They don't see hope as a viable philosophy. Their lot in life is the result of a previous life. They think they must accept it. There is no incentive to try harder, to be more than they are or to have more than they have. The project here is providing seeds, ploughs (there is a tractor on the estate now) and training for farming. We're trying to help people see that they don't have to accept their fate – that there is a better life for those who will take the initiative.'

As we walked along, Dias told us about the *kadjew* (cashew) girls on the road to Kandy. 'They sit by the road selling cashews. When the buyer is purchasing, they expose parts of themselves ... '

'They display their breasts', Peter interrupted, for the sake of clarity.

'Yes', agreed Dias, 'so while the buyer is thus distracted, they push some cashews aside and short supply him'.

'Now *that's* marketing', commented Peter.

We passed a house with a board above the door: *Dear Spirits, It is not convenient for you to come and harm our children today, please come back tomorrow.* 'Sri Lankan evil spirits are particularly stupid', explained Sunil, another local project worker, with a grin. 'They come back tomorrow, read the sign again, and it being today by then, go away to come back a further tomorrow. Thus, the children are protected from harm always.'

While in the village I heard about a new medical condition. It was called *Lime Paste Blindness*. The people everywhere ate the betel nut; they put it on a leaf spread with lime paste. The lime paste came in small plastic sachets. One corner popped open with a little pressure and the paste came out like toothpaste from a tube. But if you squeezed too hard, the paste squirted out. Two children in this project had been blinded when it squirted into their eyes. Recently the government had banned this packaging, but we still saw the empty sachets on the ground.

As our tour was coming to an end, Dias asked, 'Do you want to see the poorest family?' I felt embarrassed. 'How do these people feel if we arrive to meet them because they have been classified as "the poorest family"?'

'They don't mind', said Dias with surprise. 'Everyone knows. After all, it's *karma*. It's not their fault they are poor.

'There are some people who say that they are doing you a favour by begging', he went on. 'If you give to a beggar you will earn merit. Therefore, by being poor and allowing you to be generous, the beggar is giving you the opportunity to earn merit. He says you should be thankful to him. He has less reason to be thankful to you for your generosity.'

This was a sentiment I was to hear five years later in an Aboriginal community in North Queensland. For them, it was the mining company that was dependent on the Aboriginal people for their land. In their eyes, the company should be thankful.

On the way back to town, we drove through the 'Free Trade Zone'. Because of free education there was high literacy in Sri Lanka. The people were very well-educated by Asian standards. The government promoted this area overseas for foreign investors: *Come and set up your factories in our Free Trade Zone. Sri Lanka has well-educated workers and low wages.* Many companies came.

The wages appeared attractive – R900 (A$45) per month for female workers skilled in using the big industrial sewing machines. Many village girls tried to learn this machine to get work in the Free Trade Zone.

But there was a catch. 'Free' Trade Zone also meant free from labour laws. No unions. No ordinary benefits applied. The factories worked all the time, three eight-hour shifts. The workers were required to complete quotas whether eight hours had gone by or not. There was no overtime.

The young women rented rooms in nearby houses. They averaged eight to a room. Some landlords took advantage of shift work by renting beds in shifts too. Many women and girls were very lonely.

Village young women found it costs R900 to live in Colombo anyway. They discovered they were sending nothing home to the village. You didn't have to be too bright to work out where all this was leading.

'Prostitution?'

'Yes', said Peter. 'The city guys take the village girls for a ride.'

6 | *A Day Dealing With Death*

Sudan 1989

Aid is a business. The experience in the Southern Sudan showed that the complexity of our work required aid agencies to be as effective in planning, management and execution as any product-producing business. There is no place for mere good intentions when these fine motives are not backed with administrative competence.

In the Southern Sudan I began to understand the ethical dilemmas we face when we try to deliver humanitarian aid in a war setting. Two opposing perspectives are in operation. One wants power and control, even possession, of people. The other wants empowerment and the abundant life. This clash of world views is volatile and dangerous. Resources are wasted. People die.

Flying from Kenya into Sudan was illegal, so our journey involved a little sleight of hand. Our flight plans showed a route to Lokichokio in northern Kenya, but our actual destination was Kapoeta, 115 kilometres further north on the other side of the Sudanese border. Rebecca Cherono, our director in Kenya, had discussed our program with the Kenyan First Secretary and the government was willing to give us every assistance. The relevant people simply turned a blind eye.

It was hot, dry, dusty and very windy when we arrived in Kapoeta. The soil was sandy and the vegetation sparse. Thorn trees and scrubby bush were the dominant plant life. It was cold in the evenings and in the mid-thirties during the day. We guessed we were between 1,000 and 2,000 feet above sea level.

It was April, and the rains were predicted to come in May and last until September. Roads would then quickly become impassable.

Soon after that the air strip, a cleared area beside the main street, would become too boggy for use.

Kapoeta was built by the British sometime around the turn of the century when prospectors discovered gold. Now the town was an apparently unplanned cluster of ruined buildings. A ghost town with people. There were no roads, although there had been some attempt to mark road edges with bricks and stones. There was no central water system, no electricity, no sewerage or sanitation system. At the edge of the town, a few thousand people lived in a slum of tin, wood and grass thatch.

And there was the hospital.

If ever there was an overstatement, it was to describe this rag-tag collection of walls and floors as a 'hospital'. It consisted of a few stone buildings, many without roofs, three newer brick buildings constructed by an aid agency as wards and a child feeding centre. There was hardly anything which distinguished it as a medical facility, save the patients – a few hundred sick, emaciated and wounded people huddled together in darkened rooms full of dust that blew in all day long.

The hospital had 450 in-patients when we were there. It served alone as a medical centre in an area containing a million people. The only doctor said he usually had a 1,000 in-patients, although others reported a similar number to 450 two months earlier. Those in need of aid are likely to exaggerate – the end justifies the means.

There were few beds. Patients rested on blankets on the dusty floor. The operating theatre was in the only building with glass in the windows, though not all the windows. The wind and dust howled through one side of the room. Out of a mess of rusty surgical instruments only a few were serviceable, and these the doctor sterilised in an autoclave heated over an open fire. Hypodermic needles were re-used after boiling.

The pharmacy was a disorganised jumble of medicines crowding the room.

The doctor was also seeing 200–250 out-patients daily. He said he would like someone to build and equip a proper operating theatre, but his dream seemed unwise. The main need here was for diagnostic work and primary health care. With so many patients to see every day, there was little time for surgery. If someone needed advanced care they could be transported south overnight by road to the Red Cross hospital in Lokichokio.

'If they are too sick to make the journey, there is probably not much hope for them anyway'. said Dr Dan Carlin, an American medical adviser, matter-of-factly.

Malnutrition and gastro-intestinal problems were predictably the most significant presenting problems. Dan had some concern about the quality of diagnosis in the hospital. We saw many children with severe malnutrition, one of whom was described by the doctor as 'having a cough'. The brittle, orange hair and the puffed limbs and shiny skin spoke to me, even as a non-professional.

The doctor had to treat war injuries and the occasional exotic problem, but mostly it was malnutrition and complications from that. Malaria was common and so was tuberculosis. Recent reports suggested these TB cases were really AIDS. I worried about all those hypodermic syringes being sterilised by boiling over an open fire.

In a newer building was the feeding centre. Inside were a few metal dixies for cooking up a mixture of water, Unimix and Soyalac (these shipped in by World Vision) and plenty of bowls for dishing up. World Vision had supplied them too. There was one water pump beside the feeding centre. The town had two other pumps some distance apart.

We were told there were twenty-two camps surrounding Kapoeta. We saw one, called Matchi. It contained a few thousand people. We met some newcomers who sat in a tight, quiet group under a tree. All the children were malnourished, with maybe twenty per cent by Dan's estimate in the most advanced stage of malnutrition. He thought nearly all could be saved if the food could be distributed from Kapoeta and proper feeding regimes maintained. One child in the group was too far gone. 'A few weeks at most' was Dan's prognosis.

We had heard stories of people walking for months and found these stories confirmed. One woman said she had walked from an area near Wau, well to the west of southern Sudan. It had taken her a year. She had moved from place to place, always moving on as conditions became more desperate.

The people built circular huts of sticks and grass. A good 'long grass' hut would last two or three years, we were told, but these would last only months. The more people came, the further out they walked to find building materials from the local vegetation. One man pointed to a distant mountain range showing where they were going now. 'For a strong person', he said, 'it is about three hours walk. Most people take more than a day.' A stream of women entered the camp about three o'clock with loads of sticks, grass and leaves balanced on their heads.

As was normal, the camp was located where it was because water was nearby. A dry river bed yielded water by digging down about two metres. When the hole got too deep, they moved upstream. The river bed was pock-marked with earlier endeavour.

The water was cloudy and brackish. Dan reckoned malaria infection was guaranteed given the swarms of mosquitoes by the river.

Audrey Hepburn, in her role as UNICEF ambassador, had visited this camp a few days before. She had complained that there was no food in the camp, and we found the same. This was hard to understand because there was lots of food in Kapoeta, twenty minutes away by vehicle. We asked when the last food delivery had been. 'April 1st' was the reply – seventeen days before.

An official accompanying us from Kapoeta pointed out that the policy was to deliver a large supply and replenish it when it ran out. It was not clear whether supplies had run out, but we did not see any evidence of grain stores. Nevertheless, the condition of the people suggested that they were receiving some nourishment, probably from private stocks retained from an earlier distribution.

We were shown the base of a new grain store which the camp administrator humorously described as 'Great Expectations'.

It is fair to say that the food situation in the camp was not clear to us. We felt there were signs that the food supply being sent from Kapoeta was insufficient. One of these was the extent to which people were eating the leaves of the thorn trees. We saw these leaves being carried into the camp and prepared for cooking. It was not clear whether this food was intended to supplement the food supplies because they were insufficient, or because the nutritional balance was enhanced by the addition of the leaves.

Later, back in Kapoeta, Leo Ballard, World Vision's Africa relief director, spoke firmly to Commander Lam Akol of the Sudan People's Liberation Army (SPLA).[1] Akol was the number three man

---

[1] The civil war in Sudan is between the SPLA, representing the Christian-African south, and the official Sudanese army based in the Muslim-Arab north. But such labels are simplistic. One needs to ask what both 'Christian' and 'liberation' mean in such a context.

in the SPLA and had come with us on the plane from Nairobi. Leo urged him to get food to the camps. Leo could not understand why a Toyota Land Cruiser had not been dispatched with an interim supply.

Despite these hiccups, it was very encouraging to see that World Vision aid *was* getting through. There had been news reports that gave the impression no aid was being delivered. This was false. Of course, while World Vision supplies had been arriving safely by truck, UNICEF/WFP had not, until the day we were there, managed to get a single truck into Sudan. But they had been successfully airlifting food into some areas. The Kapoeta storehouses were full.

We were glad to feel so confident about the way World Vision was working in this theatre of need. Leo and his team were extremely well regarded. I was proud to count them as colleagues. Norwegian People's Aid (NPA) was an excellent partner. I enjoyed the 'can do' approach to the work and the obvious results.

The UNICEF/World Food Program (WFP) effort was another story. Bad luck and bad organisation seemed to characterise the UNICEF/WFP effort at the time, certainly in Kapoeta.

The night before we arrived, the first UNICEF/WFP convoy into southern Sudan of fifteen trucks rolled into town. Each truck was adorned with large UN symbols on the bonnet and doors and a blue UN flag attached to the front like a diplomatic vehicle.

I was surprised to see UNICEF/WFP in this area of the country. It was not clear that the local leadership, which wanted World Vision and NPA to be the only agencies working in this area, had been consulted. There were other places where we could not work without a substantial increase in resources, and there it was practical to spread the effort. Given the already packed condition of the storehouses, in Kapoeta further convoys here were superfluous just then.

But we discovered that this convoy was heading further east to Torit. Accompanying the convoy in four brand new Toyota Land Cruisers were the officials and the media – a five-person film team from Germany who had followed the food aid every step of the way from Copenhagen, and a three-person UNICEF film crew. The convoy was headed by a man named Gerard, a Lebanese who had previous experience in Chad.

This gallant band descended on the surprised Sudanese after

having cooled their heels in Lokichokio for forty-eight hours. Permission to enter Sudan had been at first refused by Sudanese offended by the way the Germans had been photographing local women. Most women and girls unselfconsciously dressed naked from the waist up, but, like people anywhere, they would prefer to dress up to receive guests or be photographed. How would you like to be photographed in your gardening singlet and shorts?

Our interpretation of what happened next was this:

Faced with the sudden influx of media demands, the SPLA in Kapeota could not cope.

They invented a coping mechanism – official passes.

They simply asked UNICEF/WFP for their official passes.

Since no-one had heard of such a procedure until moments before, naturally UNICEF/WFP could not produce the required documents.

Impasse.

This was resolved simply by the passing of time sufficient for the SPLA to produce some official documents, and at eleven the next morning videoing began. By this time, Greg, our own video cameraman, and I had managed to find someone who would say yes, we too could start shooting.

We had been walking around the hospital with the doctor when the UNICEF/WFP show got under way at the pharmaceutical store. Suddenly, we were asked to desist and wait until they were finished. Dr Dow, the official designated to cooperate with people like us, could not be in two places at once.

By mid-morning, the UNICEF/WFP convoy was ready to roll, and so were the cameras. Like a precision driving team, the convoy left under a panoply of blue and white. The film crews remained behind to record the dramatic departure.

Leo Ballard watched the show with obvious disgust. 'Never seen so many bloody flags', he commented. 'What the UN should do', I said prophetically, 'is spend a little less on flags and a lot more on protecting aid supplies.' This was later to become common place in Somalia and other places.

About noon, the UNICEF/WFP convoy came hurtling back into town. They formed up in a circle, wagons-against-the-Indians style. The drivers were very agitated. The lead truck had been blown up fifteen kilometres down the road. An accompanying military escort had 'disappeared' and the rest had high-tailed it back. They wanted to dump the grain right there and go home.

It had been clear for a long time that neither the SPLA nor the Sudan government forces shrank from attacking food convoys if they were intended for the other side. The SPLA attacked a UNICEF/WFP convoy heading towards Malakal on the same day we were in Kapoeta.

The local army chiefs arrived to say that the firing had merely been over-enthusiastic 'celebrations' over the SPLA victory in Bale the day before. Just soldiers shooting into the air. They urged the drivers to go back to Torit and get the supplies delivered.

The drivers would have none of it. They wanted assurances that the road was safe. Talk did not reassure them.

At this point, Leo decided that a convoy of WV/NPA trucks, which had arrived just before we landed, would not go on to Torit as planned but would off-load. It was interesting to see the difference between Leo and Gerard in the way they handled the situation. Leo felt that, in a crisis, it was important to act. 'Even a bad decision is better than no decision', he opined. Thus, by the time the UNICEF/WFP convoy got moving again, the WV/NPA trucks were efficiently unloaded and long gone back to Kenya.

At four o'clock two wounded men from the earlier convoy shooting were brought into town. They were a clerk of the Sudan Relief and Rehabilitation Association who had been shot in the side, and a Kenyan driver shot in the foot. The driver reported that his truck, the lead truck of the UNICEF/WFP convoy, had been hit by a rocket-propelled grenade and blown up. Two SPLA soldiers in the escort were also killed.

The popular theory was that the attackers were Toposa, a local tribe who were marauding convoys and towns, taking advantage of the unstable situation with captured weapons.

The clerk died within thirty minutes. At this news, the UNICEF/WFP drivers dropped their truck tail-gates and started to dump the grain in the middle of the road. Mutiny. Gerard tried to reason with them, but they had had enough.

'They're going to be real happy if it rains tonight', commented Dr Dan laconically as he watched the sacks being piled up in the open air.

Finally, SPLA military men persuaded the drivers to drop the remainder of their loads in the storehouses and they blazed off, right over the precious grain they had already off-loaded. It was, for me, a final, sickening sign of a relief program in a mess.

Later, left alone in town with an injured driver, Gerard wrote a message for me to take out to his boss in Nairobi requesting a plane to help him get the wounded man out. Gerard said that this would be the one and only try for UNICEF/WFP at trucking in supplies. After this, they would stay with air-lifts.

'It's very expensive', I commented.

'Yes, but when you add all this up', said Gerard, looking around in a way that summed up the day's disasters, 'this is also very expensive.' I restrained myself from commenting that it didn't have to be done quite *this* way.

Prima facie, it seemed that UNICEF/WFP had been carried away by the legitimate need to put southern Sudan onto the world's political agenda. But they could not match plans with outcomes, rhetoric with action. What we experienced leant weight to the view that the more agencies working in the area, the greater the security risk.

The UNICEF/WFP approach had been to set up a 'big program', using their own personnel, their own trucks, their own camera crews, and so on. I wondered if a better strategy would be to network many smaller agencies, like World Vision and NPA, who had experience and track records in aid delivery using local resources. It was amazing what could get accomplished when no-one cared who got the credit.

It was getting late and our plane had not arrived. Within a few minutes we would pass the decisive moment. Although it was still light in Kapoeta, it would be too dark to fly our plane into Nairobi by the time we got there. Fifteen thousand feet is the minimum for night flying in the Rift Valley, and our unpressurised plane was not equipped for such giddy heights.

The idea of staying overnight in Kapoeta without food or blankets was not too distressing. After all, the local people stayed here. Nevertheless, we indulgently began to contemplate the warm rooms at our Nairobi hotel.

With ten minutes to go before it was too late, we set off to walk to the airstrip. We found the plane already there, 'Twig' nervously pacing up and down wondering where we were. He had come in unheard on a wide circuit. He had been waiting an hour.

7 | *A Clash of Cultures*

The USA 1990

In the second half of the twentieth century, no nation has shaped the world of development as much as the United States of America. This would be an unalloyed good thing save for the fact that the shaping was heavily influenced by American world views, political correctness and methods.

As in South Africa, I saw in the USA how insidious is the process of creating and maintaining a cultural reality. America was, of course, a lot different to South Africa. Yet similar processes seemed to be operating – processes that invisibly created and reinforced beliefs about America's role as the definer of truth and justice. From this followed a sense of responsibility *not merely to set the agenda for the world, but to police it.*

More personally, my encounters with American culture made me realise that I carried prejudice in my own heart. This was an uncomfortable discovery since I didn't think I was a prejudiced person, nor did I intend to be prejudiced. I wondered where this came from.

January 1990 was an interesting time to be in Washington. The US President, George Bush, delivered the State of the Union address one Wednesday night and the National Prayer Breakfast was the next morning.

There was much talk there, and at the conference I had attended the week before in California, about 'the work the Lord is now doing in Eastern Europe' – namely, the collapse of the Soviet Union. Not for the first time I heard Habakkuk 1:5 misquoted:

Look at the nations, and see! Be astonished! Be astounded! For a work is being done in your days that you would not believe if you were told.

I say 'misquoted' because everyone, including Billy Graham, applied this verse to the mighty changes for good in Eastern Europe. When the Lord said it to Habakkuk, he had exactly the opposite scenario in mind. God was planning to wreak havoc.

More than one Afro-American wondered whether what they saw as a disproportionate interest in Eastern Europe reflected a white racist orientation. I thought it a personally challenging comment. Overseas aid apparently took a battering in the US budget, although I did not see anything reported on the matter (which suggested it did). Furthermore, the ANC Chaplain told me that a reduction in Africa programs would be used to fund aid to Eastern Europe. Sounded distressingly familiar. *Would the Australian government follow suit?* I wondered.

Of course, the US was taking the credit for what was happening in Eastern Europe. They had been a 'shining light of democracy and freedom in the world', and now the darkness was fleeing. I smiled in a superior way at this boastful arrogance.

But if America was winning the war overseas it was clearly losing it at home. Washington was a good place to see that. A beautiful city with great charm and architectural character and a fine sense of history and place, it also had the highest murder rate in the country. Most of the deaths were young, Afro-American and drug-related. In a town half the size of Melbourne they were killing each other at better than two a day. I met more beggars on the streets of Washington than I had anywhere in Mexico the week before. Come to think of it, I hadn't met one in Mexico.

The Prayer Breakfast scene was a stumbling block for me. First was the amount of jingoism in the event. I suppose this was not unreasonable; after all, it *was* the US National Prayer Breakfast, and it was to be expected that every speech should end with 'God Bless You, and God Bless America'. That this grated on me was surely my problem. As one new friend commented to me after a day or two, 'I think your trouble is you just don't like Americans'. This judgment shocked me, but I had to agree it contained some truth.

I didn't *feel* prejudiced against Americans, yet I could see that my behaviour and reactions implied prejudice. On the one hand, I reacted against the lack of humility and modesty I often encountered there; yet was this because I resented just how powerful, important and successful these people were? On the one hand, I saw myself as part of a *European* culture in the South Pacific; yet the USA was the country, outside of Australia, that I felt most at home in. Why would I be so surly about people with whom I felt so comfortable?

I suspected the answer was partly internal. The other part seems external to me. It had something to do with how I had been brought up, how my values and beliefs had been shaped. It was a cross-cultural prejudice.

Because of the huge number of people from outside the US at the event, more than one speaker, and not just Americans, suggested it should be called the 'International' Prayer Breakfast. This would plainly have been wrong because it was such an American event. My prejudice forced me to notice how many ordinary national American events were given international titles they did not deserve. The *World* Series, for example. Even (think about it) *World* Vision.

Having established the negatives, there was good news. The Washington Prayer Breakfast was a wonderful, inspirational event.

The program was of a consistently high standard, although the back-up, largely volunteer administration creaked and groaned at times. There were official meals from Wednesday noon until Thursday night, with the actual Prayer Breakfast on Thursday morning. The speeches were of a high standard, entertaining, thoughtful, inspirational and appealing in their statements of Christian conviction. More than once I wished our own politicians could (a) employ such good speech-writers, (b) use them so well and (c) say such profoundly important things about the Christian faith.

The line-up of talent at the Breakfast was impressive, including Miss America, Billy Graham, George Beverley Shea, the Vice President and the President. The Secretary of State, Jim Baker, gave the keynote address. It was the statement of a seeker, a believer who still needed to experience his beliefs in a profound, personal way.

They did so much so well. And I recognised envy in my own heart. I wanted to be this great. I wanted my country to be this great. But, I thought dishonestly, *I* would be more modest about it.

8 *Would You Like Fries With Your Security Check?*

Israel and the Occupied Territories 1990

Looking back, there are three sign-posts of particular significance in my journeys toward justice. The first was simply beginning to experience the world beyond Australia. The third was the encounter, described later in this book, with indigenous Australia. On the way there was a second encounter of deeper than usual significance – my first visit to Israel.

For me this represented a real loss of innocence. For a start I realised that I had been deceived about Israel. This hurt. I had believed the common Western myths surrounding the creation of the modern Israeli state. To these had been added some beliefs about what the Bible said on the matter. All of these were to come under challenge over the next few years as I tried to understand what the experiences of Israel and the Occupied Territories really meant.

If ever I had experienced the impact of social engineering, I encountered it in Israel and the Occupied Territories – on both sides.

If every I had wondered how to operate effectively as a development aid agency in a complex and contradictory world, I found more questions and fewer answers here.

If ever I had experienced that truth is not always what is presented to you as truth, I discovered it more distressingly here.

Orly Airport, Paris

'Welcome to El Al Airlines. We have to ask you a few questions for security reasons.' The man at the security counter before the check-in counter was about twenty years of age. There were five of these counters. The others were attended by women who seemed teenage. Everyone carried a clip-board.

'Sure.'

'May I see your passport, please?'

'Sure.' It went under the clip on his clip-board. He laboriously read the first page, looking up to see if my face resembled the photo. He was apparently satisfied that new glasses and a trimmed beard had not obscured my identity. He flipped through the passport pages. There were forty-eight of them, with visas on forty-four from all over the world. Even I thought it was interesting reading.

After five minutes of silence he said, 'May I see your ticket, please?'

'Sure.' It went under the clip on his clip-board. He studied the ticket. He was reading everything – even the notice that suggested one should not take hair spray on board.

'Is this your first trip to Israel?'

'Yes. First time.'

'What will you be doing there?'

'I'm a tourist.'

'What do you plan to see?'

'Well, I'm not sure until I get there.'

'Is someone arranging your itinerary in Israel?'

'Yes.'

'Who is that?'

'My office there.'

'Ah, you have an office in Israel. Do you have their address and phone number and the names of the people there?'

'Sure. You want to know that?'

'Yes, please.'

I got out my digital diary and tapped in W-A-R-N-O-C-K. I gave him this name, and the office phone number. He wrote this information down on the pad on his clip-board.

'What business is this?'

'World Vision.' I had to spell it (it was my accent for sure).

I offered him my business card. It went under the clip on his clipboard.

'And what does this World Vision do?'

'Development assistance.'

'What is that?'

'Well, you know, we work with kindergartens, health programs, agriculture.'

'And what will you do in Israel?'

'I will visit some of these places where we are offering assistance.'

'Do you have a letter from this organisation inviting you to Israel?'

'No.' Although I wasn't surprised, I tried to sound surprised. Since when did you need a written invitation to visit Israel?

'Where are these places you will visit?'

'I don't know, frankly.'

'Jerusalem? Haifa? Tel Aviv?'

'Maybe. I really don't know my itinerary until I get there.'

'This Bill Warnock will meet you at the airport?'

'Yes, and he'll know what we are doing.'

'We?'

'Yes, me and my companion.' The Rev Graham Beeston, a French citizen who also happens to be my brother-in-law, was travelling with me.

'Who paid for your ticket?' I was just getting used to the other line of questioning and he was off on another tangent.

'My company.'

'How have you come to the airport?'

'You mean right now? Or from Australia?'

'From Australia.' I was sorry I asked.

'Well, first I went to a conference in Germany, then ... '

'What was this conference?'

'It was a meeting of all the directors of World Vision from around the world. We meet irregularly, and this was one of our meetings.' I was starting to get bored. We still had a long way to travel.

'Do you have a brochure of this meeting?'

'I have the conference notebook. Do you want to see that?' I was sure he would. He did.

I laid my large aluminium Zero Halliburton suitcase on the floor, dialled the combination code and opened it up. Inside, near the top, was my bulging conference binder. I took it out and handed it to the interviewer. Amazingly he managed to get it to stay under the clip on his clip-board.

'Close the bag, please.' I closed my bag.

Now he took a long while to look over the notebook list of contents. He tried to look knowing. Then he returned his attention to my ticket. Whenever there was a lull his eyes and fingers fell on my ticket. He would scan it with his index finger as if proofreading. Suddenly he would spot something.

'How did you come from Frankfurt to here?'

'Well, that's a bit complicated.' Bad answer.

'You flew to Lyon. Why is that?'

'My brother-in-law lives near there.'

'So you stayed with him last night?'

'No, I stayed with *his* brother-in-law last night.' To his credit, his eyes did not flicker.

'So what did you do in Lyon?'

'I just got off the plane and my brother-in-law picked me up.' I took pity on him and continued. 'Then he drove me home to his place in Romans-sur-Isère, and I stayed there on Wednesday night. Then we came to Paris yesterday.'

'How did you come to Paris?'

'By train.'

'You have the tickets?'

'No, he has the tickets.' I nodded in the direction of my bon frère.

'Where did you stay last night?'

'At his brother-in-law's place.'

'Where is that?'

'I don't know. I just went with him.'

'You don't know?'

'Well, it was not far from a station called Mairie D'Issy.'

'Then how did you get to the airport?' This was even more complicated. Graham's brother-in-law could not take us at the time required, so he rang his son, Michel, and then Graham's brother-in-law's wife (following this?) drove us to Michel's place, where Graham dropped off a gift for Michel's new baby, and then Michel drove us to the airport in his car.

'His son drove us.'

'Who packed your suitcase?'

'I did.'
'When?'
'Every day.'
'No. When did you last pack it?'
'This morning.'
'And where has it been since?'
'In the boot of the car.' He seemed to understand 'boot'.

'Has it been out of your possession any time since you packed it?' Now these were sensible security questions at last. He had stopped a line of questioning that presumed I was a terrorist. Now the presumption was that I might be used by a terrorist.

'No. It has been locked. And it was locked in the car.'
'Are you carrying any gifts for people in Israel?'
'No.'
'Did anyone give you a parcel for you to carry for them?'
'No.'
'Think hard.' I thought hard. My brain started to hurt.
'No.'

Back to the ticket. A long silence. I inspected the seat allocation counters behind. Most airlines let you walk right up. El Al is security paranoid. Even if such paranoia was justified, it subtly reinforces the image of Israel as a beleaguered state. At this stage I was convinced that the security questioning was sincere, based on a real danger. Later I wondered whether other matters of a more political nature were the main motivation.

'Why are you going to Athens after you leave Israel?' I had been told to expect this question from others who had received this treatment. He was not reading the ticket as carefully as he pretended. The answer was under his thumb.

'It's on the way home.'
'Why Athens?'
'Because that is where I connect with the Singapore Airlines plane that will take me to Singapore, then to Melbourne.'
'Just transit.' Ah-hah. 'Why did you go this way?' Persistent fellow.
'I don't know. Because it's the quickest way home, I suppose.'
'The travel agent made this choice for you?'
'Yes.'
'Please wait a moment.' All during my interview he had repeatedly

checked the progress of a similar interview being done with Graham, two desks away. He noted that this interview had now concluded and Graham's female interviewer was standing in the middle of the waiting area talking to a more official, older person.

Our two interviewers huddled with this first man for about five minutes. They referred to their notes and looked back at us from time to time. I felt like I had a second-hand car as a trade-in and the salesman, after kicking the tyres and tut-tutting his way around the car, was now having a mock conversation with his manager, from which he would return to tell me, very sorrowfully, that the car was worth only half its apparent value.

The result here was similar.

'Would you mind waiting over here for a few minutes? It will take a little time.'

Somewhere in the next thirty to forty minutes the phone rang in our Jerusalem office. Bill was out. The accountant took the call from a person who asked abruptly about me and my visit. The accountant verified that World Vision was indeed expecting me. More than that he did not know. They should wait for Mr Bill.

At the same time in my office in Melbourne, a colleague took a call from a person saying he was ringing from Israel. He asked to speak to me and was informed that I was travelling overseas. The caller hung up.

After half an hour another woman came and took me off for a second interview. The questions were all the same. The interview was much shorter, and she seemed unconcerned about how I had got from Frankfurt to Paris although Graham and I thought this by far the best part of the story. After all, why had two Middle Eastern looking fellows been sitting in our reserved seats when we got on the TGV in Vallence? And why, when we went to the Buffet Car, had a third swarthy chap taken over our position? Was this a clever PLO plot to sneak a bomb into our bags?

The young woman who had interviewed Graham came over to us as we waited and apologised for the delay. 'It takes a little time', she said. Meanwhile, others were being slowly processed. The queues were getting longer. One young American was taking as long to get going as we were. But then he looked like a hippie. We seemed to be in a role play about stereotyping.

After more than an hour I was invited for a third interview. Now she concentrated only on the possibility of us 'being used'. 'You charity people are targets', she said. I agreed this was a possibility and said I was aware of the risk and was very careful. My suitcase was always locked unless I was present with it. I did not accept parcels except from family, and then only if I knew what was in them. She seemed satisfied and asked us to wait again.

At last, some minutes later, we were ushered to the check-in counter, our bags and tickets stamped with brown security stickers. We received our seat allocation and walked away. Then, loudly in French, a policeman with a loud hailer announced the area was being evacuated. Two other gendarmes held a long tape and gradually moved the crowd back. We went upstairs to the departure lounge. We never heard an explosion.

The whole process had been strangely curious. At no stage was our baggage searched or, as far as I could tell, X-rayed. I was asked if I was carrying a weapon, but they just took my word for it. Would a real terrorist be less convincing? I was not searched. Perhaps we walked through a metal detector but I cannot recall doing so. There were booths for doing body searches but they were not used.

Why had it taken them more than an hour of simple questioning to decide my security risk to El Al? If they were concerned about whether we were carrying weapons, there was a very easy way to find out. They could have asked to search our bags. We would have said yes. No-one seems to mind a little inconvenience to know that bomb-carriers have little chance of getting on board. But this was clearly not what it was about.

What if your real aim was to create in the traveller's mind an image of insecurity and threat? Since you wanted to concentrate on image creation, you must concentrate on the person. See how carefully and in how much detail they checked *me*? I was scrutinised; my bags were not. I came away with an impression of security rather than the fact of it.

After that, the flight was unremarkable. We arrived on time in Tel Aviv to find no-one waiting; apparently the message that we had changed to an earlier flight had not been received by Bill. I said to Graham, 'We'll wait until 7.30 p.m., then we'll take a taxi to Jerusalem'. I think I was more relaxed about this than Graham, but mix-ups of this kind are part and parcel of travel. Bill arrived at seven, and we enjoyed the drive in the dim evening light to

Jerusalem, where we fell into bed in a pleasant room at the YMCA in East Jerusalem.

At 4.00 a.m. the room echoed with the Islamic call to prayer from the speakers of the mosque across the road. 'Come to prayers. Prayer is better than sleep.' It is a noble sentiment, but we were humble of spirit at such an early hour.

We planned to go the next day to two Palestinian villages in the West Bank, but plans had to be changed. The day before someone had allegedly thrown a stone at a settler's car in a town named Biddu and the army put a curfew on the town. No-one could come out of their houses.

The problem for us was that this town was a key crossroads. Access to the villages on our itinerary was via Biddu. We would not be allowed to pass through.

Nevertheless we set out by bus, the driver saying we would take an alternative route – the 'World Vision' road, an agricultural road (read 'dirt') built by the community with support from Save the Children Fund and World Vision.

On the bus was 'Richard Nixon', so named by his friends because of his likeness to the former US President. Bill said the kindergarten teachers loved him because he worked so willingly at the kindergarten. Nixon had been shot in the legs during an incident in his village some months before. Israeli soldiers had fired tear gas until it ran out, then rubber bullets until they ran out, then live ammunition. One of these bullets hit Nixon. Finally, the soldiers were separated from their vehicles long enough for women to set their jeeps alight. Once reinforcements arrived, twenty-five men from the village were arrested. Four of these were still in jail. (Seven others from this village were already incarcerated.)

Richard Nixon told us he was now '100 per cent'. 'I am made of iron', he said.

We passed olive and fig groves in terraces on hills whose size surprised me. These were major hills, rivalling the Dandenong Ranges in Melbourne. Some of these terraces were 5,000 years old. The ground was very rocky and it was easy to see why the Palestinians threw stones. They were an unlimited resource.

We left the highway by an unmade road, then we joined the 'World Vision' road for a slow and rough grind up and over the hills to the village that was our destination. The journey took over an hour. 'If they had not put Biddu under curfew it would take us ten minutes', said Bill. 'Also, when Biddu is under curfew that means there is no school for the teenagers from the whole district, because that is where the only high school is.' Everybody got punished, including us, when someone threw a stone at a settler's car.

At the village we discovered the soldiers had been the day before. Women had been required to paint over pro-PLO slogans on the walls. Children had been made to pull PLO flags down from the mosque and overhead wires. Windows were broken in some houses. One soldier took a pot-shot at a roof top water tank. The speaker on the mosque was taken away. A new one had already been put up.

The children in the kindergarten were gorgeous. They sang unmelodic chants. Some words were translated:

We are the Palestinian children,
The Flag expresses who we are.
We shall not stop until we have our freedom, our state.
If the Israelites don't give us our land,
The Jews will break themselves.

I was a bit troubled by the blatant indoctrination of the children. This was a highly politicised education program. I was not surprised, however, as I had read of this in David K. Shipler's book *Arab and Jew: Wounded Spirits in the Promised Land*.[1] It appeared that indoctrination of children was an important part of the struggle both for Arab and Jew. *But is this World Vision's business?* I wondered.

We began to meet people. One man, Mahmoud, told us he had spent only three nights at home in the last year. He went out and slept in a cave or on a rock, for fear the soldiers might come and arrest him. 'The night is not special for you', he said, 'it is for everyone. Thieves, soldiers.' During the day he could see a kilometre in any direction, but at night he hid. Many men of his age did this. So far he was not on a wanted list. Later we heard he was.

I asked if the soldiers had ever come to Mahmoud's wife when she was alone. 'Yes', she said, 'and our little son, who had mumps at

---
[1] Viking Penguin, 1987.

the time, sat up in bed and said, "Go away. I hate you." And they went away!'

People had ID cards that identified where they were from. Blue for Israel. Orange for the West Bank. Green was a special card preventing the owner from going to Jerusalem.

A group of *wanted* arrived. All but one of about six men said they had been in jail at least once. Some were *bingo* people: at times the army would stop people, line them up and go along the line looking for people they wanted. When they recognised one, they said 'Bingo!' The Arabs had never seen a game of Bingo, but they understood the rules.

'How long are you staying?' asked one man.

'Five days.'

'Is it enough? You need to put yourself in the people's place.'

We asked this man if he had been in jail. He replied, 'Yes. It's normal.' I found this shocking – the extent to which life under occupation had become *normal*. Questions about being arrested, about curfew, about beatings, about harassment, about confiscation of land, about anything that seemed extraordinary to me, were treated with a perfunctory dismissiveness that was disarming and bemusing. At first I thought they didn't want to talk about it. Then I realised that it was so commonplace that talking about it was itself unusual and extraordinary.

One man told his story.

It was at the beginning of 1988, one year into the *intifada*.[2] At 1.00 a.m. there was a knock on his door. They called his name. There were twenty soldiers at the door, and another forty surrounding his house. He had one wife[3] and one child. He opened the door. The Captain, named Zuheer (they always seemed to use this name), announced, 'I have a licence to arrest you for six months'. They asked him to sign a paper in Hebrew. He was afraid they might have been settlers disguised as soldiers; they were sometimes more violent. He was in his pyjamas. They would not let him get dressed, nor to put on shoes. His hands were tied behind his back with 'American'

---

[2] *Infitada* means 'uprising' in Arabic. The idea of the *intifada* was to resist the Israeli occupation through acts of civil disobedience, strikes and stone throwing.

[3] Arab men can have four wives, if they have a good reason. Many do so without a good reason. Later I asked a man if Arab women can have four husbands. He said, 'Of course not'. I said, 'Why?' 'Because they are Arab women.'

rope that got tighter if you struggled.

His mother hit a soldier. They fired a shot in the air. He was walked (no shoes) one kilometre over sharp rocks. Two soldiers punched and kicked him as he walked. They stopped him by a pole on which was a picture of Arafat. 'Who is that?' they asked. 'I can't see', he replied, knowing perfectly well who it was. 'Do you have a light?' They produced the light. As he craned his neck back to look up, they bashed his head forward against the pole.

At the end of the village there were thirteen jeeps and one large truck. He figured he must be a Very Important Palestinian. He put one foot up onto the jeep and they threw him head first onto the floor. They climbed in and put their feet on him. Each time he spoke they kicked him. Another three were arrested at different villages. They were all on the floor of the truck now, under the soldiers' feet. Any noise, they were kicked.

At the prison they tied him kneeling with a sack over his head. The sack smelled of donkey manure and urine.

'What's that feel like?' I interrupted.

'It feels normal.'

'Good answer', his friends said, wryly. I admired their black humour – the good humour of the oppressed. 'No-one can reach freedom without some pain. So this is normal.' Here was the willingly paid price of a liberation struggle. The oppression was simply creating heroes and martyrs. It was back-firing.

He was taken to an interrogator, who began pleasantly, 'Tell me your story'.

'I have no story. No problems.'

'If you won't, I will.' The interrogator mentioned an incident in which one of the *shebab*, the young men of the village, had been killed. 'Where were you?'

'In the field working. I heard about it from my mother when I returned.'

Then the interrogator began using bad words. He described the man as the 'brother of a bitch' and 'the son of a prostitute' – words, he said, that hurt the Arab Muslim to hear much more than the Israeli Jew to say.

Next the interrogator brought his file. This contained information from 'dogs' (collaborators). There were twelve allegations – member of Fatah, threw stones, bottles, many things. His brother was out of the country and a member of Fatah. 'What do you get from your brother?'

When there was no answer, the bad guys came in. They hit him. He said there were three kinds of interrogators – the nice man, the one who hits, and the half and half. For ninety minutes they beat him. Punched his face, chest and back. Whipped him anywhere. They kicked his genitals twice.

At this point another man reminded us that this happened early in the *intifada*, so this man had been lucky. Recently, one young man had been repeatedly kicked in the genitals. Now he took one hour to pass urine.

This treatment went on for forty-one days: questions and beatings, the same every day. For six days more they put him in a cupboard about one metre square. It had nails in the walls and water on the floor. Once a day they let him out to go to the toilet, but only after he had cried out for an hour.

The story seemed incredible later as I went over my notes. Yet there was no guile or dissembling that I could discern. Here was an ordinary honest man, telling his story in an unremarkable way. It was normal.

While we listened to this story, the children were watching a video. It showed scenes of Israeli clashes with the *shebab* and of PLO marches. Whenever the images on TV gave the *V* sign, the young children responded enthusiastically. Later I discussed this disturbing politicising of the young with Bill.

'But every country politicises its young people', he said, starting to recite 'From the halls of Montezuma ... ' to remind us that the USA also has chauvinism in large part in the education system of its young people. Of course, I agreed with him. I sang badly 'Allons enfants de la Patrie', and Graham and Bill rushed to correct the melody.

'I regret that any country exhibits chauvinism and jingoism in place of a healthy national pride', I said. 'I regret it in Israel. I regret it in the Occupied Territories. I regret it in the USA; I regret it in Australia. Ultimately it divides and stereotypes rather than builds bridges between people. The danger here is that young people learn to hate rather than to love. Jesus' way would be to place love for neighbour first, and love for country second. I agree that, practically speaking, the politicising of the young is understandable for the Palestinians. Some may even argue that, given their oppression, it is appropriate. I don't suggest it is, in the world's terms, a bad thing. I just regret it wherever I see it. Of course, there is much more to regret here than the politicising of the young.'

I didn't quite realise how true this last statement was, nor how small-minded a discussion of the politicising of the young appeared in the context of the much greater issues of human rights that existed in this country. These I would encounter soon enough in my visit. But first our friend had to finish his story of being in prison.

After forty-seven days he was transferred to another prison. In all he was behind bars for six months. 'Why six months?' I asked. It was a law from the British Mandate used with convenience in the present situation. The law stated someone could be kept in detention without trial or charge if there was a severe security risk. 'You know what they do?' Of course, I didn't. 'They watch the area where you come from while you are in jail. If there is no trouble, they know you are the trouble-maker so they keep you another six months.'

'The Israeli oppression is meant to weaken us, but it does not work', the man went on. 'Instead it works the other way. It strengthens and unifies. When my village was nine days under curfew, I went to another village. They welcomed me and I stayed there, building friendships and solidarity.'

The TV was still on. There was a scene of a lone Israeli soldier with a rifle and a single Palestinian youth with a stone. The soldier cowered behind cover while the youth stood defiantly in the open, throwing stones at him. The soldier poked his weapon around the corner and fired blindly at the youth. He missed, then turned and ran away.

'See, the Israeli soldiers are cowards', someone said. Reminded of reports I had read that both sides saw the other as cowards, I asked whether all Israeli soldiers were cowards. 'They cannot stop their jeep from being burned by some women. You think they are not cowards?'

During our conversation we heard that a curfew at a nearby village threatened the lives of the chickens that World Vision had provided because the people could not venture out to buy chicken feed. Bill was angry when he heard this. 'The chickens will die', he said, bitter at the waste.

'What do you expect?' the Palestinians said. 'They do not respect humans, why should you expect they care about chickens?'

Finally, after being in this place for four hours, I asked, 'So what do you want? What outcome?' Their reply was typical of what we heard from Palestinians over the next few days.

'Negotiation.'

The Palestinians would quickly say the Israelis were all crazy. But they did not ask for revenge or compensation. They asked for peace, real peace. For Jew. For Muslim. For Christian. Of course, only Palestinians fit into the second and third categories. 'We want the UN to sponsor a peace process. All we want is to be human. That's it! To be on the list of humans. They do not treat us like humans. To them we are animals. We want to be human.'

When did they hope there would be an end to their oppression? 'We don't know. We have hope. This might be God's test of whether we are worthy of his love. Our patience is being tested. Perhaps my sons will also be tested even more, as my father was tested before me, and his father, and his father.'

When? When? When?

'Tomorrow in the season of the apricots.' The apricot season is about three days long. The saying means 'never'.

'When the salt has flowers.' Same meaning.

We went for a walk among the olive and fig trees. It was hot in the sun but cool in the shade. The hills were all terraced, although perhaps little more than half were properly cultivated. The new road was opening up old orchards again. The orchards were steep. The men asked me to throw a stone. I gave it my best shot and it sailed beyond some bushes less than a hundred metres away. Each man hurled a projectile in long impressive arcs far beyond my pathetic effort.

The next day was Sunday, and Bill arrived with the awful news that a gunman in a white Peugeot had opened fire with a machine gun on a group of Arabs going to work inside Israel.[4] Seven had been killed. The gunman got away.

---

[4] Because of the lack of employment in the Occupied Territories, Palestinians commonly found their way into Israel and gathered each day at places called 'slave markets' with the hope that they would pick up a day's work.

Later we heard that he had been dressed in military uniform, and had lined up the people, demanded their identity cards, then opened fire. A police helicopter chased the Peugeot and they arrested an Israeli man in his twenties. The news said he was not a military person. It quoted an army official saying the man was suffering from a mental disorder and that the attack was not an expression of nationalism.

This last claim took my breath away. That an army man could assess a criminal's mental condition within one hour of capture was very impressive. Over the next few days it was revealed that the man had been discharged from the army after a bad service record, that he had troubles with his girlfriend and that he had been molested a few years earlier by an Arab. An editorial in *The Jerusalem Post* said that the crime was little different from someone in the US shooting at a crowd in the local McDonald's, and that Israel should have been congratulated for its speedy police work.

Doubtless the speedy police work was commendable. But the crime could not be directly paralleled with a McDonald's shoot-up or Melbourne's 'Hoddle Street Massacre'. Incidents like this, even if they were aberrations, sprang from the context of systematic oppression of the Palestinians by Israel. They were, as the Israel Labour Federation's Council for Jewish-Arab Coexistence said, 'the fruit of the influence of nationalist hatred'. An Israeli woman, representing a lobby group, said 'It is impossible to separate the gunman's actions from the political context. He may have been crazy. Perhaps he was lovesick for his girlfriend. But he put on an Israel army uniform and killed Arabs.'

Every Arab we met dismissed the notion that this was an action unrelated to Arab/Jew relations with cynical incredulity.

'When a Jew kills on Arab, he is a crazy person. If a Palestinian were to kill a Jew, it would be a clear case of anti-Semitism.'

'There are two standards of justice here. Rabbi Levinger gets five months for killing Palestinians. The Palestinian who killed Israelis on the Gaza bus got thirty years.'

'If this man is crazy, then every Israeli is crazy.'

Although I felt this last statement generalised Israeli responsibility unjustly, I agreed that the man was crazy. Anyone who cold-bloodedly killed seven other human beings was crazy in my book. More than seven others were to die that day. That also was crazy.

After beginning the day on this grim note, we drove to Gaza wondering if there would be a curfew. Near the checkpoint there was a stream of Gaza vehicles. The workers were returning from work early. A police car drove by the column and pulled out any vehicle (like ours) without Gaza plates. We followed him, thinking this was special treatment for Jerusalem cars (another case of discrimination towards Israelis), but we were wrong. At the checkpoint the police car pulled off the road indicating for everyone to follow. We drove straight up to the checkpoint. There was a police camera and what looked like a foreign TV news crew.

Bill said, 'Shalom'. The soldier spoke to him in Hebrew and Bill lapsed into English. Meanwhile a soldier asked me, 'Where are you going?' I said, 'Gaza'. Better to be obvious; I thought this was the only place you could go on this road.[5] 'You cannot. Turn here.' Bill got the same message and he turned the car away, then slipped into a small car park right beside the checkpoint. 'Let's walk through', he said. A friend was supposed to be picking us up on the other side.

We walked briskly. Graham, looking like a rabbi, lagged a bit, and Bill hurried him along. 'Just keep walking. Don't look back.' Loudspeakers and loud hailers sprang into noisy life. Nothing was said in Arabic or English so we could not understand if they were asking us to stop (although we suspected that they were). I expected to hear the sound of army boots running up behind us; to feel a rough hand on the shoulder; or to hear a volley of warning shots. None of these happened. Once we were fifty metres away, it went quiet. Probably confusion about whether we were Israelis or foreigners, or whether we were heading for Gaza or the Israeli settlement, combined with our purposeful and confident gait to get us through.

Our friend was not there to pick us up. At a service station Bill called the hospital where he worked. The news was bad. 'The whole of Gaza is in flames.' We could see columns of black smoke. One person was dead already in one refugee camp. There were reports that the Israelis were shooting at people from helicopters. It would be impossible to get in. It was the worst day in Gaza the hospital had ever seen. People were crazy. Soldiers were crazy. We should come

---

[5] It was not. There was a turn-off to an Israeli settlement just a hundred yards beyond the checkpoint. Reasonably, the soldiers were letting through any Israeli heading there.

only at our own risk. Regularly that day we prayed for angels to go before us and behind us. Bill said, 'We have to pray whether God wants us to go ahead or turn back.'

> Then an angel of the Lord said to Philip, 'Get up and go toward the south to the road that goes down from Jerusalem to Gaza.' (This is a wilderness road.) (Acts 8:26)

Right then a Renault R4 with a UN flag flying pulled up. That was the fastest answer to prayer I ever had! I didn't even get to say 'Dear Heavenly Father'. I had a quick picture of God saying, 'I know, I know. Get on with it.' The UN official offered to take us into Gaza to the Ahli Arab Anglican Hospital where we were planning to make a short visit anyway. We accepted.

Before we left, the man in the service station, who had offered us tea and cigarettes while we waited (we accepted tea), said, 'Look at these people [the Israelis]. We ask and ask and ask for talks, for peace. And this is what they do.'

The UN official said, 'Today, ten will be killed in Gaza, I predict.'

Along the way, blazing tyres littered the road. The driver described them as 'the Palestinian symbol of protest against the Israeli occupation'. Stones were everywhere. Gaza was like a war zone. Houses and shops were boarded up. People huddled in doorways and up alleys. A couple of stones came our way, but mostly people waved and offered the *V* sign. We encountered two army jeeps. The *shebab* had scattered. The soldiers were running up an alley, crouched over, rifles pointing. We had to go another way. The driver ran the slalom of rocks and flames with skill and daring.

We arrived at the Ahli Arab Hospital by 11.00 a.m. They had coped with the first wave of emergency cases. All medical staff had been found and brought to the hospital, mostly in ambulances. Non-urgent in-patients were sent home when the news of the first massacre was heard. The hospital administrator, Jorgen Rosendal, a Dane, knew there would be trouble.

There were reports that the army was using its stone throwing machine from helicopters. They also had a water cannon that fired hot and dyed water. It burned and marked its targets for easier identification.

Now we heard that three dead had arrived at Shifa Hospital (the nearby government hospital). There were over 100 casualties in camps, but no ambulances to bring them. Two quick Fiats arrived and people scattered. Two young men with head wounds were despatched into the emergency ward.

Throughout the day we heard the boom of tear gas cannon, the occasional burst of gun fire and the calls to mourning on the Muslim loudspeakers. As we walked to Jorgen's office we saw a soldier on a nearby roof top watching us through binoculars. It felt eerie.

Why didn't the soldiers pull back? The official announcement was that they were trying to minimise the outbreaks of violence. But evidently their presence created the context for violence, if it didn't incite it directly. There was no violence in the streets we drove through unless the army was present.

'I expected this', said Jorgen as we sat down, referring to the mounting casualties.

'How?'

'For two to three months there have been clashes in the street outside two or three times a week. This is much more often than before. A curfew was imposed. The street was so littered with stones you could not see the footpath. School girls are now throwing stones at jeeps. An old man tried to stop them. Nobody can control the *shebabs* anymore. They are really nationalistic now. I am very worried.'

'Is the violence worse now?'

'It's different. The army seems more patient lately. They let stone throwing go on for a long while before reacting. But then they respond with bullets rather than beatings.'

'So the response is worse?'

'Well, I think beating is worse. Beating is more severe for the soldier. Now it's long distance violence. On 26 April, our worst day so far (today would be worse), we had ninety-one *intifada*-related casualties. Seventy-two were gunshot wounds.

'Casualties can happen any time. Gaza people are seeing no hope, no progress. The risk is that the younger radical elements will take over the PLO. The older ones will lose control – then violence will spill over to Israel. Maybe it cannot be solved in a calm way anymore.'

The standard of health care in Gaza was brilliant under the circumstances, but it was still inadequate. There were 850 beds in Gaza for 700,000 people. That's 1.2 per thousand, compared to two per thousand in Israel and five per thousand in Scandinavia. In 1967, before the Occupation, there were 2.4 per thousand in Gaza. It had halved.

It looked like there would be five days of curfew, maybe ten. This idea of curfew was stupefying. A Jew killed seven Arabs, and all the Arab towns were closed! Why did they get punished?

The phone rang, and as Jorgen spoke I wandered to the window and looked out. The birds still sang. A beautiful big jacaranda tree was in full bloom behind the hospital. It was going to look great, no matter what happened. I felt a sense of God's protection over all this sorrow.

Patients were now arriving in dribs and drabs. Two girls arrived without families. They had to be admitted as it was impossible to get them home. 'The hospital is also a hotel and a restaurant', joked one doctor.

Some children had been admitted. Mostly they had bullet wounds in the head. These were 'rubber' bullets: steel balls about the size of a marble covered with a thin layer of rubber. They had less give than a golf ball. Fired from a few metres they entered skulls and broke legs. In the hospital we saw the results on people and in their X-rays. Most of the older boys and young men seemed to have leg injuries caused by bullets. A surprising number were shot exactly in the knee. Jorgen pointed out that the more serious cases were taken directly to the government hospital.

Someone reported they heard an Israeli news bulletin that said there were only four gunshot wounds in Gaza. So far we had seen dozens and this was just one hospital among three major ones.

In the ward the wounded spoke to me. 'We want real peace – for all. Jew, Muslim, Christian.' This was from a man who was shot in the hand two days before and now had returned with a leg wound. 'Look and compare our situation with the rest of the world. Other people are protected; we are shot at. Boys this age should be in school; here they are in hospital. We should feel cared for and protected.'

Reports came in that the soldiers were using live ammunition in Rafah camp. They were insisting that the people go to their houses, rather than the army withdrawing. It was a stand-off. Stones had been dropped from helicopters.

A UN official said, 'This is the worst day of violence in Gaza since the Occupation [1948]'.

Now we heard the official figures to about 4.00 p.m. One hundred and sixty-seven casualties treated at Shifa, and 107 at Ahli Arab. We heard unofficial reports that nine were dead in Gaza and four in the West Bank. That *was* the worst day ever.

After five hours at the hospital UNRWA[6] transported us out. 'In places like this', Bill said, 'all the agencies cooperate. There is no competition.'

The army stopped us three times. The first time two jeeps wedged us between them. There were no people in sight, but rocks immediately started to hail down. Bill said, 'Drive, drive'. The calm German UNRWA woman waited to hear the advice from the soldier, so she could ignore it and tell the driver to continue. The soldier said, 'You cannot go down that road. It is too dangerous.' As we drove away the UNRWA woman said, 'Only dangerous for the army'.

A large group of *shebab* was positioned fifty metres away, hidden from the army vehicles by a two-storey building. They continued to throw stones in long arcs over the building at their out-of-sight targets. Impressively, they landed with pin-point accuracy. The *shebab* paused as they saw us, then waved us on. Only dangerous for the army.

At the second army patrol a Major asked brusquely for our German hostess's ID card. He read it and said, 'Go ahead', adding 'Welcome' as if he had learned it was good to be polite to agency people.

A third checkpoint let us through without delay. We were sure glad that God sent the well-marked UNRWA cars to help us out twice in one day.

As we got near to the Gaza Strip checkpoint, a steady stream of noisy Palestinians was flooding back into Gaza. Every car and truck was festooned with black flags of mourning. The people, mostly men, chanted in Arabic, 'God is great, God is good'. They did this right under the gaze of the Israeli army manning the checkpoint, any respect for them evaporated in rage and grief.

At the final checkpoint, where our car was parked, the UN driver could not go on because he did not have a 'metallic card' which

---

[6] United Nations Relief and Works Agency for Palestine Refugees in the Near East.

permitted exit from Gaza. Bill suggested we walk through. Was he pressing our luck? The German woman said she would wait to see how we got on and come up if there was any trouble.

Bill said, 'Walk briskly. Look like you know where you're going. Don't make eye contact with anyone.' We passed by without incident and drove away.

We had spent the day in Gaza. It was a day never to be forgotten, and an experience that had cut into our hearts and our minds. As the cut healed it would leave deep scars.

The next day was a strike day, called to mourn the deaths of the seven Arabs at Rishon Levion. The Old City was eerily quiet. We parted at Notre Dame Hospice and walked down by the Old City wall to the Damascus Gate to visit the Spafford Children's Home, where World Vision Australia supported a social worker. As we went along we saw just one man, and a woman with two children. 'Normally, it's packed', said Bill.

The entrance to the Muslim quarter was marked by scorch marks where a fire had been cleared away. Later, as we left, we saw that a burning tyre had been reinstated on the spot and was flaming furiously.

We met eighty-five-year-old Anna Grace Lind, grand-daughter of the Spaffords who established the 'American Colony' in Jerusalem over 100 years ago.[7] On the Arab-Jew conflict she saw good and bad on both sides.

On the Jews' right to the land she referred to a speech she gave to Jewish students based on Ezekiel 47. 'It says, healing comes down from the temple first. Then, in the last verse, it says you must *share* the land. They were very surprised to hear this. One young man had the Torah with him and read the passage in Hebrew. They were very impressed.'[8]

The walk up to the Church of the Holy Sepulchre was quiet also. A few Arab boys and even fewer street merchants hung about. There

---

[7] The Spaffords' fascinating story is told in the book *Our Jerusalem: An American Family in the Holy City 1881–1949* by Anna Grace's mother, Bertha Spafford Vester.

[8] 'So you shall divide this land among you according to the tribes of Israel. You shall allot it as an inheritance for yourselves and for the aliens who reside among you and have begotten children among you. They shall be to you as citizens of Israel; with you they shall be allotted an inheritance among the tribes of Israel. In whatever tribes aliens reside, there you shall assign them their inheritance, says the Lord GOD.' (Ezekiel 47:21–23)

were occasional tourist groups, and Bill was annoyed at the noise they made, along with some Arab flute sellers, on what should have been a day of sorrow and mourning. Three uniformed people, one woman and two men with walkie-talkies, hurried along almost crouching towards us. The image of rats scurrying ahead of trouble was imprinted powerfully on my mind. They were the advance scouts for a large tour group, clearing the way.

We visited a family. One son had been killed while cycling to a friend's place in the north of Jerusalem. A second son was in prison awaiting trial. Mother and father and the older sister welcomed us solemnly but gladly. The sister translated well. She was studying engineering. 'But the university is closed', I said, surprised. Yes, but about 700 students continued to study and receive help and examination in anticipation of the university reopening.

Finally we walked up to what used to be St John's Greek Orthodox Hospice. The Israeli government had paid US$2 million covertly through a Panamanian company to buy this building to establish a Jewish settlement in the Christian quarter, despite a centuries-old unwritten agreement that the Old City Christian quarter would be free from Jewish settlements. The Hospice was located virtually next door to the Church of the Holy Sepulchre, the traditional place of Jesus' crucifixion and burial. I saw how provocative the Israeli action, taken during Holy Week, was. The resulting attack on the Greek Orthodox Patriarch had resulted in his political awakening. Formerly seen as a weak and unpopular figure, he had been radicalised into another Palestinian advocate. It was an object lesson in how oppression breeds, rather than eliminates, liberation movements.

The next day at the American Colony Hotel I met Anne, a slim American woman with the intense manner of someone with important information. Over her shoulder was a large bag which she held against her hip.

Bill introduced her as the author of a Save the Children Fund Report that we had heard about. The four-volume report was called 'The Status of Palestinian Children during the Uprising in the Occupied Territories'. Anne agreed to give me the copy she had with her.

'Israel's pretty mad about this report apparently', I said. 'What will they say at the airport if they find it?'

'Put it among your papers in your carry-on luggage.'

The report revealed much about the brutal way in which Israel was responding to the *intifada*. Using official records, published statements and eyewitness accounts, it showed the error of the army's claims that children under sixteen were killed or injured 'by mistake' or were 'exceptional cases'. By the end of the second year of the *intifada* (the report covered the period 9 December 1987 to 9 December 1989) the data showed:

- one hundred and fifty-nine children were known to have been killed by gunfire, beating, tear gas, and other *intifada*-related causes;
- military personnel were responsible in ninety-four per cent of the cases;
- children accounted for twenty-one per cent of all deaths and thirty-eight per cent of all casualties;
- between 50,000 and 63,000 children, or one out of every fifteen to twenty children in the Occupied Territories, required medical treatment for injuries caused by the army;
- fifty-two per cent of the children who were killed were *not* near a protest activity at the time. Indeed, forty per cent were at home or within ten metres of home when they were killed;
- the army even disrupted the funerals of fifty-four per cent in some way;
- forty per cent of the children killed were under eleven;
- thirty-nine per cent of the dying children whose families and rescuers sought medical treatment were obstructed or delayed by soldiers.

In the late evening we drove via Tel Aviv and Haifa to Father Elias Chacour's Prophet Elias High School in Ibillin. We passed by Mount Carmel where Elijah tussled with the prophets of Baal, and the Jezreel valley in which Naboth's vineyard was situated. Ahab coveted the vineyard, and his wife Jezebel said, 'Are you the King of Israel or not?' She arranged for Naboth to be killed so Ahab could possess the land. I felt a political sermon coming on.

We enjoyed rich fellowship, story telling, a walk around the yet-to-be-completed school and a good night's sleep. The showers were cold, but the hospitality typically Palestinian.

The next day we drove back to Tel Aviv. Before leaving Ibillin we stopped by the church that Father Elias wrote about in his first book, *Blood Brothers*.[9] I found the 'baptised' grapevine now huge and covering two buildings. We sat briefly in the church in which Father Elias, as a young priest, challenged his community towards reconciliation by chaining the doors shut during a Sunday morning service. Then he waited until repentance came.

The landscape along the coast on the drive back was uniformly dull. We passed through perhaps three Arab villages where once there must have been many. Signs of lost villages remained – sometimes ruins, more often overgrown olive groves or clumps of cactus. Over 400 villages had been destroyed since 1948.

Here we were back at the airport, ready for another security check. Paranoia was contagious again; I wanted to be cautious about what I said, though I felt entirely innocent. One wondered if the mention of a name put that name in a file somewhere. The process, like mandatory drug testing, was overlaid with a heavy presumption of guilt.

'Welcome. We have to ask you a few questions for security reasons.' The woman at the security table before the check-in counter was about eighteen years of age. There were about ten of these tables, all attended by young women. Everyone carried a clip-board.

'May I see your passport, please?'

'Sure.' It went under the clip on her clip-board. She laboriously read the first page, looking up to see if my face resembled the photo. She flipped through the passport pages. She opened the leather name tags on my suitcase and carry-on bag, checking the name against my passport. She read the stickers on my big suitcase. I was particularly proud of the one from the Vintage Car Museum in Launceston, Tasmania. I hoped she would ask me about it.

After five minutes of silent reading she said, 'May I see your ticket, please?'

'Sure.' It went under the clip on her clip-board. She studied the

---
[9] Kingsway, 1985.

ticket. She was reading everything – even the notice that suggested one should not take hair spray on board.

Deja vu.

The rest of the interview followed a predictable and familiar course. At one point she asked me what I had done in the West Bank (I had told her truthfully that I went to Bethlehem). When I paused, she said, 'Everything is permitted in Israel. You understand why I am asking these questions?' I was tempted to answer 'No' to see what the standard response would be. I decided not to rock the boat as time was running out to catch my flight.

The plane was due to leave at 9.30 a.m. At 9.00 a.m. they asked me to open my bags and began to take everything out.

In the centre of my suitcase in a special pocket were the cables for my laptop computer and printer. A second security man said, 'What are these?'

'Cables for my printer.'

'You have a printer in here?' he asked in a way that made it sound like I had a communicable disease.

'Sure. You want to see it?' I asked ingenuously.

He did. He also wanted to see my computer. Then he saw my video camera. My primary interrogator sighed audibly as if it would look bad on her CV.

The Save the Children Fund report was in the documents section of my carry-on bag. The labelled spines were face down and the back of the volumes were blank. I took the books out and placed them face down on the table. No-one showed any interest in them. I was not sure whether to be disappointed.

A representative from Olympic Airways came to try to hurry them up, but he got short shrift.

I was now attended by three young women who joined me in taking everything out of my bag. Every bottle was uncapped, every tube inspected, every box opened. One sniffed my Chanel after-shave and said 'Nice'. I offered to sell it to her duty free. She declined without smiling.

So thorough was the search that we found four sweets collected in different parts of the world and wedged in different corners of the bag. I offered them around after sucking on one to show they weren't poisoned. They declined without smiling.

A man took the empty suitcase away and returned it within a few minutes. We began to repack the bag.

After twenty minutes the computer and printer were returned. The battery of the computer had been removed and a young man told me to pack it as two pieces. I was not permitted to put it in my carry-on bag. This security precaution is observed in many international airports.

At 9.25 a.m. the video camera appeared. The man said, 'You have visited a hospital?'

'No', I said honestly. I could not remember taking my video camera to a hospital.

'Let me see', I said and reviewed the tape. Sure enough, it was scenes of the Bethlehem Paraplegics Hospital. I explained that it was the 'Bethlehem Arab Society for the Physically Handicapped' and that my organisation had helped this hospital with funds for mattresses and other things. I said we had visited it on Tuesday. He seemed satisfied.

My primary interrogator meanwhile had permitted the Olympic representative to organise my seat allocation and label my suitcase. Once the video camera was packed, with its battery separated, the suitcase was whisked away. And so was I.

The interrogator accompanied me on a fast track through passport control. Now I felt like I was getting the Frequent Flyer treatment.

Near the gate were booths for body searches. I was invited into one and a serious man asked me to remove my leather jacket. He pressed it against the wall like a New York cop holding a juvenile delinquent ready for hand-cuffing. With his thumbs he felt every seam.

'Please remove your shoes.'

I remembered Elias Chacour's refusal to cooperate at this point, but I felt less principled. Chacour had finally written a complaint saying he was very sorry that all of Israel was so afraid of his shoes.

Apparently satisfied that my shoes were not dangerous he permitted me to go. Another man met me and took me on my own private bus to the plane, full of patiently waiting passengers.

'Do you work for Olympic?' I asked him.

'Yes, not for security,' he said, adding, 'Thank God.'

'I must be the favourite of Israel', I said.

'How so?'

'I am the one they want to keep here as long as possible.'

9 | *A Look into the Future*

Guatemala 1990

Earlier in Sri Lanka I had seen how it might be possible for World Vision to work in such a way that our development processes took the whole complex world into account. Not a piecemeal approach of bits and pieces, but a comprehensive process that honoured the wisdom and ability of the local people. With some colleagues, I began to talk these ideas up. One World Vision office which responded with enthusiasm was Guatemala and its director, Dr Annette de Fortin. In my heart, new hope began to emerge that World Vision's work would be increasingly effective and empowering of people.

My head ached. The altimeter in the Toyota Land Cruiser said 3,000 metres. Higher than Kosciusko. Up here it took at least two days to acclimatise. Any kind of activity left me breathless.

Geoff Renner, my World Vision colleague from Melbourne, adopted a typically Australian it-could-be-worse attitude. 'You should be on the highlands of Bolivia at 5,000 metres', he said.

No, I shouldn't. I should be home in Melbourne. Mount Dandenong is plenty high enough for me.

In less than an hour we had climbed more than a thousand metres. From the top, the *Mirador*, we looked back to the town of Huehuetenango. You pronounce this Way-way-to-nango (rhymes with mango). I amused our hosts by suggesting most Australians would pronounce it Hewey-Hewey-to-nango.

Children in their colourful Indian clothes ran up as we got out of the cars and gave us yellow wild flowers. We gave them a few coins.

The view was spectacular beyond words. Many families live and work these steep slopes. They have virtually no money, but they do have million dollar views. Unfortunately, you can't eat a panorama.

Over dinner the night before we had discussed our vision for ministry. Sitting around the table were Annette de Fortin, the World Vision field director, Javier and Hugo, two of her senior managers, Mario, the local area manager, Corrina, a Peruvian development agent working elsewhere in Guatemala who had come along as my interpreter, Julio and Liszet, the local facilitators, and the visitors, Geoff and me.

I said we wanted to be in the business of 'empowering people to transform their worlds'. (We had a bit of trouble translating 'empowering' into Spanish, but between Geoff and the rest we worked it out to their satisfaction.) Empowering people meant doing the best development ministry we could. I said we wanted people in the field to say what was needed to transform the lives of the poor. Then let us think together about how we could *create a relationship* between the people in the project communities and our supporters.

At first I think our colleagues were sceptical that we really wanted them to have a blank sheet to work on. 'Will your donors accept this?' asked Mario.

'That's part of our challenge', I replied, 'we haven't found the donors yet. We are now making some undesignated funds available so you can get started. Then as we understand what you are doing better, we can begin to develop a strategy for communicating that to our supporters. I'd like you to help us in that too. And I'd like the community to know what we are doing in the support office.'

The hotel owner came over to tell us she wanted to close the restaurant. We went to bed. I heard later that everyone else sat up late discussing our suggestions.

Next day we headed up the mountains. We talked as we bumped and slithered along the poor roads. Gradually trust began to emerge.

At the top of the mountain we came upon a high plain. At the end of the road was a small township, *La Haciendita*. When we arrived a dozen men surrounded the vehicles and welcomed us gladly. They knew Julio and Liszet.

They were open and confident. There was much to do here.

There was a lot of poverty. They knew they had the opportunity to help themselves. They welcomed our involvement with them.

What was different about this project? It was the way World Vision had decided to work – in the attitude, the approach. Julio and Liszet themselves came with an open agenda. Their first task was simply to get to know the community and to let the people get to know them.

Too often aid agencies arrive with a kit-bag full of solutions. Experience had shown us that this was actually high risk. First, no matter how good an idea, if people don't own it themselves there is a good chance it will fail. Just look at all the abandoned and useless tractors and water pumps scattered around the Third World by well-meaning but foolish donors. Second, people often know the solutions to their own problems. What they need is the opportunity or the process to spell them out, or sometimes to discover the wisdom that is within them.

World Vision's approach here was to spend time to become part of the community. At the time of our visit the project was actually a bit hard to see. It was invisible. That was because it existed in relationships.

Soon these relationships would begin to be productive for the local community as Julio and Liszet used their training as community development workers to help the community explore and discover solutions to their own problems.

Annette mentioned one difficulty in the area. For three months of the year whole families migrated to the coast to become coffee pickers. They earned about A$5 per person per day. Then they returned to the high country and tried to survive the rest of the year.

Some leading people in the community had contracts with the coffee plantation owners to provide workers. There was a complex system of exploitation.

Back on the high country they cultivated few crops. It was just too cold most of the year. They cultivated potatoes and ran sheep, but the lack and non-variety of food meant many children were malnourished. And staying warm in this part of the world was not easy either.

Down the road was another area called *La Capellania*. The houses were spread out here and we walked across some fields to one of them. A twenty-six year old man and his twenty-five year old wife lived in this one room home with their two children, a girl aged three and a boy aged one. All they had were a few bits of furniture, a pallet for sleeping on, some blankets, and some pots and pans. A chicken wandered in and out. The children looked like they had not been washed in weeks.

Annette, who was a medical doctor, discovered that the baby had a tumour of the umbilical cord. He needed to go to hospital, but the family had no money for the bus. *A child might die for the lack of a bus fare*, I realised. I asked whether we could help, and Geoff assured me it had already been taken care of during our conversation. Liszet was going to see to it.

Within a minute of our arrival seven men appeared as if from nowhere – the local committee. 'It's unusual for two cars to come together', said Annette, 'so they knew something important must be happening. Then they saw Liszet in the car and realised it must be people from head office.'

Annette made a fine speech encouraging the people to take responsibility for their own futures. They responded enthusiastically.

'It is we who will benefit, so we will try very hard', said the committee chairman.

'And we will help too', said Annette.

'Thank you very much', they said to all of us.

This was our latest field program. I felt we could not be working with a better equipped national team. Annette and her colleagues were at the forefront of development ministry. They had introduced child sponsorship into communities, not as a way of getting money into communities, but as a way of linking communities with supporters relationally. They had taken this step even before most support offices were ready to respond adequately.

It was an exciting week for me in Guatemala. I felt I had seen the future of World Vision's development ministry.

10 | *Selamawit*

Ethiopia 1991

I had discovered in the southern Sudan that war is the enemy of development. Now, in Tigray, Ethiopia, I discovered the corollary – that peace is fertile ground for the explosive blossoming of people and abundant life. Nevertheless, war and its belief system that destroyed the value of human life left a legacy of robbery and violence that one encountered every day. Sometimes the events were trivial: a small robbery or a careless attitude. Occasionally the events were more dangerous: a resort to violence or the use of a weapon to achieve power over someone.

Much of my thinking over a decade about the complexity of aid was focussed in the story of one little girl, Selamawit. Seven factors were operating in a complex way that were killing her.

People in Ethiopia were more relaxed than when I'd visited it once before, when Mengistu was still in power. I got a visa at the airport without any official paperwork when the local World Vision office mistook my arrival time. Yemane, our Ethiopia director, thought this remarkable. Another Australian colleague had been made to wait three hours because the paperwork had not arrived on time.

The statue of Lenin outside the Hilton was gone. Children had attempted to demolish it and succeeded with the help of heavy machinery.

The Ethiopian Airlines in-flight magazine said, 'Addis Ababa is a safe city. You can walk safely at night.' They were dreaming. You couldn't walk alone any time. Two thieves robbed a Canadian colleague Philip Maher one morning by the push-shove-and-frisk routine while he was walking with four others on the way to church from the Ghion Hotel. Our cameraman, Doug, received the same treatment in the early evening darkness walking between the Ghion and the Hilton, but spun around, scaring them off. My baseball cap was stolen off my head while I sat in the car in a traffic jam with the window down.

Yemane said that sometimes in the markets (which we had just walked through) someone came along behind people with nice shoes, got them in a bear hug and lifted them off the ground while an accomplice stole their shoes. I checked to see if I was still wearing my Reeboks.

I was in Ethiopia accompanying a World Vision Canada film team. My goal was to do some television segments that we would use in our World Vision Australia television programs. I also wanted to assess the opportunity for project work in Tigray.

On the flight up to Tigray, as we looked over a landscape of wriggly worm trails, Yemane talked about Ansokia in the height of the famine. (Ansokia Valley was an area featured in the BBC report that exposed the world to the terrible Ethiopian famine in the middle 1980s. World Vision began an extensive program there, and for a time Yemane was its senior manager.) He recalled how the Tigray People's Liberation Force had once killed three staff when they mistook them for government officials. The World Vision compound was next door to a club for party officials. When it was attacked some ran away, and the pursuing freedom fighters thought the people in our compound were the escapees.

Life had been difficult in Ansokia. Many were dying of starvation, and doctors and nurses were making life and death decisions about who to feed and who to leave to die. There was constant insecurity.

The day before we had spoken to the director of REST, the aptly acronymed Relief Society of Tigray. Tigray had been ignored for a generation, he said, but now the people had high expectations. War had ended and the Tigrayans had won. They expected help. But out of 900 million birr requested for Wollo and Tigray, the Ethiopian government could only find B100–150 million. And Tigray would get only thirty. It needed 500.

Many people saw the war as a way to bring social change, not just peace. If those expectations were not met, maybe the peace would be destabilised. His implied message was: If World Vision believes in peace, you will bring aid to Tigray.

He was very conscious of dependency problems. Handouts must be accompanied by education. 'The process in Tigray is very bottom up', he said.

We landed in Mekelle and two Toyota Land Cruisers took us to the Abraha Atsebeha Hotel. Resembling an eighteenth century English manor house, it was all front. Little in the hotel was working although the flat bread was tasty and the spaghetti nourishing. We thanked the Italians for this edible legacy.

I have never been too fussy about where I stay as long as it's clean. And as long as there's a working toilet. And as long as there's hot water for the shower, or at least lukewarm.

The hotel was at least clean. I shared a toilet and bathroom with guests from five other rooms; the toilet overflowed and stank. The drizzle of water in the shower seemed to have come from a glacial cave far removed from the mildness of the equatorial Tigrayan plateau. As usual, I cleaned my teeth in Ambo water, the excellent Ethiopian mineral water with bubbles that last three days. Splashing on plenty of cologne felt like covering a multitude of sins.

My logic told me that my discomfort at the lack of creature comforts was nothing compared to millions in the world who lived their whole lives without a hot shower. When a call of nature comes at four in the morning, and the only option is a stuffed loo, emotion takes over from logic.

My little troubles were soon forgotten, however, as we drove into the countryside. A desolate, sparsely treed landscape. Shale and rocks abound.

Once there were trees and a river,
Once there was grass where you stand,
Once there were songs, about rights instead of wrongs,
Once was the time of man.

We were looking at a humanly-engineered environmental disaster.

Two hours drive north of Mekelle we arrived in the town of Wukro. The hospital there was unlike any you would find in Australia: it had earth floors, no furniture and people were lying on the floor in the dirt. The staff were too stretched to do a baseline nutrition survey. They could only react to patients as they presented themselves.

I was bothered by an unfamiliar smell. Hospitals usually smell of disinfectant. This was the musty, sickly smell of unwashed bodies and blankets. There was no water in this town. Any water they could find was not for washing.

In India, my first overseas trip, in 1977. 'Willesee at Seven' reporter, Howard Gipps (right) waits while drivers and camera crew attempt to restore an ailing (but brand new) car.

World Vision India colleague, David G, sits on the door by the ruins of a church in Andhra Pradesh. Many in the community sheltered here during a cyclone. They were crushed when the building collapsed. Two people, an old man and a young girl, survived because they were standing by this door which flew open as the wall fell around them.

'Making' the news for Australian television in India in 1977.

The 'Willesee at Seven' team wait for the Hyderabad express to come through.

The Bombay Yellow Fever Quarantine Hospital where I was detained at the India government's pleasure for a few days in 1978 for my failure to read the fine print when having my shots.

Boarding for Uganda in 1979 after the fall of Idi Amin. No airlines were flying scheduled services so we went by light aircraft.

The one place every visitor has their photo taken in Uganda – on the equator.

In the refugee camp in northern Somalia, Anne Deveson and I talk with Dr Ken Tracey, Africa regional director for World Vision.

Ghanaian Ahuma Adodoadji (left) and I discovered that his being African was no guarantee that he could operate effectively in Somalia.

Talking with Masai children in the Rift Valley, Kenya, 1978.

In a kindergarten on the West Bank, Israel.

In Guatemala, World Vision national director, Dr Annette de Fortin (left), discovered that this woman's child needed urgent medical attention. His mother had not taken him to the hospital because she did not have the five cent bus fare.

left: Signing a project community's visitors' book in Vietnam.

right: Rebecca Gibney hosted a number of World Vision Australia television specials. On this occasion her 'duties' included tea with officials in Vietnam.

below: The 'crew' who make the World Vision Australia television specials. On location near Da Nang, Vietnam.

above: I made two visits to Beijing with World Vision International presidents. On both occasions our hosts made sure we saw the Great Wall of China. This visit in 1991 was with Graeme and Fran Irvine.

left: They were flying kites in Tienanmen Square, Beijing, when we visited in 1991, a year after the massacre. I am standing in front of the monument to the martyrs of the Communist Revolution.

In Tigray, Ethiopia, with Don Scott, president of World Vision Canada.

This landscape in Tigray, Ethiopia, was once heavily forested. This generation, through careful harvesting of the water, hopes to restore the environment.

Jean Penman and I participated in the dedication by the Archbishop of Canterbury of the David Penman Memorial Centre in Zebabdeh on the West Bank.

With Luba Relic, a Serb migrant to Australia, who told her own story of oppression, hatred and pain in the midst of the Israeli–Palestinian reality.

Steve Levitt, World Vision communications fixer, demonstrating the standard issue bedroom suite for World Vision people on field visits. This 'hotel' room, complete with missing hand basin and plumbing, was in Battambang, Cambodia.

One of the many 'killing fields' sites in Cambodia – this one near Battambang.

Enjoying Hanoi's equivalent of the one-menu-item restaurant in 1992. World Vision Australia board member, Rev Dr Noel Vose (centre left), and colleague, Boyne Alley (centre right).

Acting the part in the Cu Chi tunnels outside Ho Chi Minh City, Vietnam.

One of the strengths of the sponsorship scheme is that children, families and sponsors can write to one another. Here in Vietnam 1992 I enjoy reading letters sent from Australian sponsors to their sponsored children.

Riding in a 'technical' with the *Sixty Minutes* crew in Somalia. The reporter was former Prime Minister, Bob Hawke.

Bob Hawke with Nurta Haji Hasan, the lawyer wife of Ali Mahdi, one of the claimants to the Somalia presidency, in a refugee centre in northern Mogadishu, Somalia.

left: Bob Hawke with Alistair Dawson, local UN rep in northern Mogadishu, who ran feeding centres in a refugee centre.

right: Bob Hawke found that World Vision's Africa communications expert, Sudanese Jacob Akol, was also a better than average golfer.

below: Visiting with Renamo, the rebel group in Mozambique, included accepting pillion rides from General Dhlakama (man riding the motorcycle on the left) and his officials. Ladies went first.

The World Vision base headquarters in Baidoa, Somalia, was a converted hotel.

World Vision workers often have their own challenges to overcome. This woman came to work as usual in Bur Hakeba, Somalia, despite receiving the news that her missing husband had been found to have been shot dead.

'Gift of Australia' has many uses. The packing for high energy biscuits is recycled as roofing material in camps for internally displaced persons.

above: The Piazza del Commune in Assisi, Italy.

left: The Basilica of Saint Francis of Assisi in Assisi, Italy.

Broadcasting on indigenous radio. Ray Minniecon (left) and I were guests on the breakfast program in Townsville, Queensland.

Kevin May (left) and I talk with Doug Walter, coordinator of CAAAPU – Central Australian Aboriginal Alcohol Programs Unit – in Alice Springs.

The staff introduced me to a little sick girl. Her name was Selamawit. She was two years old and weighed just five kilograms. What was the problem?

In Wukro malaria was an epidemic. In the previous two months in Selamawit's village of 800 people, 147 had died – 137 under fourteen. At first glance, then, I came to the quick conclusion that Selamawit's problem was malaria.

It was not that simple.

Selamawit might yet survive the malaria if she hadn't been so weak. And she was weak from malnutrition. So the problem was malaria *on top of* malnutrition.

Proper food was in such short supply that even in the hospital there was no milk for the child patients, only bread and tea. The nurse said that without proper food Selamawit had no chance of surviving the malaria. We offered to buy milk for Selamawit and the three other under-fives in the clinic. The nurse said it is 'very expensive' – A$1.55 per litre. We left A$190 for milk for four children for a month (one litre a day).

So the problem was malaria on top of malnutrition. There were two factors working inter-dependently. Right?

Again, it was not that simple.

The reason there was no food was war. War had prevented the family from farming. They had run away for their own safety, becoming refugees in a place 200 kilometres away from home. Now they had returned, but *after* the short rainy season. And if you didn't get your crops in before the rains, you must wait another whole year for the next chance. So no harvest that year.

Malaria, on top of malnutrition caused by war and seasonal rains. Four factors conspiring to threaten Selamawit's existence.

Well, it was not that simple either.

Less than 100 years ago, so the older men and women told me, this area of Ethiopia was covered by forests. Now it was a desert with barely a tree from one long horizon to another. In two or three generations, *every* tree had been cut down. As the trees were taken away, the water table sank. Crop yields plummeted. Grandfathers talked of harvests big enough to feed a family for a year or more. Now they harvested enough for a week. And for fifty-one weeks of the year they were dependent on food aid.

So the problems were malaria, on top of malnutrition caused by war, seasonal rains and environmental destruction. Five factors that would kill Selamawit.

Sorry, it was not even that simple.

I began to ask questions like these: Who owns the land? How is produce marketed? Who makes the profits? The answers revealed a slowly changing political and economic system that had been weighted against the farmer and in favour of the mythical State. The residues of communism, African style.

Malaria, malnutrition, war, seasonal rains, environmental destruction, bad politics and economic structures tilted unjustly against the poor: seven factors that would kill Selamawit.

During the day, someone said that the problems seemed too huge. 'No', I replied, 'we just need a sense of proportion. There's lots of money around, if we only want to spend it on the things that will make a difference. World Vision – and the world – needs a sense of proportion on a range of things.'

Someone worked out that the poverty problems of the world could be solved if less than thirty billion dollars a year were spent on the right things. In 1992, more than 300 billion dollars were spent by the United States, the European Community and Japan simply protecting their own farmers from competition.

If we wanted to solve the problems of poverty, we could not use the excuse that the world did not have the resources. The world simply lacked the leadership with the willpower.

11 | *Flying a Kite*

China 1991

In 1991 I visited Beijing for the second time. I was part of a small group with the president of World Vision International, Graeme Irvine. I was included in the party because of involvement over many years with World Vision's work in Hong Kong, and more particularly because I had been part of an initial survey team which had designed World Vision's response to serious flooding earlier that year in An Hui province.

The visit impressed on me the complexity of revolution. First, Beijing itself had changed physically in the nine years since my previous visit. We had then stayed in a lovely old, rambling guest house surrounding a beautiful Chinese garden. Now we were in a tall glass international hotel run by a Swiss-trained Singaporean.

Second, I was surprised at the frankness of some of our discussions. In formal situations, China's position might be clear and consistent. But informal conversations revealed other streams of belief and action. Perhaps I had thought that the tanks crushing the student protest would have crushed all comment. I discovered that dreams and aspirations are tenacious and enduring.

They were flying kites in Tienanmen Square. Mary Cheung, World Vision's communications director in Hong Kong, said, 'They're very symbolic. The people fly them because they have an appearance of freedom but they're still attached to the ground by strings.'

This day in Tienanmen Square the young official accompanying us, tall, in his twenties, said, 'This is the place to take a photo because it is the place of the martyrs'. We were standing in front of the statue to the martyrs of the Communist Revolution, but he had more recent martyrs in mind. The ones who had used this statue as the centre for a peaceful youth protest that ended on the night of 4 June.

When I didn't get the point he indicated that this was the place where '*we* had gathered'.

I asked him if he had been here on the night the tanks came. He said, 'No. If I had been here on that night I would be in jail now.' As we walked away from the Square he said, 'Change will come in China but now we just have to be patient'.

David Ngai, the executive director of World Vision Hong Kong, pointed out the place where the steps of the martyrs' memorial had been replaced. The new stone obscured the damage done by the tanks which had driven up the steps.

It had last been in the Chinese capital nine years earlier in 1982, when I also accompanied another World Vision president, Stan Mooneyham. It was his last official duty before finishing with World Vision. I recalled how impressed I was with the way the Spirit moved to create friendship between Dr Mooneyham and the officials.

On this second visit I met one man who was in that earlier series of dinners. I think I can find his face in the photographs taken then – Mr Zhu. We greeted each other as old friends. Being an 'old friend' in China was a special honour.

Since I was first in Beijing a lot had changed. Most noticeable was the number of high-rise buildings, especially hotels. There was no suitable international hotel in 1982; now there were dozens.

The fashions had changed in the streets too. People were wearing all sorts of clothes, with both young men and young women smartly dressed. In the old days it was just the Mao suit, grey, green or dark blue. Now there were many colours.

The mood too may have changed, although I could not recollect very strongly what the mood had been nine years before. Certainly people didn't discuss events outside China then. You didn't have frank discussions like the one we had in Tienanmen Square that day. So many people were speaking openly about change now. I felt that the Chinese leadership was quite out of touch with the mass of public opinion. Ordinary people were just being patient, waiting for change to come.

One of our hosts, Mr Jiang, described the different nationalities he worked with. 'The Australians were number one', he said, 'open and easy to make friends.' Of course he would say that to us.

'The Americans are too talkative', he opined. 'They just say

"Hello, hello," "How are you?" and "Goodbye" and act like big brothers.' The English and New Zealanders were too formal: 'High-nosed people'. The Germans were friendly with a sense of humour: 'Very demanding but fair'.

The Chinese are renowned for indirection. Straight answers, for which Australians tend to be unfairly well known, are not part of their make-up. I think the most frightening way to begin a sentence in an official meeting in China is with the words 'Speaking frankly ...'

Much of our official discussion with the Chinese concerned World Vision's earlier response to a flood in AnHui province. The United States contribution to AnHui was only $25,000, this being the Ambassador's limit. At many millions, World Vision's contribution was the biggest international response.

Graeme Irvine pointed out that 'World Vision is a small agency'. Madam Wu of the Ministry of Foreign Affairs said, 'We don't judge a hero by his size'.

Beijing was a beautiful city, reminiscent of Paris and Melbourne. Very wide, tree lined streets. Quite modern. Bicycles everywhere. A lot of vitality and a sense of progress.

Graeme contrasted Beijing with Moscow. In Moscow nothing worked. There were no products in the shops. You could not make international phone calls easily. Faxes did not arrive. The hotel plumbing was ineffective. The laundry service did not work. There was no food. Moscow was very drab, Graeme said.

Beijing by comparison was full of life. People apparently had more freedoms – there was a more free feeling even than in Singapore.

The national strategy was to put economic before political reform. The open policy to the West continued, and openness to restructuring the economic side of Chinese life continued too. One had to say that the Chinese were taking a pragmatic approach.

Of course, issues of political reform were not being dealt with by us, and issues of human rights were definitely not on our host's agenda.

We noted that people who were formally in the progressive reform area of politics were now beginning to emerge again in lower positions. They had been demoted but one suspected they were on their way back. At least this was better than in the old days, when such people would have lost their lives or been put in jail.

Again we saw there was a great deal of hope for reform as long as people were patient.

For one day of our visit we were treated as official tourists, just as we had been a decade before.

The Great Wall and the Ming Tombs had changed quite a lot. Nine years previously one could simply drive up to the Great Wall and start walking. Now it cost money.

They had built a cable car which you could ride for A$5. When you got to the top, you had to pay another few dollars to walk along the Wall. Locals paid much less.

The real price was in pain. The walk was unremittingly downhill. By the time we entered the tourist market at the base of the Wall, our knees were in serious decline.

The Ming Tombs were now the same kind of commercial corner. It cost a few cents to enter the park, but a few dollars to go down into the Tomb. While the admission charges were very low by international standards, it was an indication that the Chinese were doing their best to make the most of the tourist trade.

12 | *If You Were Here, Would You Be Different?*

South Africa 1991

During 1991 I began to realise consciously that I was experiencing an inner journey. The way I wrote in my diaries began to change. I began to write about the places I visited and about how events also had implications for me.

This visit to South Africa led me to reflect on how I might have reacted if I had been born in South Africa – as a white or as a black.

I realised I had more confidence in the ability of my culture and upbringing to shape what I was, than I had in my own ability to shape my culture. How trapped was I in what my society and upbringing said I should be? Would I ever be able to break through and find real truth independent of this socially constructed reality? These were questions I now consciously began to explore by placing myself into the shoes of six of the impressive people I met in South Africa.

At the end of my visit to South Africa I joined the privileged few. I boarded a jumbo jet, silently complaining about another long flight in 'the big bus in the sky'.

What would I leave behind in South Africa? A nation sitting on a powder keg. A country of astounding wealth and privilege, yet unparalleled poverty, oppression and injustice. There was change coming in South Africa, but would it come soon enough to avoid a violent catharsis?

As I prepared to leave, I found myself wondering where I would fit if I had been born South African rather than Australian. If one were born black, options were limited. If one were born white, options were limited in different ways.

Would I be like the sixteen-year-old waitress at Mike's Kitchen? She told us she had been born in Ireland and come to South Africa as a small child. We told her we had just spent the day in Soweto.

'Oooh', she said, her pretty eyes widening under her long blond fringe, 'we took a wrong turn into Soweto last year. I was *so* scared. I just covered my eyes and screamed until we got out of there.'

Then the clichéd comment of the alleged non-racist. 'Not that I dislike the blacks, mind you. I'm not a racist or anything. I work with them here every day.'

We obligingly filled out the form entering her in the Waitress of the Year competition. If she won, one of us would go to Mauritius.

'From Australia?' I asked.

'Maybe not', she replied. Such privileges depended on where you live.

If you lived in Soweto you didn't think about holidays in Mauritius. Or anywhere.

Could the luck of birth have found me like Tabo, the young father who sold marijuana for a living? Well, I guessed he sold marijuana. What I actually asked him was 'How do you earn money?'

'I buy and sell', he replied – the common euphemism for pushers of low-grade escape drugs.

'How much do you earn?'

'I buy for about 120 rand and sell for 350. About twice a month.' A good mark-up and enough to keep his wife and two children fed and clothed.

Fifteen years ago he abandoned school. Everyone did. The government was insisting that their education be conducted in Afrikaans instead of their own language. The education was second class anyway. Classes were boycotted, schools and books burned. Only a few went back to school when it became quiet.

Tabo was typical of this third generation of apartheid blacks. They knew no other world except enforced racial and ethnic separation. They had no education. They had few analytical skills and no world view beyond Soweto. They distrusted de Klerk and all the 'settlers'. Worse, they were losing faith in Mandela and other black leaders.

The general view in the West was that de Klerk was a hero, Mandela a saint, and progress towards a multi-racial New South Africa inevitable. The view from Soweto was different, even if the hope was equally optimistic.

'How is life different for you since the changes in South Africa?' I asked a group gathered for cards and beer in a Soweto home – a *shebeen*. A vivacious young woman with a big smile framed between huge gold earrings stood up to me.

'What changes?' she demanded. 'Nothing's changed here. There is still no employment. The garbage collection doesn't work. People are killed.'

'Do you think war is inevitable?'

'Inevitable? It's already here. We are being killed right now. The hostel people [the Zulus] came to this corner' – she pointed at the street corner 100 metres away – 'and attacked us. We had no arms. So we threw stones.' It began to sound like the Gaza Strip. 'Then the police came. Did they disarm the hostel people? No. They shot at us! My cousin was killed. Right here.' She pointed out into the street. More than sixty people died in one weekend that month.

'But', I said defensively, 'Mr Vlok, the Minister for Law and Order, told me that this is definitely against policy. He said if they find police taking sides, they take action to deal with them. Transfer them. He said this sort of thing is a mistake.' There was a loud communal groan of derision.

'Is it a mistake when you kill someone? Aim the gun and pull the trigger?' she asked, tears of anger rimming her eyes. The question hung in the air. It seemed impossible to answer.

If I were her, would I have been any different?

What if I had been born in Adriaan Vlok's shoes? Would I have been like him?

Vlok, the Minister responsible for police and internal security for the previous four years, was charming. Soft-spoken and reasonable, he smiled easily and accepted any question with disarming humility. I thought we must have attended similar schools for *How to Handle Tricky Interviews*. He avoided the direct answer by generalising.

'Two World Vision workers in Queenstown were detained last week under the police powers to detain without charge. I wonder why the police need such powers in the New South Africa?' I asked.

'Well, I am sorry to hear that. I do not know the particular details, of course.' Well, not *of course*. We did mention it last week when setting up the interview, and we did fax details to your office a few days ago, but we know you are a busy man. 'The police only have this power to detain people suspected of being involved in terrorism.'

Terrorism? Excuse me, we are talking about World Vision field workers.

'Frankly, I hope we do not need this power much longer. For the time being it is necessary. I look forward to the day when everyone will be safe and the police can get on with their real job of catching criminals.'

So say all of us. He had the technique down pat, and I am not Jana Wendt.

While we set up some concluding camera shots, the Minister moved to another part of his office. He had his photo taken with a slim, muscular woman with short blond hair and a nervous smile. 'This lady is a captain in our police force', Vlok informed us as his PR photographer went about his work. 'She has just completed her doctorate and I am receiving a copy.'

'We don't have such attractive police captains in Australia', quipped our cameraman.

'Or as well-educated', I added, attempting to balance the sexism.

There was good-natured laughter. Such nice people. Such nice surroundings. So easy to like. Would I have been any different in their circumstances?

Circumstances at the African Methodist Episcopal Church in Pimsville, Soweto, were quite different. The road was muddy and pot-holed. We needed a guide for directions and personal security.

On the way to church we ran a police speed trap. They pulled us over. My colleague, Cathy, the only black person in the car, began to explain to the junior officer that she was taking three Australian visitors to church. He was very polite but lacked authority to do anything except issue the ticket.

Steve, our cameraman/director, stepped out of the car. He was wearing a military style raincoat over a white collar and tie. 'I know how to get out of a car like a policeman', he bragged. He stood upright and glared fiercely down the road at the senior man in charge. When the senior policeman saw him, he stiffened and waved us on.

'South African justice', Steve commented cynically. Cathy was saved from embarrassment towards her guests, but I felt we had just re-cemented one loosening brick of apartheid.

The church service began at ten o'clock with two-thirds of the congregation still to come. A choir of all ages assembled in the courtyard. They began to sing in harmonies that invaded every pore and brought thrill and pleasure. It was like being immersed in a warm musical bath. The music massaged a troubled soul and relaxed a mind occupied with too many things. I was there to worship, and suddenly God felt very close.

This service was unlike anything in Australia. Music occurred at every turn of the prayer book page. The preacher stood to preach and launched into song after his fourth sentence. All joined him.

A woman led in prayer. Her prayer was in the local language, but her passion communicated universally. Her voice rose in volume and pitch, and her breathing degenerated to asthmatic grunts. The pain and brokenness of her prayer pierced every heart.

The preacher preached – man, did he preach! The method was fire and brimstone, exhortatory, loud and energetic. The content was the opposite – reconciliation, forgiveness for the past wrongs of the oppressors. David's love and forgiveness to his rebel son Absalom was compared with the father's forgiveness of the New Testament Prodigal Son.

Preacher and translator alternated. Sometimes the preacher led in the local language, sometimes in English. The translator never faltered. They maintained the rhythmical dance, lifting us higher and higher to the point where the preacher asked if we can be like Christ who, while nailed to a cross, could still say, 'Father, forgive them, for they don't know what they are doing'.

It was a political message undoubtedly. It was a message of justice and hope for the New South Africa. If I had been this preacher, would this have been my message?

Not far away was the home of Walter Sisulu. He welcomed us at short notice. Interviews with ANC leaders were hard to get in those days, but Sisulu responded through the approach of a mutual friend. The home was modest, small and typical of Soweto. There was a small Mercedes in the driveway. Since I coveted it, I did not accuse others.

Sisulu was grandfatherly and slow in manner, but his mind and his commitment were strong. After we had talked for almost an hour I asked him, 'Despite everything that has happened to you, how do you remain so positive and peaceful?'

To me the moderate peacefulness of this echelon of black leadership was simply miraculous. Despite the death of many friends, despite decades of imprisonment, despite the apparently unending hopelessness, they kept their dream alive. It was perhaps the finest story of hope this century.

Sisulu's answer was a commercial for the ANC dream of a just and fair, multi-racial South Africa. This dream had sustained him. It still did.

The response was unsatisfactory to me. What inner force, what external force, can maintain such strength? Surely this was beyond ordinary humans. Surely this was the work of God. Sisulu made no such claim.

Would I be like Sisulu if I had been born in his shoes? At last here was one question I could answer with accurate candour. No. I was simply not that strong and good a man. I was too sinful. I coveted his motor car. I was pleased when an unjust system permitted me to run speed traps with impunity. I was glad I didn't have to live here and wrestle with the day to day realities of injustice and privilege. I was leaving tonight. I would be glad to escape.

13 *Interludes*

London and Assisi

One great blessing of my work has been the privilege to travel, but very often travel can be a burden. A jumbo jet is not nearly as comfortable as your own home, no matter how much the advertisements dress it up. Also, much of my travel is to places lots of others would not particularly want to go. And the things I do there are often hard and painful – physically and emotionally.

Nevertheless, if you travel from Melbourne, you will often find yourself 'in transit' through a tourist destination. I have had many such interludes. A few hours or a day or two. Sometimes I pack things into an overseas trip to try to get the most value out of the considerable cost. During such trips, a day or two break in the middle is essential for the health of the body, mind and soul.

Here are notes from two such interludes, the first in London, England, the other in Assisi, Italy.

At first it may seem unclear why I include these in a book about an inner journey. There is a reason. I don't want to give the impression that my inner journey towards justice was planned and organised. In truth, I did not seek it. Nor did I willingly embrace it as I discovered that something was going on in my soul. Often I was in denial.

Besides, there were many easy distractions. It was easy, as I did in London this day, just to switch off, enter the present and fully enjoy it. These accounts are included to show how much I enjoyed the opportunity to escape. There was nothing bad about this; indeed, it was necessary therapy. Yet too much of this kind of sheer tourism could become indulgent.

The visit to Assisi began with the same escape motif. Yet I realised that more was going on in my soul. I could not simply be a tourist in a place which commemorated the life and work of this great saint of the Christian faith. My diaries fail to record the mystical nature of this visit, and perhaps that is inevitable; nothing specially different happened, and my diaries tend to record only what did happen. Yet later I saw the Assisi visit in a special light. The souvenirs and books I bought are prominent around our house today, speaking to a special and needed kind of spirituality.

London, 1992

It was the fourth or fifth time I'd stayed at the Alexander Hotel, which was really just a series of tenement houses that had been converted. I presumed they were built sometime last century in South Kensington, not too far from Harrods and the Kensington Palace. You could walk into London from there if you were not in a hurry, but the tube was handy and only 80p.

The hotel had three stories and my room was on the top, with a window that peeped over the wall into the street. It was not well ventilated and rather humid, so I was sweaty soon after my morning bath.

I sent a long fax to Judy and wrote some postcards, then at 10.30 went to the tube. I had no particular aim for the day. Originally I thought I would go to Windsor Castle, but that could wait another time.[1] After a week of being organised almost every second of the day, it would be good to *waste* time productively.

I looked at The Maze (otherwise known as the map of the London Underground) and decided to buy a ticket for Piccadilly Circus.

En route to the station I bought a paper and looked up the movies. The Swiss Centre was showing a mixture of foreign films. They had a new print of *Belle du Jour* and a 1991 film *La Double Vie de Veronique*. This won the Best Actress award for the lead, Irene Jacobs, at the Cannes Film Festival. I thought I might see one of these in the afternoon.

The Underground disgorged me at Piccadilly Circus by the 'Eros' statue. Actually, it isn't a statue of 'Eros' at all, but of the 'Spirit of Charity' in the likeness of some bloke who used to own all the land round these parts. But the locals had clearly placed a more carnal interpretation on the statue and it had stuck.

I was surprised at the huge number of people around. It was

---

[1] *Carpe diem* (seize the day). The fire at Windsor Castle changed the look of the place forever. When you think of doing something, do it.

obviously the height of the summer tourist season. All day I kept hearing accents from European countries, and from America, Japan and Australia. Hardly a Brit in sight.

I wandered into a huge fun parlour with a galaxy of video games. Among them was the latest rage, 'Virtual Reality'. For £3 you could put on a thing like a motor cycle helmet and be transported right inside a game. In one of them you 'drove' through a video city shooting at huge robots. The action was visible on six television monitors so you could see what each player could see. Everyone played against the others. I remembered watching the Natalie Wood movie *Brainstorm* in which they predicted this exact phenomenon.

At midday I sat at a table in a pizza restaurant and ordered mushroom pizza and red wine for lunch. I watched the passing parade of tourists and young people. The youth of London looked like the youth of most other places. But then, maybe they *were* the youth of other places.

After lunch I wandered down the Haymarket and soon found myself at Trafalgar Square. What a crowd! There were more people than pigeons.

The vendors with the bird seed franchise were cleaning up. For 50p they gave you a little cup of seed so you could tempt pigeons to come and excrete on your shoulders, claw holes in your cashmere and peck blood out of your fingers. The tourists were lapping it up.

I wondered why I hadn't brought my camera. Perhaps it was that it had been three years since I'd been in London during the summer, and all I remembered was grey boring streets, none of which I wanted to photograph again. Here there were wonderful shots of people all over the place.

I sat on the rails opposite the National Museum and consulted my map. A woman in her twenties came up to me and said, 'Excuse me, do you know the way to Oxford Street?'

She had a German accent (or was it Icelandic? I always get them confused) and another woman hovered in the background with one of those I'm-not-game-to-speak-English expressions on her face. I recognised it immediately since I have seen a similar expression from the inside. I was tempted to say, 'No, but I know the way to San Jose'. However, valour conquered indiscretion, and I said, 'Yes', pointing out on the map where I was sitting and where Oxford Street was.

'You just go down there to Piccadilly Circus, then keep going around to the right.'

'I go Piccadilly Circus?' she asked, looking at the map as if it were instructions for assembling a nuclear accelerator.

'Just down there', I said, pointing down the street.

'Sank you', she said and wandered off in the general direction of *down there* explaining things to her friend. I'm sure they got lost.

I wandered into the first of half a dozen book stores that I poked around during the day. I found two interesting word books. One was a dictionary of problem words and phrases that are often misused – for example, Hamlet says, 'Alas, poor Yorick, I knew him, Horatio', but for some reason everyone says, 'Alas, poor Yorick. I knew him well'. The other was a book of difficult words, like *imbroglio*. Did you know the 'g' is silent? Nothing to get into an imbroglio about.

Next I found a market with lots of craft shops selling local and overseas crafts, including the same things you can buy in World Vision International Clubs handcrafts program but much dearer. Things looked cheap until you realised £20 was really $52. A Gaelic trio played music that sounded like it was being dragged through a tea strainer.

I stepped into a lane of seventeenth century houses and found a peaceful place away from the tourists. It was only about two metres wide and all the houses had bay windows bending outwards. I guessed they were all offices now.

At the end of the lane I was back among the crowd, and heading towards Covent Garden. I could hear music and applause. I could not have planned a better place to go on a summer Sunday.

Covent Garden was pulsing with vitality. Here people of all types, colours and designs mingled like cassata. A shirtless guy had green, yellow and red hair that stuck half a metre in the air. A giggle of Japanese girls squashed into a doorway eating frozen yoghurt. A girl with a French accent (or maybe it was Icelandic) said, 'Sir, can you make a picture for us please?' Fortunately her camera made the picture. I just pointed it and pressed the button. Beautifully framed.

Little kids were having their faces painted. Bigger kids were having multi-coloured strings woven into their hair. All sorts were having their profiles sketched by sidewalk artists. And everyone was flowing past hundreds of street stalls with every imaginable kind of craft. Ceramic animals. Jewellery made from anything. Pens lathed out of wood. Even baskets woven by Kurds out of telephone wire.

There were food stalls and restaurants, but few places you could buy a Coke.

In and around all this was street theatre. Robotic dancing. A Glynn Nicholas type doing all sorts of indescribable things with kids in the crowd. A man who twirled on his head (wearing a crash helmet). Jugglers. A man who picked pockets and whipped a bra out from under one lady's T-shirt (not her bra, although she wasn't sure for a moment).

In another book shop I stood beside a woman who folded up a soft cover book she had been inspecting and put it casually into her handbag. I wanted desperately to turn her in. I watched as she walked out of the shop to join her husband and daughter waiting outside. If I'd been sure that I wouldn't be required to appear at the Old Bailey later, I would have said something. But I was too selfishly concerned for my own unimportant agenda and let the crime go. Why do people do this? Unfathomable.

I bought an ice cream from a counter where a shop assistant cut her finger as I waited. A drop of blood stained the Rocky Road so I asked for plain chocolate. *Can you get AIDS from ice cream?* I wondered.

I decided to make for the Swiss Centre in Leicester Square. The square was always a hive of activity on the weekend evenings, with its cinemas and many restaurants. Drunks and ordinarily happy people sat around, with foreigners arriving on the hour to see the Swiss Centre clock play its many bells. Extremely kitsch, but that brings in the tourists.

It was now almost six o'clock, so I found the cinema with the Bunuel festival and decided to see *The Double Life of Veronica*. It was most mysterious and very spooky. I really enjoyed it.

I joined the madding throng at the Bella Pizza restaurant and had Tagliatelle Bosciajola and a small bottle of Valpolicella. Thus fortified, and feeling like some real escapism, I went to the nine o'clock screening of *The Universal Soldier*, an entirely gratuitous and mega-violent movie about robo-soldiers manufactured out of dead Vietnam vets.

I crammed into the eleven o'clock train to South Kensington with the rest of the Saturday night movie crowd. You certainly can't be alone in London on a Saturday night, although you can still be lonely.

It rained during the night and I awoke to a grey, rainy day. Ahead of me was a flight to LA. A hire car took me to the airport for around A$65. I think London is the only place in the world where hire cars are cheaper than taxis.

Assisi, 1993

I arrived at Rome around 8.15 p.m. and the fun began. I had to pick up a rental car then drive to Assisi, about 120 kilometres away. I had been studying maps and reckoned I knew the way. The problems turned out to be of a different kind. I knew one road was a tollway. I had on my person 6,000 lire, or about A$6.00. Someone had told me the tolls in Italy were big, so I was hardly sure if this would be enough.

No problem, I thought, *I'll just change some money*. All the automatic *Cambio* machines were out of order. At the one teller open at the bank there was a line of at least fifty Japanese waiting for change. I decided to go elsewhere, found the rental car courtesy bus and proceeded to Hertz.

They gave me a Fiat Uno and informed me that if I wanted change I would have to go back to the airport. I got on the bus again and retraced my steps. Eventually, after walking around the terminal, I found a machine that was operating and got some lire. Back on the bus to Hertz, into the car and off.

The little Fiat buzzed along efficiently and reasonably quietly. It would sit on 110–120 except on the steepest hills. I went towards Rome, found the ring road (a huge motorway that circled Rome about twenty kilometres out) and about thirty kilometres later found the A1 north towards Firenze. Soon I came to the toll gates, took my ticket and drove on.

For the next sixty kilometres the slow lane was a constant stream of semi-trailers heading north at around a 100 kilometres per hour. I had never seen so many trucks in one place. The stream never stopped. It became mesmerising. Just as remarkable, there was a similar stream coming south on the other side of the tollway. Clearly goods moved by road in Europe, and at night.

After a while I came to one of my scheduled turn-offs and the exit toll gates. Fortunately this was just like those in France, where they ring up your toll on a display, so I didn't have to try to translate *Cinque mille cento loggio autelegniatto quadriphonico ravioli, gracie.*

It was 4,500 lire, about $4.50, so I would have had enough after all. Never mind; it saved me changing money later.

Now I was on an ordinary highway of good standard, sign-posted with logical signs that were easy to read. I went for about seventeen kilometres before coming to a sign that said *Peruggia/Assisi* and turned off. About eighty kilometres further on another sign said *Assisi* and I was almost there.

Although it was dark I saw plenty of civilisation on the way. Towns and commercial areas hugged the road in most places. Occasionally I would break free for a few kilometres but soon I'd be in the next town. The compactness of Europe is always a surprise to Australians.

Eventually, I saw ahead of me, up on a high hill, the Basilica of Saint Francis at the edge of Assisi. It was still flood-lit at 11.45 p.m.

Now the hard part began. Although I had a map of Assisi and thought I had committed it to memory, I was soon bamboozled. The road was full of twists and turns and hardly any street had a name on it. I drove around for fifteen minutes, stopping about four times to re-orientate myself. Each time I thought I had it sorted out, but then got confused again.

Eventually I asked a man who was closing some shutters on a hotel where the Hotel Giotto was. He took three steps back and pointed up over the top of the nearby buildings. High on the hill, about 200 metres away, was the roof of my hotel.

He explained how to get there. 'Out the gate, the road turns around a bit until you get to the traffic light. Then go straight ahead and up the hill.'

I found my way out the gate (the city is walled) and down a stretch of road that twisted like spaghetti for 200 metres. At the traffic light – just one, permanently red, next to a sign which I translated as *No Entry* – there was a narrow fork. Both directions seemed 'straight ahead', but only one went up; and since I had actually gone down the other one twice already that evening, I went up. Beyond the *No Entry* sign (which fortunately also said, in English, *Except for residents and hotel guests*) I found my hotel.

The night porter took my passport and car keys and gave me a room key. The check-in procedure at Italian hotels was the fastest in the world. The room was simple. It had a painted concrete floor, a single bed with teak laminex bed-head, a wardrobe, a desk and a vinyl covered lounge chair. There was no room for a second bed. The ensuite had a shower but no screens or curtains, so when you showered, the whole bathroom got a spray.

It was 12.30 a.m. by now so I didn't need encouragement to sleep. Although the bed was banana shaped, I slept well until noises on the solid floors outside woke me just before my alarm around 7.40 a.m.

I pulled up the shutters and the view took my breath away.

I looked over the roofs of Assisi. In the foreground was a jumble of stone buildings in local pink and white stone, tiny gardens and a few tall, slim pine trees. Beyond was a wide, wide valley with farms and towns spreading into the distant haze. Just beautiful. I wanted to stay forever.

I spent the morning bringing my notes up to date. It seemed a shame to work rather than go sight-seeing, but I felt better getting my responsibilities out of the way first. Every now and then I could look out the window and say, 'I am really here'.

By the time I'd got everything done and faxes sent, it was almost noon. I wandered out and found my way to the Basilica of Saint Francis. Not surprisingly it was just closing for lunch, to re-open at 2.00. I bought a local guide book and wandered along until I found the city square.

On the way a man in a black trench coat looked at me as if he was trying to get my attention. A few minutes later I spotted him again and he made eye contact with me. A minute later I was standing by a stone wall admiring the view when he came up beside me. He was in his early 50s.

'Lovely view', he said in an American accent. 'Where are you from?'

'Melbourne', I replied, then added 'Australia' in case he hadn't noticed the word written in 500 point type on my cap.

'Yes, I saw the word *Austria* and realised it was in English.'

I thought this a funny thing to say, and I noticed he was looking at me in a decidedly funny way. In fact, he was *leering* at me. Suddenly I became convinced he was trying to pick me up!

I was surprised at how revolted I felt by this. If you'd asked me whether I would have been disgusted by such an approach, I would have said yes; but I was *really* disgusted. My stomach turned and I felt deeply insulted that this jerk would think whatever he was thinking about me.

I had attained an insight into another aspect of injustice.

I said, 'It *is* a lovely view' and turned and walked away. Out of the corner of my eye I saw him follow, but when I turned down a side street, I saw him no more.

The rest of Assisi was magnificent, wondrous, inspirational.

I had lunch at a restaurant on a first floor verandah overlooking the main town square. Many buildings were from the time of Saint Francis, the eleventh century and before. The place was full of tourists and so many teenagers. It seemed that every second person was carrying a back-pack.

After lunch I found the Church of St Clare. She was a follower of Saint Francis and began an order called the *Poor Clares*. Her tomb was downstairs. As usual, the relics of the saint were buried under the high altar, but steps led down to a crypt from where one could view the coffin.

I meandered back in the direction of the Basilica and stopped briefly in a church which had been built over another church that dated from Roman times. Unfortunately the steps leading down to these Roman foundations were closed.

While walking I realised that I spent a lot of my life writing things to Judy in my head. Whenever I travelled, I was constantly shaping things I wanted to tell her. I hadn't realised how much this made me think about my family. This was therapeutic for me – another way of being with loved ones when not actually with them.

Around 3.00 p.m. I came to the Basilica of Saint Francis itself and spent the next hour and a half looking it over. There were two churches, one built right on top of the other. That meant there were actually three, since there was also a crypt under the lower one.

Soon after Saint Francis died in 1232 they built the lower church to house his tomb. By 1239 the Pope had arranged for a larger church to be built on top of the first one. Last century, the Pope arranged for a crypt to be excavated under the lower one so that the coffin of Saint Francis could be viewed. They also checked the contents and confirmed (they don't say how) that the relics were indeed those of Francis of Assisi.

Naturally, the lower church was gloomy. Like many old churches it had a bunch of extra chapels leading off left and right, each with its own elaborate decorations. There was no doubt that regular worship in such a place could be a rich experience. So much had been put into the surroundings that you could reflect on different elements of the artistry every time you came. My see-it-all-in-one-afternoon approach couldn't do justice to the work of the builders and artists involved.

Downstairs the crypt was bare. The sides of a stone coffin were displayed behind glass. Upstairs the upper church was tall and light by contrast. Around the walls were twenty-eight large frescoes, mostly by Giotto, depicting events in Francis' life. It was quite interesting to make the life journey – even if some of my reflecting was interrupted by a monk explaining the frescoes to a German tour party.

I bought some souvenirs and wandered slowly back to the hotel.

14 | *A Country on the Mend*

Vietnam 1992

By 1992 my diaries had begun to reflect the complexity of the development situations I encountered. Every conversation was a chance to get a new insight into cross-cultural communications. Every project activity became the signal for another question or observation.

At first I had only understood things as they were presented to me – "Here is the dam, Mr Hunt" and I would see a dam of water. Now I would wonder how the dam changed the power balance in the community, whether it caused environmental damage by changing the grazing patterns of the cattle, how it might change the role of women and children who used to see themselves as water carriers.

Vietnam in 1992 was a rich place to make such explorations. It was exploding into the world, and struggling to come to grips with the rigidity of a Communist system against the freedom of markets.

Welcome to Economy Class again. World Vision Australia had an enlightened travel policy which predated my leadership. Most people travelled Economy Class. All flights within Australia, and international flights under ten hours, were taken in Economy Class.

However, the organisation had learned that there was a trade-off when longer flights were involved. Someone who travelled twenty hours in a plane was going to be very tired at the end and all the more so if squeezed into a small seat, and surrounded by the West Los Angeles Baton Twirlers Club making their first visit to Australia. That happened to me once. One pre-teen girl was cute. Twenty-five of them were a cacophony.

With lack of sleep and jetlag, long distance travellers were usually unproductive when they arrived. Some wallowed in a daze for days. Our experience was that the extra investment in a Business Class seat (never in First Class, unless some generous airline offered a free upgrade), often made our people more productive more quickly. If it was going to cost money to get people overseas for a conference or project evaluation, we wanted to get the best out of that investment.

I had been delighted over the years to discover how many World Vision people flew Economy anyway, even when the policy entitled them to the extra comfort.

On this journey Thai Airlines brought us safely to Hanoi. With me were colleagues Roger Walker and Boyne Alley and World Vision Australia Board member, Noel Vose. Our Vietnamese colleagues, Mrs Lan, Esther and Victor, were at the airport to meet us and see us safely into the Lotus Hotel in town.

This was a pleasant dive with a black and white TV, working fridge, hot water, flush toilet and clean linen. Apart from the eight flights of steps up to the room in thirty-five degree heat, it was fine. The simple 'Guide for Visitors' produced by the local World Vision office recommended that one not leave one's shirts on the floor as friendly mice would eat small holes in them. 'The mouse', said the Guide, 'comes with the room (no extra charge)'.

The Guide also said that there was no need to tip in Vietnam. Yet the porter stood still when he dropped my suitcase and said the only English that sprang to mind: 'One dollar'. Since many Vietnamese would not earn one dollar a day, I felt that price was a bit steep. But what could I do? I gave him a dollar, thus contributing to the distortion of the local economic order.

Roger threatened Noel and Boyne with his 'special gift for first-time visitors to Vietnam' – snake liquor. This is the vile concoction that has the full body of a snake curled up in the bottle.

The drive in from the airport was a non-stop interrogation. Boyne and Noel asked questions about everything that moved and most things that didn't. Why is that there? Who built that? Why? How big? When? Why? These were questions that, for the most part, the local people had never thought to ask. (How would you answer someone who asked, as you passed the Melbourne Cricket Ground, 'Why did they build it there?')

At four we went to the Australian Embassy. The last time I was here we had lunch with some people from Son La province. This had been an utter surprise to me as I had been totally unaware of our involvement in the province. Yet here were these people thanking me and giving me gifts for something World Vision Australia had done for them. I graciously accepted their thanks, praising God for colleagues who didn't need to ask my permission to help the poor.

This time I was better prepared. No-one turned up to shower gifts upon us. Indeed, the Ambassador had heard we were coming and left town. The First Secretary had suddenly found reasons to be out too. We were met by an AIDAB project officer who had been in Hanoi a mere week.

We stopped by the Metropole Hotel for refreshment. The afternoon was hot but not unbearable. Rain seemed close by. Bob Seiple, president of World Vision US, had stayed at the Metropole in the early days. Roger thought Bob may have had the original bed; it had such a sag in the middle that he and his wife Margaret rolled together and the mattress touched the floor. How Roger knew this, decency prevented me from asking.

The Metropole had been transformed since then. It was very French in the best colonial style, right down to a chef named Didier. As we walked in Boyne looked at me accusingly and said, 'Were *you* the one who chose that other hotel? This seems more like it'. Of course, he protested, he was only joking. A room here cost US$265 a night – more than the average Vietnamese earned in a year.

Mrs Lan walked us around like a tour guide showing off a local historical site. Then she directed us to the lounge bar where we sank down into a rich black leather Chesterfield.

'What would you like?' asked the waiter.

Mrs Lan said quickly (as if she had been preparing all day), 'Ice cream'.

Now there was something you couldn't get in Hanoi last time.

Roger wanted to buy some water so we decided to go for a walk in the city centre. Hanoi was still a place where you could walk free from badgering. The same could not be said of Saigon, where hordes of street kids were likely to descend on you en masse, emptying your pockets with such daring that you were left gasping at their audacity.

Regrettably, the begging industry was beginning to take hold.

And it was an industry. Equally regrettable was the fact that it was, comparatively speaking, lucrative. A few dollars a day earned from foreigners was more than a worker might earn from more productive enterprise. Two or three beggars encountered us but they were not persistent in their advances.

More insistent were the newspaper boys anxious to sell me a copy of *Vietnam Investment Adviser*. This was not a newspaper for which I had much fascination. I asked one newspaper boy if it had a girl on page three and he showed me instead a magazine with a dull faced naked woman on the cover. Served me right for trying to be funny. I didn't buy it, either.

A man sat on a corner with two air pumps, a hand pump and a foot pump, providing a service to cyclo owners and other bicyclists. Dozens of people were set up with two square feet of groceries for sale. Bigger shops were only a metre or two long. A jewellery store also sold lacquerware and ancient fob watches with names like Omega, Longines and Skuda. Skuda?

Noel decided to buy a four-section lacquerware set with intricate inlays of duck egg shell for just $15. A silver bracelet was only $10, but I wasn't sure whether it would go over my daughters' hands. 'Too big for me', said the shop assistant, sliding the bracelet over the slimmest hand in the Orient. *My signet ring would slide over that hand*, I thought to myself.

As we walked along women rushed over to greet Roger. Former paramours or his Vietnamese wife's cousins? 'They remember me because I bought some maps from them', he explained. 'Sure, Roger. And I bought some chewing gum once at a shop in Knox City, and the owner remembers my children's birthdays now.' Pull the other one.

The ladies did try to sell us maps. We bought postcards instead. Ten thousand dong for ten – about ten cents each. The 'Hanoi' set was 15,000 dong. To a finance man like Boyne, 15,000 anything is a number to be decimated. He steadfastly refused to purchase the set at 15,000, trying to beat the shopkeeper down to ten. She was already offering her 'best price'.

The impasse was resolved in the usual fashion. Boyne walked away. She didn't call out. At the next shop, another cousin greeted Roger and offered the same postcards for 14,000. 'A veritable bargain', pronounced Boyne. He'd saved himself ten cents.

We drove around Hanoi the next morning. Many women wore conical cane hats tied under the chin with colourful silk; Boyne was later to discover that such hats were scratchy if worn by bald men. Many men wore green pith helmets.

We were on the way to meet Dr Ngo Van Hop, Director of International Cooperation in the Ministry of Health, and Dr Vin, who travelled with our film team last time I was here and was head of the government department that related to foreign aid agencies.

Dr Hop's top priority was community health centres. Thirty per cent were good, he said; forty per cent were OK; thirty per cent were bad.

'Why?' I asked.

'The salary from the community is low. It has not kept pace with other incomes and local costs, so it is hard to get people to staff the centres. The State has agreed to pay two-thirds of salaries at clinics in remote mountainous regions. Local district committees have the control now. So about half have adequate salaries.'

Another of the unintended consequences of the move to a free market.

I found myself wondering, *Where is the safety net for the poor?* The changes in the economy were the right ones. Many of the formerly poor had now entered the economy as entrepreneurs and small business operators. They had moved from poverty into the new middle classes. This was good. But many others were still unable to make the leap into the middle classes. Their capacity to contribute was not utilised. For them, conditions were getting worse.

Private medical services were growing rapidly. For the poor, who could not afford the new private doctors, the State-run medical system was deteriorating further from already impossibly low levels. Unless something was done to provide a safety net, life would become increasingly intolerable at the bottom of society. As the average level of wealth rose, and as the average quality of life improved, the gap between rich and poor would grow – not merely because the rich would be getting richer (that would be tolerable) but also because the poor would be getting poorer. And their ability to participate in the benefits of an increasingly vigorous economy would diminish. This was intolerable.

There were 4,000 private pharmacies already and they were growing fast. Pharmacists were opening chains of stores with the only link being the name of the qualified pharmacist. The rich could have any medicine they liked now. Not so the poor.

We left Dr Hop and drove through the bicycle-infested streets to visit the Cancer Institute. An Australian cobalt radiotherapy machine, superseded at home, was to be installed.

The whole place was full of incongruity. Dickens with lasers.

We were shown the existing radiotherapy machine in a concrete bunker out the back. Czechoslovakian technology from 1973. The machine was so old, we were told, that treatments which should take forty seconds, took four minutes. I found it hard to tell how well they were dealing with this technology, but then I was totally untrained. I trusted the experts we had sent to ensure they did it right. But my intuition was flashing 'Danger!'

With confused feelings about the quality and direction of health care in Vietnam, we motored across town. We were going to have 'Kentucky Fried Fish' for lunch.

We stopped in a narrow street, climbed a thin staircase and squeezed in with half of Hanoi. The whole front of the house was open to the street below. The buildings opposite were close and the branches of huge trees between filled the view. It was noisy but comparatively cool.

The menu consisted of just one dish: Yellow Fish. And an amazing (and secret) collection of herbs and spices.

A frying pan was placed on a terra cotta flower pot with a charcoal fire in it. Some greens were thrown into the pan; it looked like some kind of aromatic grass. Special oil. Fish sauce. Spring onions. Peanuts. Sticky noodles on the side. *Deee-licious*.

After lunch we visited the School of Pharmacy. We met Professor Do. He was very enthusiastic about the Drug Information System from Iowa University. One CD ROM disc held all references from 1/85 to 4/92. A complete library he could hold in his hand.

This was an American product, and American companies could not trade with Vietnam – it was still the enemy in 1992. But it was 'sanitised' by coming from Curtin University in Perth.

'The help from World Vision is very precious', said Professor Do.

We had misgivings. Not about the quality or importance of the work there. It was excellent. However, whereas two years before we were training pharmacists to go into the health system to help the poor, now the graduates were going into private practice. I admit that in their position I would have done the same.

Doubtless Vietnam needed more private pharmacists. They would be good for the economy. But the only system available to the poor was the State health system. We questioned whether providing this training was World Vision work anymore.

Moreover, the new free market in pharmaceuticals meant that hospitals had to compete with the private pharmacies and the many unqualified people selling drugs. And many expatriate Vietnamese in other countries were sending drugs home as well. 'Free market has a good and a bad side', said the Professor. In the market there were even blind people selling drugs. God knows what you got when you asked for Paracetamol.

Everywhere we went we were offered tea and lychees. The lychees were deliciously sweet and juicy. It was impolite to refuse a drink although it was not impolite to leave it untouched.

Next we visited an Evangelical church and Bible school. We met the seventy-nine-year-old pastor, Dr Thu.

Pastor Thu liked to tell the story of how Roger came with the first cheque of $8,000 to rebuild the church. Twenty-five churches had been destroyed. Now they were rebuilding eight. But there had been no help from World Vision since Roger handed over the cheque.

It was tempting to authorise $40,000 to rebuild a church. It would have been a monument to my generosity. I could visit it; 'I made this possible'. But it would be a bad idea, and not just for my soul. Noel said the rebuilding of a church with outside money often created jealousy within the community which inhibited the effectiveness of the church. I wanted them to have their church buildings, but there were better things to do with World Vision's money.

Pastor Thu said, 'Soon we shall have our first graduates from the Bible school. They must have churches to go to.' But what's a *church*?

The going was getting tough, so the tough went shopping. The market streets of Hanoi were marvellous. In those days it was safe to walk. No thief picked our pockets. No shop-keeper charged outrageous prices (just two to three times more than normal). Beggars didn't follow you for blocks saying, 'Father, father, father ... ' like a cracked record.

It was pure joy for all your senses. The shops spilled onto the footpath in a panoply of packaging. Every nook was a shop, every cranny a kiosk.

In the silver shop I mentioned 'bracelets'. Three women thrust dozens of bracelets at me. I put one down. They picked it up and showed it to me again. Soon I was not sure what I'd seen already and what I hadn't. It was an effective sales technique. Did they have 300 bracelets, or ten bracelets which they showed me thirty times?

Boyne succumbed to temptation and bought one of those ludicrous conical hats. He put it on. His appearance had all the elegance of a human lamp shade.

Later at dinner, Noel tried again to find out how the changes in the economy were affecting the poor. 'How can the poorest of the poor be protected?' he asked a professor. Again he got no answers.

On the flight down to Da Nang, Roger discovered a sticker in his box of Uncle Toby's Muesli Bars. It was a mug shot of Susan O'Neill, a member of the Australian Women's Hockey Team bound for Barcelona. Roger stuck it on the aircraft bulkhead. I wondered if Susan ever imagined, when she took up hockey, that her visage would one day adorn a Vietnam Airlines Tupolev aeroplane flying between Hanoi and Da Nang.

In Da Nang, Roman Garcia (ex-Philippines) met us with the rest of the World Vision team. Dr Anne Mattam from India had been there a month.

We checked into the much-improved Bach Dang hotel overlooking the river. Last time I was there we checked in then checked out thirty minutes later. This time everything worked, although when you showered, the whole bathroom got wet (even the toilet roll).

Roger tried the phones next morning. 'Use that one', said the receptionist, pointing to one of two phones on the counter. She looked away, distracted by an American guest who was flirting with her.

Roger dialled the number we wanted in Bangkok. As he waited, the hotel phone rang and the receptionist answered in Vietnamese.

'Hello', said Roger into his phone, 'may I speak to Bryan Truman?'

'Hello?' said the receptionist into her phone. Roger looked up at her and said, 'It's me.'

The receptionist looked confused, then looked at the phone Roger was holding in his hand. 'Oh, sorry', she said, lifting another phone from under the counter. 'Wrong phone.'

Later that day our cars bounced along a rural road to a local health clinic. The clinic chief told Dr Anne that he needed a new birthing table. 'But you have three already', she observed.

'Yes, but only two are working.'

'And how many births do you have a month here?'

'Twelve.'

'Twelve?' said Anne. 'Sounds to me like you already have more birthing tables than you need. You're not likely to ever use more than one at a time.'

'He also wanted a dozen iron beds', she told us later. 'It's just empire building.' Tin generals exist everywhere.

Wherever we went, we endured set pieces of speech making. Everyone was 'so honoured' to have us here. And for our part we were 'so humbled' to be permitted to be in partnership with such a dynamic people as the Vietnamese. Repetition undermines sincerity. It seemed that it was impossible to be too glad to receive us, and it was equally impossible to be too humble in response. You could not overdo humility in this society.

Over dinner that night with Mr Nguyen Dinh An, the Vice Chairman of the People's Committee of the Quang Nam/Da Nang Province, our hosts waxed lyrical about Ho Chi Minh. He was portrayed, in turn, as the best in the world in the following categories: teaching, cooking, soldiering, managing, as a kitchen hand, philosophy, economics, politics. The myths have created a legendary figure.

On the present changes in economic logic our hosts reminded us that Uncle Ho said, 'If socialism doesn't help the poor, it's not worth persevering with'. 'Jesus would agree with that', I offered. 'No *ism* is just if it fails to bring justice to the poor.' This proved a bit hard to translate.

We caught the early flight next morning to Saigon. Roger arranged for a driver and guide to take us to Cu Chi then left to visit the family of his wife, Lien.

At Cu Chi was Saigon's best tourist attraction: part of a network of 200 kilometres of tunnels and underground rooms built during the various wars. A short video presentation prepared us for a tour of the network. The video was a propagandised introduction to the greatness of the people of Cu Chi, who single-handedly drove off, in turn, the French, the Americans, the malaria and the common cold.

Heroes and heroines abounded. Here was Lam, who dug four kilometres of tunnels, on three levels, despite arthritis and a crippled left foot. And here was Truong, who at thirteen was already competent with rifle and rocket grenade launcher, yet too small to stand in the trenches. So she balanced across the chasm, ruining the prospects of hundreds of American young men every day. She was credited with thousands of enemy dead, many destroyed by antitank mines she whipped up in her backyard kitchen along with the rice and chocolate cake she made for her fellow soldiers.

Well, not quite. But you get the idea.

Despite the propaganda, the true story was incredible enough. The tunnels were fascinating and showed quietly and clearly the amazing endurance of these people. They indicated the extent to which they suffered and the privations they accepted. They presented the indomitable spirit of people who wanted freedom and self-determination. They still deserved better than they had got.

15 | *Drinking From Ancient Wells*

Israel and the Occupied Territories 1992

There are few better places in the world to explore the relationship between Occupier and the Occupied than the Middle East. In Israel one encounters a vigorous debate around justice that is much more open and free than in many countries. One can quickly see the implications of stereotyping and myth-making as tools for creating and maintaining race hatred. And, as I had discovered in my earlier visit, one can come under personal attack without too much provocation on one's own part.

My next visit to Israel and the Occupied Territories was prompted by the desire of the Archbishop of Canterbury to officially open a West Bank community centre that World Vision Australia had funded and which was to be dedicated to the memory of the late Archbishop of Melbourne, David Penman.

Again there were plenty of incidents on which to reflect. World Vision's own response to development now clearly recognised that the roots of poverty often lie in oppressive structures. Our president reinforced the need for World Vision to respond by standing with oppressed people.

The experiences culminated in an extraordinary visit with a Serbian-Australian sponsor to see her sponsored child. As we spent the day together we heard her own story about oppression at the hands of Croatians that, for me, resonated with the Israeli/Palestinian experience. Yet I was amazed to discover that, while it was possible for her to see the prejudice of oppression in someone else's story, it was harder to see it in her own.

On the flight north from Australia I read *From Beirut to Jerusalem*,[1] a big thick book written by Thomas Friedman, an American Jew who was *New York Times* correspondent in Beirut and Jerusalem in the 1980s. The writer was both a political journalist and a Jew who had bought the whole Israel myth as a young man, but then had to face the reality of the way the Israel dream was creating injustice for the Palestinians. His viewpoint was uncommonly relevant.

At Zurich the connection to Tel Aviv was on Swissair, so I was spared the kind of interrogation I'd experienced when travelling with El Al two years before. Nevertheless, State Security conducted a security check of all checked-in bags, which required plenty of time before the flight. They opened my bag and held over it a machine that looked and sounded like a giant hair drier with a spotlight on the front of it. God knows what it was looking for, but they didn't seem to find anything. Except a pair of smelly socks and a windscreen chamois that I tried to explain was a towel. Very funny people, these Australians.

Bill Warnock, our Jerusalem representative, was at Tel Aviv airport to meet me. We offered a lift to part of an American consulate family whose driver had not turned up. The roads were clear, but snow drifts a foot deep lay by the roadside.

The next day we were supposed to accompany the Archbishop of Canterbury, George Carey, to a service at St George's Cathedral. By 11.00 a.m. he had not turned up. We discovered that the Archbishop could not cross into Israel. The bridge at the Jordan was under three feet of water. There was speculation about how they could get him there. Sensible people would have sent a helicopter (I suspect the British embassy suggested this), but only a neutral helicopter would be acceptable to both Israel and Jordan. I didn't happen to have one with me.

We sat in the home of Kamil Nasser, head of the YMCA, waiting for news. The big talk in Jerusalem was the Israeli government's provocative action of arresting twelve alleged conspirators and planning to deport them. One of them was Ghassan Jarrar, the Deputy Director of the Outreach Program of the Beit Sahour Rehabilitation Centre run by the YMCA and supported by World Vision (we visited it the next day). For three years, said Kamil, Jarrar had said

---

[1] Farr, Straus & Giroux, 1989.

nothing which could be considered inciting – even to his wife, Kamil joked.

'It is just an excuse', he said. 'Just three days earlier the authorities changed his green card to an orange card. This effectively gave him an absolute clearance to travel between the Occupied Territories and Jerusalem and even overseas if he wanted to.' In order to get this change in card, he must have been given an absolute security clearance; yet three days later he was a security risk worthy of deportation. It was a joke, and a very cynical one.[2]

Fortunately there was more than one way across the Jordan (but only if you were the Archbishop of Canterbury) and he arrived four hours later. The service went ahead then at 2.00 p.m.

The Archbishop seemed a down-to-earth chap; I thought he'd fit in well at my Doncaster Community Church of Christ, although I sensibly refrained from saying this to him. Jean Penman[3] was present with her chaplain, the Rev Jenny Rockwell. Special seats were reserved for visitors and dignitaries at the front of the congregation, although visiting clergy of bishop rank and above were seated in the choir stalls inside the sanctuary (St George's is a small traditional cathedral with a sanctuary separated from the body of the church by a see-through stone screen). I was seated in the third row of the visitors by the central aisle, so I had a good view.

The processions were impressive. The organ was well played and a young Aussie trumpeter from West End, Brisbane, was on hand to add drama to some of the hymns. They even had a fifteen voice choir. The organist was a European woman who taught music, including pipe organ, to Palestinian children. She played a thrilling Bach Prelude and Fugue as a recessional.

English and Arabic blended in the service and the program read the Arabic way (we would say 'from back to front').

Archbishop Carey preached on Matthew 2, the visit of the Wise Men. He emphasised two words: *mission* and *joy* (although only the word *joy* actually appears in the passage). He said that the Christian faith was about God's mission to the world. 'If human rights are

---

[2] Jarrar was tried and sentenced in secret in a military court. No-one knew what evidence had justified the deportation order, although there was international pressure at the time on Israel to produce it.
[3] Jean and David Penman served in Lebanon from 1972–75. David later became Archbishop of Melbourne. He died, too young, in 1989.

violated, the poor oppressed, the Christian must speak out and take the consequences ... The Christian mission is universal – to every one.' I remembered that he was speaking in a multi-faith community in which Christians were well outnumbered by Jews and Muslims. 'God's way of evangelising begins with a generosity of spirit that is inclusive. The Wise Men represent the Gentile world. The message is for all people.' I noticed, too, that he never used any name for the land. He talked neither about Israel nor Palestine but referred to 'this land' or 'this Holy Land' – smart politics.

About joy I remember him saying that there is no joy without pain. He described 'the Jewish people who have passed through so much pain, and still fear', and spoke in a similar vein about the Palestinians. 'Both communities have a right to exist', he said, echoing the moderate line.

Once the Archbishop had been installed as a canon of the cathedral, the local Bishop, Samir Kafity, brought him out into the congregation to pass the peace. But before that he took the opportunity to make a mini-sermon himself. I found this very moving. He was a dynamic speaker (even better in Arabic, I sensed) and master of the moment. In the middle of his speech he waved to someone at the back of the church and two Orthodox bishops floated down the aisle. Samir didn't miss a beat but welcomed their late arrival, tying it into what he was saying. Then he commented, 'This is a welcome interruption. Rather better than when Bishop Tutu was here.' On that occasion they had cleared the cathedral during the service because of a bomb threat.

Bishop Samir reminded us that the angels came to a field just a kilometre or two from where we were sitting. I was amazed at this obvious reality. Their message, Kafity said, was two-fold: one, glory to God; two, peace and goodwill towards all people on earth. 'There is only one kind of peace', he thundered. 'There is not two kinds, or three kinds, of peace. There is only one kind of peace. It is a kind in which people are equally honoured.'

For the first time during my two visits to Israel I had a real sense of this being the place where Jesus walked. My earlier visit to Golgotha and other places had an artificial and surreal feel about it. These sites were no longer what they must have been in Jesus' time. They had become 'churchified' and converted into symbolic places. But to look out across a bare, stony field away to the west and think that one night, 2,000 years ago, a night much like last night, clear, cold, star-filled, a bunch of angels appeared to some shepherds and announced the glory of God and wished peace and goodwill towards all people – I could imagine that happening, and it seemed very real and close.

The next day we were to participate in the dedication of a community centre on the West Bank to the memory of the late Archbishop of Melbourne, David Penman. We met for breakfast on the top floor of the YMCA.

Graeme Irvine, the international president of World Vision, was worried about our video crew arrangements. A naturally modest man, Graeme did not take to the whole television idea with ease. He also thought that taking a television crew into the West Bank sounded a mite foolhardy.

When the crew turned up, all our fears were justified. They arrived in a dark four-wheel drive car festooned with aerials. Two Israeli men peeled out. They were wearing leather jackets and gold-rimmed sunglasses.

Our Palestinian hosts audibly drew breath. One of them whispered in my ear, 'If they go into the West Bank they will be target practice'.

Quietly, we thanked them for their assistance and sent them home.

Although Shechem itself is not mentioned in the New Testament, an important event took place there and it is recorded in John 4 – the meeting of Jesus with the Samaritan woman at Jacob's well. It was here that Jesus first revealed to someone that he was the Messiah, and, of course, it was to a Gentile (lest there be any doubts that the Good News is meant for all nations).

So our first stop was at this exact well.

Saint Helena discovered the site in the fourth century. She built a church there which was destroyed by the Persians. A second church was destroyed by somebody else, and a third by an earthquake. At the end of last century a start was made on a fourth, but work ceased on it in 1914 when the walls were, as they were still, about ten feet high. There was no roof.

The well was now underground as other building and the general change in terrain had covered it. Twelve stone steps took us down to a small room which barely contained our party of about forty people. A tiny stone well was in the centre of the room. It was deep, but only wide enough for the bucket to go down. A sanctuary had been built behind it.

Bishop Samir read John 4.

Father Eustinius, the Greek Orthodox priest who acted as warden, told the story of the death of his predecessor, Father Philemonos. In 1971 religious orthodox Jews killed him while he was saying his evening prayers. Armed with axes, they first chopped off his hands, then his genitals. Then they chopped the sign of the cross on his feet and on his bald head. After this they killed him by chopping off his head.

For three years, no-one would come to be warden, then Father Eustinius volunteered. He had an elaborate alarm system set up in the nearby village in case he was attacked. He had needed it. Three times he had been stabbed. Three times bombed. Once attacked with an axe. In all there had been fourteen attempts on his life. The first time he ran after the criminal and caught him; the man confessed to the crime and the courts declared him insane. Six times the priest had appeared in court and each time the person who came to attack the holy site was declared insane.

After telling this story, the priest launched into a vigorous denunciation of the Israeli Occupation and support for Palestinian aspirations. While sympathetic, Bishop Samir finally pointed out that time was moving on, and we were invited to drink from Jacob's well. It was flat, bland, cool and clean, and apparently quite healthy. Unlike Jesus, the water was offered to me in a wine glass!

From here we went to St Luke's Hospital, where Bishop Samir commented, 'People talk about dialogue between religions and people, but we are living it. We are all Palestinians here, but we are Christian and Muslims living and working together in a common ministry of love and health.'

The new hospital was due to have been finished in 1989, but since the *intifada* the labourers had only worked three hours a day. The hospital was quite small and a bit drab and old-fashioned, but looked to be effective and well run. Seven thousand in-patients had been dealt with the previous year, sixty-five per cent of them treated free (or nearly so).

Here I met a member of the Palestinian negotiating team. They were supposed to be in Washington but were refusing to go, along with all the Arabs, in protest at the Israeli deportation orders against the twelve Palestinians.

Here I also briefly met Fr Bilal Habiby, the priest of parishes in Nablus and Zebabdeh – a lovely young man from Galilee who trained in Australia under a program set up by David Penman.

At the church service which followed in Zebabdeh, Bishop Samir talked about his personal connection with David Penman. David had come to Jerusalem for Samir's enthronement. Samir also spoke of the gifts of Australia to Zebabdeh in Fr Bilal – the gift of a priest and a theological education. During his speech there was a series of sonic booms. The only way I could tell they were sonic booms and not bombs was that no-one else batted an eyelid.

We left the church after the Archbishop preached a fine sermon, finishing with the famous quote from Saint Francis of Assisi, 'Go into the world and preach the Good News. Use words if necessary.'

Right next door to the church was the almost completed David Penman Memorial Clinic. Bishop Samir gave instructions about who should stand on the steps as the official party: he and Archbishop Carey first, Fr Bilal next with Jean Penman, then the Australian Ambassador, then the World Vision people, including 'Paul Hunt'. This was a change; usually they call me 'Peter'. The Bishop announced that Jean would speak, then the Archbishop would pray, then we would have lunch.

Neither Graeme nor I was bothered that we didn't get to make our speeches. As I said to Graeme later: 'Our speech is a living testament in bricks and mortar. Our speech is the David Penman Memorial Clinic. It is an eloquent speech that will be here long after we are gone. Remember, as Saint Francis said: Tell the Good News. Use words if necessary.'

We began the next day with the staff in the World Vision office. January 7 was Christmas Day for the Greek Orthodox, but one Orthodox staff member came in anyway. When Bill said how naughty this was, I commented that it was rather typical of World Vision people. Even in Australia dozens of staff and volunteers came in on the night of Christmas Day to answer phones for a television special.

We drove to Beit Duqu, where I had been before. Last time one young man, Fahad, had walked with a couple of friends over the hills to meet us and have lunch. Fahad was jailed a few weeks later when he helped organise a display at Ibillin of handcrafts from his village, some of which, naturally, included colours representing the Palestinian flag. He was in jail for some months and his case was followed by an Australian journalist who happened to be in Ibillin with Bill at the time.

There was a lively discussion in the house of Fahad's parents, who brought us coffee and biscuits.

'Each visit by James Baker [the US Secretary of State] there is a new Israeli settlement in the Occupied Territories', someone said. I had in fact photographed a new settlement nearby that had been established even while the Madrid talks were going on. Israel's provocative action in scorning world opinion and defying political process on their claims to the Occupied Territories was breathtaking and bemusing.

I asked whether there had been much change in the activity on settlements since I was in the country twenty months before. Yes, they said. There had been many more settlements in the last year, and further land confiscations. Some suggested it was really a way of provoking Palestinians to stop the negotiations.

Land confiscation was in fact advancing even while Israel discussed peace. I was reminded of the Japanese delegation in Washington discussing peace even as the bombers flew across the Pacific towards Pearl Harbour. A smartly dressed, handsome and articulate young man was introduced to me as a lawyer working with a group fighting land confiscations. This seemed futile and ironic to me.

'Surely, if they want the land they will just take it', I suggested. 'It is a military administration and they can do what they want.'

This was true in the end, he explained, but there were ways of fighting it. In 1979 an area of twenty acres near the village was taken 'for military purposes'. In 1989 a new survey was done by the military and an order was issued to confiscate twenty-five acres – but if no objection was lodged the order would automatically extend to 250 acres. This is why the people were lodging objections, because failure to object was a de facto acceptance of the confiscation.

What kind of justice was this? I wondered. Someone makes a claim on my land, and the onus is on me to fight him off. It was the morality of the school yard bully.

Once a confiscation order had been published, the people had forty-five days in which to object. During the Gulf War curfew, some areas of the West Bank were curfewed for fifty days. Confiscation orders continued to be issued, effectively in secret. People under curfew had neither the opportunity to know, nor the opportunity to object.

There was even a plan implying that the whole of the mountain on which this village stood would be confiscated.

The sheik of the village described these things as 'stones [obstacles] on the way to peace'. They suggested to him that the Israelis didn't want peace. In the latest budget, 5,000 new houses were planned for West Bank and Gaza that year. 'They want us Palestinians to negotiate for our rights', he said. 'But why should we negotiate for something which is our right?'

We discussed the responsibility of the whole world for creating the problems in the first place. Graeme said we needed to reawaken the conscience of Britain, the US and others. They must take more seriously their responsibility to find a solution.

The sheik asked for the people of other nations to stand with the Palestinians in the same way they stood with the people of Kuwait – nothing more, nothing less. One standard, not a double standard. The UN had made resolutions; well, he said, let them be implemented, *then* let's talk. That was what they said to Sadaam Hussein: first implement the resolutions, without negotiations, then we shall negotiate. For Palestinians it was the other way round. Was this justice?

The question was no longer whether there could be justice and only justice. The question now was whether there would be partial justice or a continuation of no justice at all. Then the question was the extent to which the Palestinians would be willing to accept what they saw as partial justice. Of course, from the Israeli side, any erosion of their Occupation would seem like partial justice for them, too. Many were so committed to having the whole of the land that they would feel it an injustice to have less. Whether this was just or not depended on where you sat.

The village had wanted to put in a water system. They had the money and the plans and the labour. They asked permission of the military authorities (ironically called 'The Civil Administration'). The authorities said they would give permission if they could tell the media and invite journalists and TV crews to come to the village to see them sitting with the people, drinking coffee and discussing plans. In other words, they wanted to create a publicity stunt to show how good things were in the Territories. The village refused to prostitute itself in this way. Permission for the water supply was held up for four months.

We visited their egg raising project where I was a bit dismayed to see hundreds of hens, two to a cage, being treated as production line fodder for their output. The irony of my dismay was not lost on me or my hosts. I told them how, in Australia, we paid extra for 'free range eggs from free range hens'. 'I wish people would care as much for free range people', someone commented.

As we walked towards the village kindergarten, Graeme said, 'This is strategically important for World Vision. *We need to stand with oppressed people.* Practically, we cannot solve the whole problem of world hunger.' Therefore, he implied, we need to work where we can have most impact for the Kingdom of God.

This was immediately and poignantly reinforced when we met Dema, a little girl of about four with beautiful blond hair and big brown eyes. But behind the angelic face was a tragic story. Dema's father had been in jail for seven months. He still awaited a proper trial. Three times he had been before the courts and each time the judge had postponed the trial to allow the prosecution more time. His little girl had grown a lot in seven months. She played with plasticine and Lego at the local kindergarten while he languished without trial.

We travelled on to Qubeiba (perhaps the site of Emmaus), where World Vision's photographer, Anwar, lived. Anwar had been married three weeks before to his cousin but because she was from Jordan she was not permitted to come to live with him. Some people in this situation were given permission to reside in the West Bank. Most were not.

Anwar's mother had been killed in the massacre at the El-Aqsa mosque, two hours after the shooting had started. Anwar was protecting her when he was struck by a ricochet. Eleven fragments hit him in the back. His mother turned to help him and was shot in the head from almost directly above. Someone, a soldier or a settler, fired from a roof, a wall or a helicopter. Half her face shattered.

Friends carried them both to one gate of the Old City but found a soldier spraying the ground with machine gun fire. They carried them to another gate, found a taxi and set out for a hospital. Near their destination soldiers prevented them from going in, despite seeing the mother's wounds. They continued to another hospital where they were admitted, but it was too late. This hospital ran out of blood and soldiers delayed shipments across town. (Later World Vision helped to establish a blood bank at this hospital.)

At Qubeiba they told us about Ra'ad, aged sixteen (later we met him at the Beit Jala Rehabilitation Centre). Three months earlier at 9.00 p.m. he had been shot just outside Anwar's house. He was walking home from his grandfather's place. It was cold and dark. The soldiers probably saw his shadowy figure and fired. Five bullets entered his legs and pelvis. He limped to his grandfather's house and the soldiers followed him and arrested him, accusing him of wearing a mask (probably it was a scarf). The soldiers brought him back to where they had shot him and beat him, asking him questions. Where had he been? What had he been doing? With whom? After some time they took him to a hospital in Ramallah.

Graeme commented, 'We must call for the protection of these people. This is the first basic thing.'

We drove Fahad into Jerusalem. He told us the story of trying to get a pass to visit the city so he could help in the World Vision office, stuffing envelopes. After the Gulf War all West Bank people needed permission to travel into Jerusalem. Some had been issued with green identity cards which forbade them entering the city.

To get his permission Fahad put in an application and was told to come to Ramallah for an interview. He arrived at 9.00 a.m. for his 9.30 appointment. At 2.00 p.m. the secret police interviewed him. They asked him about his village: Who were the leaders? Who were the trouble makers? Who were the ones who made decisions? Fahad claimed to be ignorant of such matters, although anyone in the village could have answered. The policeman resorted to bullying and intimidation. 'I could arrest you right now and throw you into jail', he threatened. 'If I have done something wrong, I should be arrested', said Fahad. 'No. When I arrest you I want to come in the night so I can see the look in your mother's eyes.'

All this to get permission to travel seventeen kilometres to stuff envelopes.

We arrived a little late at the Bethlehem Arab Society for Rehabilitation — for me, a return visit. It was an impressive institution, beautifully designed and built to a high international standard. The colours were bright, the care obviously full of compassion. I could imagine how welcoming it would be to a paraplegic who had been stuck at home wondering whether life was worth living.

Some who had visited the Society had felt the quality of the facility inappropriate for the West Bank. What an irony. Surely the poor deserve the best. If this can be justified anywhere, it can surely be justified amid the squalor and wretchedness of life under occupation.

Edmund Shehader, the director, was an urbane, sophisticated, upper class Palestinian. From an old Bethlehem family, he lived in a century-old manor overlooking Bethlehem and drove an old Mercedes. In Melbourne he would overlook the sea at Brighton and drive a brand new Merc. His salary would be astronomical. Here he stood out as a rich fish in a poor pond, yet his annual salary was the equivalent of just A$25,000. Ten years after he had started to work for the Bethlehem Arab Society, his salary was still much less than in his old job.

Edmund and his wife, Hilda, entertained us for lunch with his twelve-year-old son and twenty-four-year-old niece, recently returned from studying in America. There was a sense of how pleasant life must have been — and how pleasant it might yet be again — for those Palestinians who had the opportunity to make the most of their skills and resources.

The centre struggled to find its running costs. It got no tax breaks from the Israeli government: it paid taxes just like a business and received not one shekel of support in return. Similar Israeli institutions in Israel received substantial government funding.

Around 4.00 p.m. we arrived at the Beit Sahour YMCA Rehabilitation Centre which concentrated on psychological and vocational counselling for the *intifada* victims.

Akram had been studying at Hebron University in comparative

religion. One night at 9.00 p.m. he was jogging near an Israeli settlement when a settler shot him three times. He was taken to hospital in Israel where he had six operations in six weeks. They wanted to charge him US$40,000 for his treatment. Then he was shunted around a few hospitals and finally taken to Jordan for rehabilitation.

Akram was not a major participant in any *intifada* action at the time of his shooting. The settler who shot him said he did so because he thought Akram was going to pick up a stone. The settler is not in jail.

Akram was an easy target. Leila, a Palestinian woman who was the senior counsellor at the Centre, said that most of the people they treated were not involved at the time in stone throwing. 'In any case', someone chipped in, 'there is a principle of proportionality, isn't there? Of course, we know that people throw stones. Maybe they should, may they should not. But do you fire bullets at a child who throws stones? There is a question of whether the response is in proportion to the crime.'

Majid was another victim. A twelve-year-old shepherd boy in a town near Zebabdeh, he went through the rocky side of the mountain to home after curfew one night. He heard a noise, went to see and found soldiers. One soldier called out to him so he went down. 'Do you want a drink?' asked the soldier. He seemed friendly. 'No.' 'Are you hungry?' 'No.' The soldier left and he turned away. The soldier threw something. He picked it up; he didn't know what it was and it was dark. The thing exploded.

The incendiary grenade burned Majid's entire body. His face had been restored by superb plastic surgery. His hands and neck remained scarred.

Leila, who held a Master's degree in education and psychology from the USA, talked about post-traumatic stress disorders. People had flashbacks, extreme depression and anxiety. For two to three years after their injury they often did nothing. They slept late, perhaps only getting up if their friends came around. They fought with their families, broke things, had anger fits and then regrets that left them wondering whether they were going crazy. *Intifada* victims were at first treated like heroes, and they had to act out their roles. They could not easily show anger or sorrow over their injuries.

The Centre would tell them this was all normal and common for people who had experienced trauma. The therapy was to help them to see what they had *not* lost — to be assertive and to say what they *could* do, preventing others from making them dependent. People realised they were not crazy. They were helped to improve their communications skills.

The Beit Sahour Centre was located on the Field of the Shepherds. This is the place (although there were two other nearby sites claimed) where the angels came to announce God's glory and peace and goodwill to all people. How lovely that a Christian ministry of restoration and hope operated now from this field.

Three hours later a group of Israeli soldiers, with guns drawn, surrounded the Centre, entered the premises and began searching and interviewing those present. On one patient they discovered a small piece of paper with the word *Fatah* written on it. The soldiers took him away.

The next day, 8 January, was another strike day. Bill rang at 10.00 a.m. to ask whether it was all right to take an Australian sponsor to Ramallah to visit her sponsored child. The way he said it made it sound as though he wasn't sure it was a good idea, but I wasn't going to say no to a customer.

Sixty-seven-year-old Luba Relic was a special sponsor and well known to many in the Donor Service Team for New South Wales. The sponsor of ten children, she worked at the Menzies Hotel in Sydney for more than twenty years after coming to Australia from Yugoslavia in 1949. Remarkably loquacious, we discovered that Luba could recount whole slabs of European and Middle Eastern history, especially if it involved the Greek Orthodox Church of which she was a deeply committed adherent. She was a lady with an amazing faith, confident of God's protection to the point of foolhardiness. Determined and stubborn, she also tended to be short to the point of rudeness.

Our first problem was that we could not take Bill's car with its Jerusalem plates. The solution was to find a West Bank taxi which would take us to Ramallah. Ramsey from the office went down to find a car and driver. The only one available had Jerusalem plates, but the driver thought it would be OK. 'Things are not so bad for taxis in Ramallah', he said. Ramsey actually knew the driver and it turned out that Bill had known his father and brother for more than four years. In the end he stayed the whole day with us, visiting the school and the family of the sponsored child and helping us to translate.

Luba's personal story was profoundly moving. Towards the end of the War she was twenty-one years old and living in Yugoslavia. She was married for about a year when her husband ('He called me a princess') was killed by the Germans in an ambush. Her daughter had just been born, but her husband had never seen her.

Luba was a Serb. After almost fifty years she still seemed unable to forgive the atrocities committed by Croatians against the Serbians. She talked about how the Croatians 'killed the mothers and children and threw them in the river to float up to Belgrade'. Later, when Bill mentioned an Israeli group that was helping the Palestinians and commented that not all Israelis were bad people, she said, 'The Croatians are all bad. They are Ustashi, every one. It is bred into them.'

Here, I thought, was the post-traumatic stress syndrome. Some acts of atrocity are so grave that people can only continue to live if they demonise those who commit the atrocity. Only an evil people could do what Luba knew had been done by some Croats to some Serbians. In Palestine there were many for whom the pain of the occupation could only make sense if they believed all Israelis were the devil incarnate. Such deeply held prejudice was hard to dig out and change.

What caused this kind of prejudice in Luba's life? The Croats forced her brother to dig a grave into which were thrown the bodies of Germans and her own grandmother. But her grandmother was not dead. When her grandmother cried out they hit her on the head with a shovel. Then they forced the grandfather to fill in the grave, burying his wife alive. Who could live with such a memory?

Soon after, Luba learned her husband was dead. She collapsed and was in a coma for five weeks. The nurses pumped milk from her breasts for her baby girl, but the child grew progressively weaker and then contracted pneumonia. When Luba came to, her little daughter was under one kilogram in weight and near death. Luba did not want to see her, but the nurses brought her anyway. They thought she would die soon. Luba was afraid, but once in her mother's arms the baby smiled, and Luba prayed for God's forgiveness that she had rejected the child.

Within a few days Luba was well enough to leave the hospital, but the prognosis for her daughter was grim. One day walking to the hospital Luba slipped on the icy footpath and fell to her knees, hurting herself. Angry at one more experience of pain, she looked up to the sky and said, 'God, what more do you want to take from me?'

Suddenly there was a bright light. Luba felt that the light came into her body and filled her. She didn't know what was happening to her or what the light was, but she knew she was being filled with the Spirit of God. In that same moment she knew her daughter had been healed.

At the hospital she saw the doctor and he smiled as he turned to face her. 'It's a miracle', he said. 'I know', Luba replied.

Later Luba saw an advertisement for immigration to Australia. She went to apply but the official asked, 'Where is your husband?' Only married couples were being accepted for immigration, and especially not widows with a dependent child.

Luba was disappointed and upset. Seeing her distress, the senior Australian immigration official – a man named Billie Sneddon, who would later be Speaker of the House of Representatives in the Australian Parliament – invited her into his office. She told the story of her circumstances and he was choked with tears. He ordered the officials to speed up her case despite the policy, and three days later she was on her way to Australia.

Luba sponsored Rameez at the Ramallah Evangelical Boys' Home, run by Audeh and Patricia Rantisi. On arrival we discovered that we would have to go on to Beir Zeit if we wanted to see Rameez. Owing to the strike, no-one was yet at the school, and there was no communication. Taking the boy's name, we headed off to Beir Zeit and stopped the first man we saw in the village. He climbed into the car to direct us. Sure enough, in a town of 15,000 people it wasn't hard to find.

More surprisingly, we discovered that they had been accepted into Australia's immigration program. Rameez's mother had two sisters in Sydney. On Saturday they would fly to Amman, get their papers from the Australian embassy there, and then fly on to Australia by the end of January.

Next morning I visited Yad Vashem, a large memorial to the Holocaust. It was impressive and moving. I found it incredible that such a thing could happen and that it could be done by thinking human beings. And the world stood by, probably because of a combination of ignorance and disbelief.

The memorial left me with the impression, perhaps unintended, that the Jews were the only ones to suffer at the hands of the Nazis. But many others, also running to millions, were their victims – homosexuals, communists and many whose main crime was their potential danger to the Nazis themselves.

The first part of the display concerned the rise of Nazism and discrimination against Jews in Germany. But what struck me were the many parallels with the present activities of Israel against the Palestinians. It amazed me this was not obvious to more Israelis. The very first panel stated 'an underlying element of the Jewish Tragedy was their fundamental powerlessness, as an isolated people bereft of a sovereign state, in the face of the Nazi onslaught'. One may have equally said, 'an underlying element of the Palestinian problem was their fundamental powerlessness, as an isolated people bereft of a sovereign state, in the face of the Israeli onslaught'.

Among actions taken against Jews in the early days were the Reich Citizenship Laws, which meant that only people who were of the Aryan race could be citizens. These laws 'reduced Jews to being second-class citizens'. Again the parallel hit me. Palestinians are second-class citizens, on the basis that only people of the Jewish faith could be full citizens of Israel. Of course, the German laws went further than Israeli law; but the Germans confiscated Jews' property, and this was also happening to Palestinians every day in Israel and the Occupied Territories. People were arrested on flimsy excuses, and administrative obstacles of all kinds were placed in their path. Reading the list off the boards was like reading a list of present activities in the Occupied Territories.

Of course, in Germany it got much worse. I could not believe it would here, but then one had to reflect on history and say that few would have believed that the actions against the Jews could have been possible in a modern, sophisticated and liberal state like Germany in the 1930s.

Here was the modern dilemma: How could a nation which had endured all this allow the actions being taken against Palestinians to continue, let alone be responsible for them? Human nature is very strange.

16 | *Happy Birthday in Cambodia*

Cambodia 1992

Land mines emerged as one of the key factors affecting the poor in Cambodia. Once again I discovered that the things which make people poor are often external and imposed. On this occasion, the Nine Network current affairs program, Sunday, *decided to do a feature story on the land mines problem in Cambodia. My colleague Steve Levitt and I were there to help them get their story.*

Around this time, World Vision became serious about campaigning for a complete abolition of land mines. This visit firmed up my own resolve about the rightness of this crusade.

The situation in Cambodia was changing every day. A measure of serious attention was being given to the appalling problem of mines. Nevertheless, the UNHCR plan was still to bring some 370,000 people back from the border camps within a few months.

Our work in Battambang province, the main area to which the returnees would come, revealed that this was a very dangerous proposition. At best, the returnees would be confined for a long time to holding camps designed for one week's stay. At worst, they would return to land still dangerously mined. The result would be death and injury.

Few organisations were giving attention to the *development* needs of the people after they arrived. The recent resignation of the local UNHCR representative had something to do with this concern. Plans for demobilising the various militias were also inadequate. I feared this would lead to former soldiers turning to banditry. There was already evidence of this.

Communications inside Cambodia were difficult – outside Phnom Penh, impossible. Some aid agencies had installed their own communications facilities. I was very impressed with the development work I saw being supported by World Vision. The level of local ownership of the process was very high and I felt we were truly 'fighting poverty by empowering people to transform their world'.

After a restless night in Bangkok I got up at 3.00 a.m. to shower and check out. David Chandler, World Vision's regional adviser for Indo-China, had asked me to be at the airport at 4.00 a.m. for the 6.00 a.m. flight. Mark Janz, from the Relief Department of World Vision's International Office, was also going in on our flight. David's advice was based on the slow processing of Thai Immigration: on the way in it took an average of five minutes to process each person (I timed them!). If you were last in a line of a dozen people, you could expect to stand there for an hour.

As it turned out we picked the one morning when the airport was deserted. This gave me a chance to have a long conversation with John Holloway, the Australian Ambassador to Cambodia, who was also on our flight. John knew me and World Vision well. He had been Ambassador in the Philippines when Ruth Henderson was field director there before her marriage to Harold Henderson (chief executive of World Vision Australia 1976–1988). He was the sort of ambassador who disliked the party round of diplomacy. *Too much vapid talk with people who have more money than morals.*

The flight was a little late but otherwise uneventful. There was a brand new terminal at Phnom Penh built for Sihanouk's return the year before. Judy Moore, one of a number of Australians working for World Vision in Cambodia, had wormed her way around the officials to be waiting for us at the edge of the tarmac. A Khmer woman slid us by the immigration and customs officials.

As we drove into town, Judy pointed out some boys filling a tank of about 200 litres with murky water from a hyacinth-infested pond. 'They take it into town and sell it to restaurants.' Advice: don't drink the water. Bottled water is available, although a colleague advised me to be suspicious if the bottle had been opened before it came to the table. I had brought bottled water from Thailand anyway.

We checked into the Monorom Hotel. My room was as good as any I had used in Vietnam, with one working light, a hot water heater in the shower and an air-conditioner in the wall.

Although the air-conditioner worked, the weather was too cold to use it. I had left my jumpers in Thailand thinking they would be excess baggage, but in the evenings it was almost cold enough to have pulled one on. Even the locals were concerned at the 'cold snap'. Mind you, I doubt it dropped below 20°C.

Another surprise was the Cambodiana Hotel where we went for dinner on the first night. It was a fully-fledged five star, international class hotel, with bars, marble floors, spic and span staff, good food and a swimming pool. I was glad not to be staying, there frankly: while its room rate of about A$150 a night was not very expensive in world terms, the hotel was a bit over the top in this place.

In contrast, the room rate at the Monorom was only about A$40 a night. David and Mark told me that the rats in the roof top restaurant at the Monorom were 'as big as cats'. I decided right away that I wasn't eating there.

A few people asked me what my impressions of Phnom Penh were — the kind of question I always find hard to answer. I said I thought it would be quieter and smaller. I imagined a country town feel, whereas it felt more like Da Nang or Hue in Vietnam. It was busy and noisy, with a constant thrum of vehicles and the emasculated squeak of countless motor cycle horns. There didn't seem to be any known road rules, and since many of the drivers and riders had only become mobile in the previous year we had a nation of L-platers (although L-plates were non-existent too).

On arrival I had discovered that Steve Levitt, a freelance communications expert working with World Vision, was up country in Battambang investigating the possibility of taking the *Sunday* film crew there. In this area there was a mine in the ground for every man, woman and child in Cambodia, and plenty more left over for the 370,000 people who were on the border and planning to return that year, beginning in April. When they arrived, unless these mines were found and removed we could have a *human* mine clearing operation. Already in this country it was easier to get blown up by stepping on a mine than to catch chicken pox in Australia.

A start had been made on mine clearing but recent experience in Afghanistan was not encouraging. Most mines had been laid without proper records. People going about their ordinary daily life in the rice paddies, grazing cows, collecting firewood, were being maimed every day.

In Australia, I reflected, manufacturers had some measure of responsibility for the proper use of their products. If General Motors built a car that had the unfortunate habit of blowing up in the neighbour's driveway, they would be made to recall it. What we had in Cambodia was a defective product. It was creating an environmental disaster much worse than if someone sailed an oil tanker up the Mekong and spilled its contents over the countryside. And it was not cormorants and baby seals that were being killed, but seven-year-old kids looking after the cows and pregnant women bending down to pull up rice stalks.

What responsibility had the countries and companies who supplied these cowardly and obscene devices? They should invest properly in their effective *recall*. The USA, UK, China, the former USSR, Vietnam and the ASEAN countries all supplied these disgusting mines. They did so, they said, because they had the future of Cambodia at heart. If they wanted to avoid being labelled hypocrites, they needed to fund the mine clearing operation to an effective level.

Understanding Cambodia must begin with some appreciation of the 'killing fields', so while I waited for Steve to return, Clinton Moore, the teenage son of Peter and Judy, took me to the Toul Sleng Genocide Memorial.

Toul Sleng was a school which Pol Pot turned into a torture centre. Thousands went through ritual torture here before being sent to their death. Once inside there was no reprieve. Photos covered wall after wall, taken by the officials before and after torture. Whole families were interred together to ensure no-one was left to complain.

It reminded me of the similar 'school' in Kampala where Idi Amin had imprisoned the victims of his paranoia. One telling difference here was the methodical manner of the processing – more like the Nazis. I had seen much of the darker side of humanity in these past few years.

The school was right in the middle of the city, but fifteen kilometres south of Phnom Penh was a killing field. Here they had exhumed nearly 9,000 bodies and piled their skulls into a gruesome pagoda. It gave a gruesome sense of awful suffering.

The early start had left me quite tired, so I went back to my hotel and had a snooze. Steve arrived during the afternoon and we agreed that the real story for *Sunday* was up in Battambang. This would mean a flight up country and an overnight stay.

In the evening we went to the Cambodiana for dinner with Jayasainker, the local World Vision operations manager, and Justin Byworth, the relief manager. After that we went around to the Moores' again and Frank Webster (the finance manager, but temporarily in charge) arrived with a bottle of champagne to celebrate my birthday. Judy Moore had baked a cake too. Frank was quick to point out that World Vision had not spent money on buying champagne. A supplier had given us this bottle as a gift and he'd been waiting for an appropriate excuse to use it.

We met Paul Lockyer and his *Sunday* crew and agreed to fly up to Battambang the next day. This called for Steve and Judy to do some scouting. Phones didn't work in town, so arranging a plane trip meant endless cyclo rides trying to find people.

There was only one small plane for hire in Cambodia and that was a single-engined Cessna. It was run by an organisation called *Aviation Sans Frontières*. There must be some relationship with *Medicins Sans Frontières* (the French group 'Doctors Without Borders'). This group had recently moved office, so Steve nick-named them *Aviation Sans Address*.

In the late afternoon, I made a short visit to the National Paediatric Hospital. I was glad to see this institution that has been so much part of World Vision's history in the country. As in any hospital, many patients are in heart-breaking situations, but I was comforted to see that the facility was of a good standard, especially for Cambodia. It contrasted dramatically with the appalling hospital we would visit the next day.

Gilles Guillard, a French-born Aussie who was our hospital administrator, met me and said, 'So! This is the Philip Hunt who keeps sending me postcards from strange places.' It was my habit to send postcards to Australians working overseas during my travels. Of course, I hadn't met all of them.

Once in Romania, a colleague happened to sit next to a pleasant young man on the flight into Bucharest. His name was Philip. Imagine her romantic surprise when a postcard from *Philip* turned up a few days later, wishing her well. Over the next few months, she received some more postcards from *Philip*. These only added to her confusion.

'He's not very romantic', she commented one day to a colleague.

'That's because he's your boss.'

The flight to Battambang next day took one and a quarter hours and the plane was equipped with a new-fangled tracking computer which took its bearings from satellites. The pilot, Claude, was an ageing Frenchman wanting to do something for Cambodia. *Aviation Sans Frontières* just served the aid agencies and did not accept commercial charters. Steve had described Claude as 'having a face like a map of the Swiss Alps', so I easily recognised him when he entered the coffee shop at the airport.

At Battambang air strip a white Toyota Land Cruiser arrived with a very large blue World Vision flag flying from the back. Inside were Paul and Helen Davies from Britain, who were then living in Battambang preparing our new program there. They were a young couple in their twenties who met in the border camps in Thailand when Paul was working for Christian Outreach and Helen was nursing there.

Our first stop was the Military Hospital. Most of the seventy-two patients were amputees caused by land mines. The place was appalling: run down, dirty and almost totally without resources. The operating theatre, where they carved off legs and arms, had the wind blowing through it and a floor stained with blood.

'What are you lacking?' I asked Paul.

'Everything. Antibiotics, antiseptics, anaesthetics, bandages.' I stopped him before he got to the C's.

Our hotel was called the October 23; I'm not sure why. A driver said it was 'a French day'. It was a four-storey building in the middle of town wedged between apartment blocks of similar height. My room on the third storey was mouldy and stained, though reasonably clean. Outside at the end of the corridor were two squat toilets. As the irreducible minimum for me is a clean, operating flush toilet – I'm just too Western for less – this hotel didn't pass muster. It turned out to be amazingly noisy too, with voices echoing around all night.

Next day we checked into the January 7 hotel. At least we knew that January 7 was the day Cambodia was liberated from Pol Pot.

This seemed like a palace by comparison, although the differences only amounted to en suites (with working toilets and cold showers) and a mirror on the wall.

The riverside cafe provided breakfast – omelettes – but I stuck to *café au lait, et du pain avec Vegemite*. We headed off for Rattanak Mondol, a district towards the Khmer Rouge-held hills where returnees were supposed to go. We stopped at a camp for Internally Displaced People (you are not a 'refugee' until you cross a border).

Paul Lockyer did a 'walk' and an interview with me for his report.

One thing frightened me at this camp: the number of uncovered wells. They were an open invitation for a child to drown in. The wells were about a metre wide and five metres deep, and if anyone fell in, it would be very difficult to get them out. I mentioned this to Paul and, although World Vision didn't have administrative responsibility there, he hoped to take it up with whoever did.

From there we went to an area down the road where people were trying to re-establish themselves on their original farms, having fled the Khmer Rouge the previous year. The place was littered with shrapnel, bits of shells, mines, rockets and so on. If I had gathered all that I saw there it would have filled the front foyer of our home back in Australia.

I spoke to one woman. 'Uncle goes out into the nearby mine-infested woods to cut firewood', she said. 'He stacks it and sells it to people who come looking for firewood. He'd like to take it to the market, but we have no transport. We have gradually sold everything to buy food.'

'Isn't it dangerous in the forest?'

'Yes, but he treats it like an adventure. Anyway', she said, 'he has no other occupation. There is nothing else he can do.'

Resettlement in this area was a very high risk proposition. The governor had surveyed the area and estimated there was enough safe and farmable land for 500 families. He was expecting 34,000!

Paul's report made it clear that there was now no plan to put the returnees back on their farms. Although the official scheme was for them to go to transit camps for a week, they would have to stay much longer. There was simply not enough good land available. UNHCR's job was to bring them back. Who picked them up then?

The biggest amount of money and effort would be required *after* they returned. Our plan, titled the Returnee Re-integration

Program, involved providing a mobile health team, agricultural development for all three groups (locals, internally displaced and returnees), renovating some medical facilities (such as the military hospital) and re-training (providing new skills for demobilised soldiers, the disabled and novice farmers). Some of these activities would be directed to internally displaced people, some to local communities. Some would be quick impact projects of less than $20,000, such as the building of a school. Our rehabilitation efforts would be concentrated in Phnom Penh because that was where most of the amputees were.

We had lunch in a dubious little restaurant in a little village market, then visited a mountain, on top of which was the remains of a temple turned by the Khmer Rouge into a killing place. A pipe had been stuck through one wall so that blood caused by head injuries could be more easily drained away.

A few metres away down a pleasant path were two spectacular limestone caves full of bats, spiders and sinewy tree roots. In the first a bench had been built, and skulls, bones and bits of clothing were piled up on it carefully – the remains of people killed by the Khmer Rouge. In the second, a small pyramid had been made with the same grisly material. Draped over it was a decaying corpse, its clothing still attached.

While the TV crew filmed it from every angle I went back to the temple where the view was spectacular and the air fresher. 'Except for what happened here', said Helen Davies, one of our Battambang project managers, 'this would be a lovely place to come'.

17 | *The Reporter was a Prime Minister*

Somalia 1992

Over the years, programs like Sixty Minutes *and* A Current Affair *have been useful allies in telling the stories that matter to World Vision. It could never be said that these programs ever ran a 'World Vision' story. They always retained a firm grip on editorial control, and were always determined to tell the story their way, whether or not it suited World Vision. I have never objected to this, nor wanted it any other way, even though in a business as complex and risky as ours there have inevitably been some bad stories to complement the good ones.*

In this visit to Somalia, this alliance had an important extra dimension because the reporter for Sixty Minutes *was the former Australian Prime Minister, Bob Hawke. Now, for the first time, I was able to walk alongside people who were, or who saw themselves, as the leaders of nations. I was not surprised to discover them all to be both extraordinary and ordinary. They were humans with faults, yet they carried around them larger-than-life myths and charisma. Such power could be used for good or ill. A ready smile, and a winning manner, were no guarantee of sincerity or authenticity.*

I had to admit I was lucky. I was staying at the Norfolk Hotel, Nairobi with the *Sixty Minutes* crew. It was the nicest hotel I'd been to in Nairobi – far better than the musty place I'd stayed in the time before, the name of which was now extinguished from my memory. Unlike the other rooms in my block, mine had a balcony with large airy French windows and a view over the pool. The weather was overcast, occasionally drizzling rain and quite cool.

I connected with Jacob Akol after someone from World Vision's Kenya office called home in Melbourne to see where I was. Jacob admitted that the fax with my flight details was probably under a pile of papers on his desk. He was busy, poor fellow. I hoped his state of ragged-edge harassment didn't show in the briefing he was planning for me and the crew at 12.30 p.m.

Just after noon, I called Andrew, the *Sixty Minutes* director/writer/producer, and arranged for the briefing to be at five. Jacob was relieved. The problem was Bob, who was off with someone from the High Commission – shopping. Then he was out for a game of golf.

Andrew said, 'You know Bob. He's got to get his game of golf in.' Yes, I had heard that. At least the man had priorities that were likely to lead to a long life.

Besides Jacob and myself, there were four people in our crew: Andrew Haughton (producer/director), Paul Boocock (cameraman), Ben Crane (sound) and Bob Hawke (reporter). The briefing went very well and the relationship among the six of us began to take good shape. It was quickly clear that Andrew had an appropriately high opinion of Jacob, describing him to Bob in the words our office had given him: 'The man who told the world about the Ethiopian famine'. This was true; it was Jacob who had persuaded Michael Beurk of the BBC to go (without Ethiopian government permission) to the famine valleys. The government had been trying to pretend they didn't have a problem.

I soon discovered that Bob Hawke swore quite a lot and I began to wonder how this was going to go. To his credit, he soon got onto the World Vision wavelength, especially by the time he was living in the Mogadishu compound with a dozen World Vision people. His expletives became less frequent but more effective.

During the briefing Jacob mentioned that Ali Mahdi (who was claiming to be President of Somalia) had been deputy to General Aideed (who was claiming to be in control of most of Somalia). Bob commented, 'That's the trouble with bloody deputies. They're never satisfied.'

Around 6.30 p.m. Bob was due to leave for the Australian High Commission for the fortnightly 'free bar'. He insisted we all come along. We were soon engulfed by a hundred or so people of various colours, creeds and states of inebriation.

Lacking Bob's social skills, I spent most of the time chatting with the Deputy High Commissioner, Peter Hooton, whom I had met before and who knew World Vision well. He told me that you could buy a Kalashnikov automatic rifle in the Eastleigh market in Nairobi for about US$20. He suspected they came from Somalia. He also revealed that each day, five plane loads of *khat* flew out of Wilson airport for Somalia. This was the drug the people chew. It made them crazy.

Such trade was just obscene. To a country starving for food, there were still unscrupulous people who would supply drugs for a profit. They showed no concern for the impact on a country in which one drug-crazed person with a rifle could quickly become a mad murderer. The pilot who later flew us into Mogadishu said the daily number of flights was more likely to be ten.

We were up at three for a four o'clock departure to the airport. Our plane was a Cessna twin-engine ten seater, so there was plenty of room. The pilot was Peter, an Aussie originally from Hamilton in Victoria.

Hitching a ride with us was a professor from Canada. A large Somali man, Professor Siad Togane taught English Literature at Concordia College in Montreal. He was coming to Somalia to represent the Somalia Peace and Consultation Committee, a group of expatriate North American and European Somali intellectuals. The steering committee carefully had five members, each representing a clan faction, 'since Somalis are obsessed with clans'.

Togane had previously been in Mogadishu in June 1991 but had left after eight days because he was afraid that someone might kill him by accident. They had even shot at his plane as he was coming in to land. We anticipated no such trouble this time.

It took just over three hours to fly up to Mogadishu. The city was divided. Part was controlled by Ali Mahdi who called himself President, having been elected by some clans in an interim capacity. This was what triggered the war for Mogadishu, because General Aideed refused to accept their declaration. He shelled the city, already almost destroyed in the war to get rid of the previous dictator, Siad Barre. It resembled Beirut, although since there were fewer high-rise buildings the damage was not as dramatic.

Our first appointment was with Ali Mahdi in the small area in the city's north that he controlled under a cease-fire agreement. Thus we overflew the main Mogadishu airport and put down on a deserted sandy airstrip north of the city.

It was due to be a busy day for the leaders. James Grant, head of UNICEF, was in town. The next day, the first of the UN peace-keeping soldiers were due to arrive. Many thought this would trigger violence, since Aideed had objected to an expansion of UN military presence. Also, John Schenk, a member of Jacob's communications team, told us soon after he met us at the plane that two bodyguards of the Ministry of State had argued and shot one another!

All this had made it difficult for John to get vehicles for us. But he had good cooperation from Alistair Duncan, the head of the UN in the north of Mogadishu. Two UN vehicles came, accompanied by two utility vehicles with large machine guns mounted on the back and festooned with young men carrying machine guns. These were called 'technical vehicles' and the people on them were therefore called 'technicals'.

We charged off at a dangerous rate over the sand-dunes and past an old battle ground with the rusting hulks of shattered tanks and personnel carriers littering the landscape. Fatuma, the young woman who was organising everything, said it was a place Siad Barre had fought and lost.

John said the women do all the business here. 'If you need something done, you find that the women make it happen.'

I asked Fatuma how long there had been peace in North Mogadishu.

'Six months', she said. And indeed, it did seem peaceful. There were few people carrying weapons, and those who were appeared to be soldiers acting in a policing role. There was a traffic policeman at a roundabout who saluted sincerely as we skidded around him.

As we drove through the busy but orderly streets we noted the occasional business springing back to life. There were many one-table shops, and one or two restaurants or bars. Jacob said, 'This place needs life, not death. It's important for life to come back. It needs parties, music.'

Our convoy, with enough weaponry to guard the coast of Queensland, drove directly to meet with Ali Mahdi himself. He was a pleasant man with a friendly manner who appeared to have accomplished the international public relations task better than his opponents.

His problem was that he controlled an area about the size of Fitzroy, Melbourne. It might be peaceful, it might be starting to return to relatively normal life, but it wasn't Somalia.

The crew filmed a long interview with him, and I got the impression that Bob thought him rather shallow. There was not a lot behind the smile and the easy manner. Just the same, most of us were buying the 'we're the good guys, Aideed's people are the bad guys' line. Later encounters taught us things were not that simple.

We were treated to lunch – a spaghetti and meat sauce entree followed by a very tasty fish main course. Rather too much, really, and totally out of proportion with the situation. Just the same, hospitality is something to be received in the generous spirit with which it is given; after all, God's generosity is itself rather more extravagant than any meal anyone ever offered.

Alistair Dawson, UN rep, joined us for lunch. A white Kenyan and the former manager of five-star game park hotels in Kenya, he now owned a successful restaurant and bar in Portugal. John said he was really getting things done. He was also putting his hotel experience to work by ensuring that UN staff ate lobster and fresh fruit at less than the cost of regular rations. Some miracle of knowing where to go and whom to encourage.

After lunch we visited what might have once been the Saudi Arabian embassy. Now it was a dilapidated three-storey shell with an empty swimming pool and a bitumen tennis court. Hundreds of people lived there in temporary refuge. Their general health seemed reasonable despite the crowded and basic living conditions.

Ali Mahdi's elegant lawyer wife, Nurte, guided us. Bob came across some who were in much worse condition. 'That two year old won't last another day', he suggested. 'You'd be surprised', I counselled, 'how fast kids bounce back if they get proper intensive feeding'. It was not clear, however, that they would be getting what they needed.

Next we went to a Red Cross Refugee Centre on the outskirts of town. An old naval academy stood on a large allotment near the sea. It was a bare, four-storey building with tiled floors and scarcely a splinter of woodwork left inside. The banisters were gone from the stairs. The window frames were gone. Only the wooden doors remained on some rooms.

The reason? The shortage of firewood for cooking.

The building was a landmark in the area, so it was also a target. It was spattered with shrapnel damage and several large shell holes. Families lived in the rooms and corridors with their goats and cooking fires.

But inside was better than outside, where thousands crammed into stick and cloth hovels with hardly room to walk between them. Another epidemic time bomb waiting to ignite. *Please, God, allow no child to get measles here.*

John Schenk remained in constant contact with the UN office via one of their walkie-talkies. They called us up by our initials, 'WV', except it sounded rather odd to hear World Vision called 'Whisky Victor'.

All morning there had been debate about how we should go from the north to the south side of town, where World Vision had pretty much taken over the World Concern compound for the weekend. The south was controlled by Aideed's United Somali Congress (USC). A more direct route by the coast was preferred, but finally word came through that it was not safe. Too much shooting. So we went the long way round.

As we moved along a wide street, our technical vehicle stopped and waved us on at a road block. This was the end of the Ali Mahdi zone. Nothing distinguished the strategic change in leadership; it was just another streetscape. But our technicals dared not continue. Two hundred metres away was a second road block beyond no-man's land. Another technical vehicle awaited to take over our protection.

Actually, the protection was more for the vehicles we were travelling in than for us. No-one had so far taken pot shots at foreign workers or journalists. We were welcome here. But cars were precious and valued. An unprotected car was easy to steal if you had superior weapons.

We did not go immediately to the World Concern compound but stopped for a moment at UNICEF. Here Leo Ballard, the manager of our relief program for East Africa, joined us with some interesting news. At breakfast time there had been a fire fight right outside the compound gates. It was a demarcation dispute. One clan was providing protection for the compounds – one of their technical vehicles sat in the yard and a dozen of their well-armed men were at the gates. But another group wanted the work. There was a brief skirmish and the newcomers vowed to return 'tonight' to do 'our' boys over.

Leo thought it was all bravado and that there would not be any return visit (his judgment proved to be correct). On his advice we went on to the compound.

Two identical houses stood side-by-side. World Concern occupied one; Swedish Church Relief the other. Each had a pair of open-air rotundas by the front verandah. Leo spent most of the next two days sitting in one of these negotiating deals, setting up the World Vision program in Baidoa.

We met the World Vision people. Leland Brenneman from Mozambique would be the project manager for the next month or so; he was from Virginia and proud of it. With a dry wit, natural charm and apparently unending patience, he had good things to say about the Australians working in Mozambique.

Todd Stoltzfuz (German for 'Proud Foot') came from the Sudan program. He was also American, but younger and quieter, almost shy. He smiled a lot and served everyone quietly and well.

Susan Bander was a woman in her late thirties, a nurse from Alaska, although originally from California. She was certain she had met me before, and eventually realised it was a few weeks earlier in the foyer of the Holiday Inn, Monrovia, California, where she was doing orientation at our international office.

Susan's boss was Dr Hector Jalipa, who served with great distinction in Mozambique before going (with World Vision Australia sponsorship) to Harvard to complete his Master's in public health. He returned even more committed to World Vision and would undoubtedly make a good impact. A quality man with a big heart.

James Schofield (ABC Africa Correspondent) was also there. He wanted an interview with Hawke, but Andrew wouldn't have a bar of it. 'I don't trust reporters', he said to me behind his hand, without any awareness of the irony. He seemed worried about *Sixty Minutes* getting scooped.

James was not put out by being refused and we chatted. He had objective comments on the aid effort so far. 'CARE are doing a good job, if a bit thrown together', he said. ' Nearly all of CARE's first shipment into Baidoa was looted.' I didn't recall this being reported. 'The Red Cross have great coverage, but many kitchens are not supervised.'

John said he'd asked Red Cross what they supplied and was told, 'Rice, beans and oil'. But when he visited a Red Cross feeding centre, the kitchen staff said they only had rice. He presumed the rest had been sold. This was a common pattern, not just a Red Cross problem. Anyone delivering food faced the same difficulty. There were few reliable local partners.

James asked me what I thought of Ali Mahdi. I said I was impressed with the peaceful life in his area compared with the visible display of weaponry down here in the south. Every man was carrying a gun here. Schofield replied by suggesting that Aideed was the only person with 'the capability of governing Somalia'. 'Ali Mahdi is only a banker', he said.

'Seems a better qualification for President than soldiering', I commented. 'Not too many soldiers who became presidents in Africa turned out to be any good.'

'I suppose you're right', conceded James generously.

Two or three times an hour we jumped as an automatic rifle let off a few rounds. Clearly most of this was either frightening carelessness or boredom. Pity the local cat population. Soon we stopped jumping when we realised no rounds were sailing over our heads.

We heard the crump-crump of shells landing somewhere distant but it stopped as soon as it started. During the night there was a fire fight that seemed to go on for three minutes or so. We were told in the morning that it was simply people manning the road block at the end of our street. They had fired warning shots over a vehicle which took a wrong turn.

The real worry was being hit by accident. The week before, a guard in the Swedish Church Relief compound picked up his rifle by the barrel and it went off. The bullet went through his top lip and exited in a bloody mess out the back of his head. He died instantly, a victim of his own carelessness.

Leland Brenneman suggested someone should invent a gun virus. 'You know, there are these computer viruses', he explained. 'They get into your computer and ruin it. Well, someone should invent a round that can be smuggled into ammunition. When it goes up the barrel, it renders the weapon useless.' I thought it was a very good idea. Perhaps we should get Australian Defence Industries working on it.

One of our guards was just fifteen years old. Jacob asked him, 'Why are you not in school?' He replied, 'There are no schools. I can only learn to use a gun.'

The generators ran in the compound from 6.00 to 9.30 p.m. After that it was lights out. This seemed an early time to retire but I was ready by eight. The early start and remaining jetlag conspired to get me down while the lights were still on. I bunked down on a stretcher (they called it a 'camp bed') while Leo slept on a double bed in the same room.

Obviously we could not continue to impose on World Concern for accommodation. They did not appreciate the amount of traffic World Vision was generating, although to their credit, they tried to conceal it. Our involvement with World Concern and Swedish Church Relief was not without problems for these partners. Our methodologies were quite different. They planned to take things slowly, remain small. This was commendable, but Somalia at that moment also needed the more dramatic World Vision approach – an approach that helped to put the issues on the world's agenda and generated more response. Nevertheless, the USC asked questions about the relationship when they saw us coming with film crews and journalists. It was an additional strain that World Concern could do without.

The next morning we made a courtesy call on the headquarters of the USC. A man came over and asked me, 'How many UN troops do you think it will take? 10,000? 20,000?' He was an ex-pilot with long defunct Somali Airlines. We said we did not know, but his question was rhetorical. No number would be sufficient in his view.

'No-one can impose their will on me. People come to Somalia with *their* solutions. The solutions must be found right here in Somalia. *I* am the problem', he said, holding himself up as a metaphor for Somalia. '*I* am the solution. The BBC asks people who have been here two days what is the answer. They don't ask me. They should ask me. The solution is to get Somalis to dialogue. The UN can assist, but not by imposing answers on me. No-one can enter my house and take my gun away.'

Bob asked the Secretary-General whether the USC were interested in talk and negotiation with Ali Mahdi.

'He will have to come as just another party leader. He cannot claim to be President', replied the Secretary-General. 'I was one of twenty-seven people who mediated between Aideed and Ali Mahdi. In May, they said, "Aideed is Ali Mahdi and Ali Mahdi is Aideed". They signed an agreement. Next morning Ali Mahdi renounced all the agreements and attacked Aideed's headquarters.'

Jacob said in my ear that this was just not true. Ali Mahdi had nothing with which to attack anyone.

'We heard that Ali Mahdi was importing money for his war against us so we fired over the airport to prevent the plane carrying this money from landing'. the Secretary-General explained.

Jacob asked about the 'election in Djibouti' where Ali Mahdi was proclaimed interim President.

'This was not an election', said the Secretary-General. He claimed the Italians were behind it. When in doubt, blame an outsider. Xenophobia is a favourite weapon of the powerful coward.

'When Siad Barre's forces returned within seventy kilometres of Mogadishu, Ali Mahdi did not attempt to join the fight. He *wanted* Siad Barre to come. Even though he was supposed to be a member of the USC, he did nothing to help.'

I asked Andrew whether he was planning to deal with the issue of the UN's responsiveness. Had the world been slow to respond? Why? What should have been done? What was required now?

Andrew described this line as 'worthy but dull'. His approach was to show the need, to say that despite all the difficulties the humanitarian aid effort was important and worthwhile.

Bob wanted to add another dimension and Andrew went along with this gladly. Both Ali Mahdi and the USC Secretary-General had shown a desire for dialogue. There appeared to be some common ground. If we could get Aideed to say he would talk, Bob said he would take this message back to Gareth Evans. We could probably bring international pressure to bear to hold them to their word, especially if we had both statements on film. Ali Mahdi's was already in the can.

Andrew was keen to see the gun market. No-one was keen to take him there. It was dangerous 'because of test firings'.

He also wanted to film in the port, which had been closed for two weeks. Everyone was leery about taking a camera crew there. 'It's the worst place'. said John, but agreed to ask the Secretary-General.

He said, 'No problem. We can help you do that.'

We presumed this meant sending his own militia for protection, but as we left he said to John, 'The best way you can do this is to discuss it with CARE'. CARE was responsible for port administration. This statement proved that the USC had no real control over the port. We soon discovered that neither did CARE.

Around 10.30 a.m. we were back at the World Concern compound, and I was sitting in one of the rotundas eavesdropping on Leo's negotiations with a thin, middle-aged lady dressed in flowing bright red robes. She was Annab Osman, who owned the compound houses and was organising everything else World Vision needed locally. Suddenly there was the sound of shells exploding some distance away.

Annab said, 'It is just protest about the UN troops.'

'But they are not coming today', corrected the young man who was helping her.

'I know', she replied, 'they'll protest anyway.'

Then she turned to Leo with some advice. 'Don't trust my people, Leo. Don't give them a chance to loot or kill. If anyone goes into your home without invitation, fire them on the spot.'

Time dragged slowly as John tried to find out whether we could film in the port or the gun market. I sat on a swing seat with Bob and our conversation covered a wide range.

On John Kerin (then Minister for Trade and Development): 'He's an honest, decent guy. Despicably treated by Keating. Kerin has an odd sense of humour. He tells the worst jokes. So bad you don't even laugh.'

On Gareth Evans: 'Best Australian Foreign Minister ever. A great mind. Quick. You never need to explain things to Evans. He catches onto ideas immediately.'

On Graham Kennedy: 'He has a social conscience, you know. I've been to his house and when it's just him and Bob he opens up. I think he's reluctant to show his social conscience because he thinks it's at odds with his public persona.'

On Mugabe: 'There's a harshness, a ruthlessness about him'.

On Museveni: 'Far and away the best African leader I have met'. Jacob was surprised to hear this.

John was back from CARE. They had said the port may open tomorrow, but they said that every day. It was overrun by unconnected groups of bandits. 'CARE said they would take us down there, but they really don't think it will be possible to do anything', John said.

Andrew decided to go and try for some establishing shots and an interview with the CARE guy just saying all the above.

But first we went to the hospital on the outskirts of Mogadishu, La Folle.

Wait a minute, I thought; didn't this mean 'madness' in French? *Des herbes folle*, the *mad herbs*, are weeds. A coincidence? Or a deep irony?

Graeme Irvine had once interviewed the doctor here. She seemed a modern saint giving refugees shelter on the extensive property she owned. Now she was away, and no-one was quite sure where she was. No-one was alleging wrongdoing, but there was an odour in the air.

World Vision had put in 300 metres of cotton sheeting here because the previous sheets had all been torn into bandages.

We toured the hospital briefly and noted that there were few patients. The reason was that no-one felt they had the authority to admit patients without the doctor present. Susan Bander planned to correct this.

Bob was shocked to see the people's condition. It was much worse than in the north of town. We met one young boy, about ten years old, extremely bloated by fluid retention.

I asked questions about a young mother with a frail child. She was a widow at nineteen – the same age as my daughter! Her name was Filei Nur Ibraham. Her husband died in the fighting. Many days previously (she couldn't remember when) she had begun to walk into Mogadishu from her village sixty kilometres away. She had arrived the day before. Her child, a boy, Ahmed Mohamed, was eighteen months old. They had started feeding the child yesterday and were also feeding the mother so she could improve her milk.

We returned to the compound and Bob interviewed Jacob. Paul tried to get gunmen into the shot but they were reluctant to cooperate. So he resorted to subterfuge, pretending not to be filming when he was, and pretending to be filming something else when he was filming them.

Bob asked Jacob, 'We are sitting here in a compound with World Vision people, and we are surrounded by guns. Why?'

Jacob replied, 'We don't like it. But it is the only way you can work in Somalia. Aid needs protection. The only alternative is not to come here at all. Then you help nobody.'

After this, John and I remained while the *Sixty Minutes* team went off to the port with the CARE people and Jacob. Their authorisation papers from General Aideed's people got them through two checkpoints and into the port proper. They were just setting up the camera tripod when a young man appeared. He had a gun and was very angry.

They suspected he was high on the drug, *khat*. No Somali-language capability was required to understand what he wanted. He wanted the cameras off his port. And he wanted it now.

Bob was quite shaken by the experience. He talked it through when they returned, retelling the story as other World Vision people came around to find out what happened. 'Crazy', he said with a dramatic and disbelieving shake of the head, 'he was just crazy'.

It was quite clear that whatever General Aideed controlled, no faction controlled the port.

Meanwhile, Leo and Leland had been negotiating. Leo had spent over $10,000 in a day and he seemed a bit shell-shocked. 'Here's a test for WVI Finance', he said. 'We need $10,000 deposited in a Djibouti bank account. We need it next week or Leland will be in deep trouble.'

A gun went *blatt* just outside the wall. Leo looked casually at his watch and said laconically, 'Aah. The four-thirty gun.'

Bob was interested in talking with Annab Osman, the wheeler-dealer. She had lived half her life abroad when, from her middle twenties, she worked for the Siad Barre government. She was self-taught in English and came from a huge family, most whom had moved overseas during the war. She had stayed to look after the houses. Her former husband was an ambassador and they moved from the Rome mission to New York, Canada, Senegal. In Canada she divorced and her present husband was a businessman, but now jobless.

'World Vision heard I was someone they could trust', she explained.

She organised the trucks that were carrying World Vision aid supplies. Each vehicle came with its own security and driver provided by the vehicle's owner. Trucks she rented from a local company.

Bob asked her about the future.

'You cannot foresee what will happen because it might start with two guys and a stone and blow up to the sky. If the problem were only Aideed and Ali Mahdi maybe a future could be foreseen.'

Had the world been slow to respond to Somalia's needs?

'Almost everybody has been slow.'

Do you think the UN peace keeping process will succeed?

'If they succeed, it will be the most beautiful thing for Somalia. I know my people. I served Siad Barre for twenty years. Somalis are by nature soft-hearted. Even those who killed, they will cry and regret it. I don't know who to blame, but people don't know how to talk ...

'Many young men say they are going to hell anyway. They have nothing to lose. They have no merit with God ...

'We Somalis are impatient. We want to come from the bottom to the top in one jump. We don't count the cost. Whether people are killed is not important ...

'I get depressed. I don't sleep enough. I'm hyper-sensitive. I become hopeless. But the young people are fresh. They come from the bush. They are not educated, not rich. They had nothing even before there was a civil war in which to lose things. They now find in the towns that in half a day they can make millions with a gun. The rich and the older people want peace. These others do not want peace. They say "We are here to mess things up".'

Bob asked her about Somali Fruit, the only unscathed business he had seen in the country so far. He had heard that it was protected. Although it hadn't operated for fifteen months, it was untouched.

'No, it operated until six months ago', she said. 'They are just lucky. The shells have no guidance. They just pull the trigger. Where it goes, it goes.'

'Lucky?' Bob responded. 'But it's entirely undamaged.'

'Just lucky.'

'Was it a big company?'

'Very big. It functioned beautifully. The Somali grapefruit is the second best in the world. And our papaya is near the top.'

Bob thanked her for talking with him. When she left, he turned in disgust. 'There's the biggest load of bloody hypocrisy you ever heard.'

We were planning to fly to Bardera the following day. We were told we would see the worst of the famine there, and we had been promised an interview with General Aideed.

In the evening, before the generators expired, we played Liverpool Rummy. Then Bob and Andrew had a game of Honeymoon Bridge and we retired with the news that our lights were going out soon. My Bible fell open at Psalm 23. Verse four read, 'Even though I walk through the darkest valley, I fear no evil; for you are with me; your rod and your staff – they comfort me'. Were we going to walk into the 'dark valley', the valley of death, tomorrow?

In the morning I noticed this was the verse of the day on the wall calendar. More than coincidence.

We went to the airport. It was the only part of Mogadishu I recognised from my earlier visit a decade before. John had a long negotiating argument with well-dressed people who wanted to charge landing fees and journalists' tax.

Journalists' tax? At the USC they had assured us that there were no fees for using the airport. Here was another place the General did not have control.

John's ambit claim was that none of us were journalists – that everyone worked for World Vision. Bob showed them he was not a journalist by flashing his purple diplomatic passport. They wanted to inspect it, but he refused to let it go. Wise man. They wanted to inspect our passports to see what our occupations were. We pointed out the elementary information that passports do not normally reveal this. Certainly none of the passports we had did.

The negotiation was important. Agreeing too readily would establish the currency for all those who followed. Finally we agreed to a $100 landing fee, and $20 for three journalists, whoever they were.

John and I discussed movies all the way up to Bardera. It was therapy against the day that was to come and we admitted it.

Bardera loomed up and we circled it twice to allow Paul to get some shots. It did occur to me that this was a little foolhardy. A lot of people down there had guns, and some might not appreciate being buzzed. I was just preparing to say this when the pilot straightened up for his approach.

Clearly some food distribution was going on in the centre of town. A vehicle with a CARE flag on it was waiting for us. General Aideed was expecting us and we went to his headquarters in a two-storey house. The countryside was bare and sandy. Thorn bushes abounded but they had no leaves. It was a desolate place.

Aideed kept us waiting for over half an hour, and Bob and Andrew became increasingly impatient. Jacob wondered whether the reason was that retired politicians in Africa have bad reputations, since few of them retire gracefully. But the reason proved to be the time taken to prepare a statement that the General wanted to read to camera.

This was not only dull television, it was also a history lesson for us. The crew shot a "strawberry" – the filming you do when you're not really filming. After twenty-five minutes (a magazine lasts only ten), the General stopped and Andrew said 'Change magazines, gentlemen'. Paul took the magazine off, put it back on again and they shot Bob's questions and answers.

Aideed was a trim man in his sixties with an easy-going manner but an air of power about him. Aideed told us that he had been Ambassador to India and had got to know the Aussie Ambassador well at the time. He resigned his ambassadorship to lead the struggle against Siad Barre. So much was undoubtedly true.

He told us that the world was very confused about the true nature of the Somali crisis. Too many outsiders wanted to impose their solutions. They were sincere but mistaken. The problem was not simply that there were clans vying for power.

As we filmed, a Hercules aeroplane droned in with the second food delivery of the day. Today they planned four deliveries. This was only the third day that food had come.

Hoping to dispel the confusion, Aideed sheeted responsibility home to Siad Barre, with justification. 'He introduced a communist police state with instruments of torture and death.' There was a lot more along this line.

Finally Bob asked his key question about reconciliation. 'What process will you engage in?' We got a litany detailing Ali Mahdi's mismanagement and culpability in response. Bob pressed and Aideed said, 'If Ali Mahdi officially renounces his claim to the Presidency [we already had him on film saying he would be so prepared] then we will consult our partners in the new coalition. We will be flexible.' It was not exactly total commitment.

A Canadian reporter was having a frustrating morning trying to get an interview with the General. He told me the Red Cross had two trucks stolen at Baidoa the previous day. Here in Bardera the USC tried to take ten per cent of the food aid as 'security charge', but to his credit Aideed quashed the plan. The reporter finally got his interview when Andrew wanted to shoot reverses with Bob alone. We offered him a lift back to Nairobi as he had been hoping to get out on the Hercs, now well gone.

The General wanted to show us Bardera and insisted on accompanying Hawke personally. If he had a low opinion of retired politicians, he had just revised it.

In the market square, food distribution was taking place. It was immensely crowded and chaotic. Shots were fired over the crowd for control. I was standing on top of a stone wall trying to get a view over the crowd but the rounds mercifully went a lot higher.

One group of officials gave up trying to distribute food in the open market area and started to carry bags into a stone room. A man showed me an exercise book with a list of names and numbers beside each name. People argued with the officials with profound anger and ferocity. It felt like a riot, but it got no worse.

Bob did a stand up. 'This is the tragedy of Somalia. The aid is making a difference, despite the enormous difficulties. It is getting through somehow. And we have seen people recovering. But more is needed. Peace is needed. Stability.'

At the hospital, three wards contained men, women and children respectively. The floors had been swept clean, but little else commended this as a place to treat the sick and dying. There was no furniture. No medicines. They had some Unimix, a little food. No milk for babies.

A group of three small emaciated children lay in a quiet, listless clump on the floor. 'Where are their parents?' I asked.

'In the other wards. They are just as bad.'

These children needed to be fed intravenously. Food by mouth they were throwing up immediately. Doctor Mohamed Kulan from Mogadishu had been there for two months. He said he had the needles but he did not have the solutions for the drips.

'We can at least feed some of them and they recover. For the rest?' He shrugged his shoulders.

Before he came, forty to sixty were dying a day. Now it was down to ten to fifteen. I reckoned I had just seen tomorrow's group.

The doctor and I sat by a young mother with a baby at her breast. She was Yustor and her boy, Isaac, aged nine months, was the size of a newborn. They had nothing to feed him but fortunately the mother did. The doctor was feeding her to bring her strength up. Mother and child were very thin, but she had spirit and strength.

Andrew announced, 'Righto lads. I have my story.' We returned to the aeroplane. He did not need to go to Baidoa and so we went straight to Nairobi.

On landing Bob asked if he could donate his *Sixty Minutes* fee. Could it be used to supply medicines to the Bardera hospital? I said thanks. His generosity was considerable and appreciated. But I was not surprised. So many people who visited World Vision's work responded in similar ways.

We arrived back at Nairobi around 5.30 p.m. and I managed to get the same pleasant room at the Norfolk Hotel.

Jacob and Bob were playing golf the next morning. Bob dropped hints that they would not want any novice golfers slowing them down. Jacob had a fifteen handicap. Bob said his was twenty, although it must have been less. He said that golfers always lie about their handicaps.

I heard that Bob 'played terribly' on the front nine, but improved a lot on the back nine. Jacob won the front nine. They squared the back nine.

I never did work out whether Bob's back-nine turnaround was the result of Jacob having an attack of public relations common sense, or whether Bob really did get it together.

18 | *A Crack in the Door*

Mozambique 1993

Somalia was a country being torn apart by a war led by uncompromising generals. Mozambique was just emerging from this same nightmare after seventeen years.

Here again, the pattern of over-powerful leaders and oppression of the poor was easily recognised. Here too I met another of these so-called leaders, General Dhlakama, the head of the anti-government forces, Renamo. Here was a leader for whom power meant more than anything. Such people were anathema to a development approach which valued people and worked to liberate the best in them for the sake of community.

Here too I saw World Vision working with integrity and talent. And I discovered, in one particular incident in which a colleague had the courage to ask a naive question, that compassion for the poor required an ability to see what was happening right under your nose – and enough humility to say you didn't understand it.

Mozambique was so fertile. There was no excuse that it could not feed itself, really. In a similar way, Baidoa was the bread basket of Somalia. Yet there were no crops there either.

John Yale, our Mozambique director, welcomed us at Maputo as 'the mother of all delegations'. Graeme Irvine, the president of World Vision International, had asked the heads of World Vision offices in Canada, the United Kingdom and Australia to accompany him on a trip to Mozambique and Somalia. Both countries were coming out of relief mode into development mode, and he felt we needed first hand knowledge to formulate new strategies. Together with our communications people and others we were a group of over a dozen.

John briefed us on the local situation. He said there had been profound scepticism about Renamo's ability to deliver peace. But virtually overnight in October 1992, three months before, the warring stopped, suggesting Renamo really did have better control over its people than had been widely assumed.

Much of the food for World Vision's aid program was being purchased locally: in the last year 8–10,000 tonnes of food were local. John mentioned Australian rice being sold in Tete and the money being used to buy local food for the hungry. The sale of some donated food into the local market was a common practice.

He spoke proudly of World Vision's commitment to accountability. Food monitors were a feature of the program. A complicated commodity tracking system worked. An Ernst & Young audit tracked food from donor country to beneficiaries. I was very impressed with the integrity of the audit trail.

The main concern, John said, was *food security* – not in terms of preventing food from being stolen by bandits, but in terms of the capacity of ordinary people to have secure food supplies to feed themselves. So the World Vision' program was more than just feeding. From day one distribution of Ag Paks had begun. Each of these cement-bag sized packs contained locally suitable seed, a digging implement and farming instructions in both pictures and the local language. Even in a full-scale emergency feeding situation we had started working for agricultural recovery.

The next morning, four of us climbed aboard a twin-engine Cessna 402 to fly to Caia in the centre of the country. The others left in a King Air, a much larger plane. It was faster and passed us on the way.

Caia was not a huge place, but probably because there was once a thriving cotton or sugar business there, it had an excellent surfaced runway. Thus it had become the staging point for aid deliveries into the nearby towns along the huge Zambesi River. It was already hot when we arrived, and we sheltered in a concrete bus shelter (that's what it looked like, although this town had seen no bus for a while).

We were met by a line of local officials, but our formal visit there was not scheduled until the next day. We transferred almost immediately to five smaller Cessnas which could take off and land from the small dirt strips that most towns have. Our next stop was to meet the President of Renamo, Dhlakama.[1]

Dhlakama was at Meringue, which it surprised me to discover was pronounced *merr-ing-way* with the emphasis on the *ing*. This was about a forty minute flight away. As we flew towards a large dirt strip we saw the King Air already on the ground. Apparently it had another job, to pick up someone from Renamo.

No-one was around. There were no crowds lining the strip. No cars. No soldiers. As we circled to come in, all I could see was an ordinary looking village – nothing that resembled a headquarters.

The planes taxied to a stop and two trail bikes came roaring down the strip. On the first was a youngish looking man in a military uniform with four stars on his epaulettes. He was wearing fashionable glasses with thin mock-turtle shell frames. This was Dhlakama himself. On the second was a man in a smart pin-stripe suit. It was already in the high thirties, but he looked more comfortable than the rest of us.

Dhlakama got off his bike and greeted us with a huge smile of perfect teeth. Apparently seventeen years fighting from a jungle hideaway didn't keep you away from the dentist.

'The other two bikes crashed on the way', he said cheerily. 'I'm afraid we have no car here yet. We shall take you on the bikes.' All fourteen of us.

The International World Vision president, Graeme Irvine, along with Margaret Jephson, my Australian colleague, were the first to be pillioned. Before they left, the other two bikes arrived. I wasn't riding with any two guys who had 'crashed on the way' so I volunteered to walk. 'It's about a twenty minute walk', they told us as we set off down the strip.

The bikes returned from each trip to find us closer to base each time, and gradually everyone was shuttled off, with me being one of the last volunteers. I waited until I could ride with the General. 'He has the most to lose', I suggested. He also looked to me to be the best rider.

The reason we could not see any official buildings became

---

[1] No-one could remember how to spell his name so I suggested we think of it as D-H-L [the air freight courier] Also Known As MA. It took a while for most of the group to work it out, but Don Scott from Canada laughed immediately and loudly. 'That's mad', he said. I decided this was a compliment.

apparent soon enough. The site was cleverly hidden under the canopy of trees. A large area was mottled with shade and swept clear. Nearby were a couple of meeting halls and several living quarters made from jungle material. Incongruously, several young men in white shirts and ties walked from place to place.

The General sat at the head of a table in the open air and offered us Coca-Cola. Of course.

I had long ago learned that some commercial companies can do what development agencies cannot. I recall spending a whole day travelling to a village. We flew for an hour, then drove until the car could go no further, then walked through the jungle and across streams, including one that was waist deep. Finally we arrived at a spot which seemed to have no connection with the outside world. A truly remote place.

And you know what they offered us to drink? Coca-Cola. In a village that didn't even have clean drinking water.

This simple example puts the lie to any suggestion that the world does not have the ability or know-how to solve its problems. If one company can bring its product to the ends of the earth, it is certainly possible to put clean drinking water into every village on earth. We do not lack the resources. We lack the will.

Dhlakama's Coke was not cold, and it got hotter as time passed until it tasted like tea. The flies were thick and I put my cap over my Coke can to keep them off.

'The war is over', the General assured us. He claimed that it was Renamo which had been the great champion of democracy, fighting the Marxism of Frelimo to establish a peace based on true democracy.

This bare-faced revisionism was stunning in its audacity. Renamo was set up by the Rhodesians without any real ideological mandate of its own. It was part of Rhodesia's, and later South Africa's, regional geopolitical strategy to keep the neighbouring black states weak. Even when I was in Mozambique four years before, it would have been stretching the imagination to suggest that Renamo had any clear ideological system. It was a guerilla movement engaged in a stupid, power-mad, disgusting campaign of destabilisation, destruction and damage – for its own sake.

Still, Dhlakama was so innocent-faced it was easy to believe him.

I found myself wondering if my interpretation of history was correct after all. At least, I thought, it was much nearer the mark than this 'we're the hero' stuff. Some local commentators said the real motive for Renamo taking this position was pure, self-preserving political opportunism. The country was so heartily sick of the war that Renamo had no choice if they were to survive but to find a place in the new, peaceful Mozambique.

We sat for well over an hour, with the hot sun mottling us as well as the ground around. We talked about the need to get access to the people who were streaming out of Renamo areas. Too many were coming into the towns. Better to get food and Ag Paks to them where they were, otherwise the towns would be crushed. And the people would suffer further deprivation because they would be unable to plant adequately. Or they would be victims of epidemics.

Finally we prepared to leave and the general revealed that there was a shorter walk back to the air strip. Apparently security considerations had prevented them from bringing us this way before. The walk took around ten minutes, and we arrived at the same time as those on motor bikes who had gone the other way.

From Meringue we flew to Quelimane, and it seemed exactly as I remembered it from 1989. Perhaps there were more people on the streets.

'One hundred thousand more', reported Leland Brenneman, who had returned from his stint in Somalia. That was a huge increase. Perhaps it was a deliberate hyperbole. I doubted that there had been more than 20,000 people there in 1989, and Leland figured that would have been right.

The Chuabo Hotel was as ever; I think I even had the same room. This time there was no running water so we ladled ourselves for the next two days. My room had an air-conditioner in the corner, but it struggled against the extreme heat.

In the evening we enjoyed the unique restaurant on the top floor. Here in the middle of nowhere they abided by one of the strictest dress codes in Africa. No thongs. No shorts. At least you could wear a T-shirt over your moleskins.

Our table had huge prawns and lobsters, while I had grilled steak. The fried chips were cold, which is the Mozambican way (hot food is bad for you).

I watched the street dwellers from my fifth floor window as they stirred in the morning light.

A small girl moved on her cardboard bed under a shop awning. She raised her head and looked about, then dropped it again. A minute or two more rest before another day.

Her mother was already awake. She sat over her tribe waving a cloth over them to cool them with morning air. The temperature was already in the high twenties and it was steamy. The girl stirred again, conscious of her duties, rose, folded up her bed and walked off. Soon I saw her scrubbing a pot at a tap in the neighbouring church yard.

An adult man shuffled along the footpath. Holding his elbow was a blind man. They met a friend and talked. The blind man was not included and stood at an awkward angle to the conversation.

A man stood and stretched. A cat played with his feet. Beside him, under a blanket, a teenage boy poked at the cat around him.

The mother swept. By the time I looked again she had swept the whole area in a fine pattern in the dirt. She was making this place habitable. A sense of pride for her surroundings was not lost just because she had become a refugee from hunger in her own country.

A fire was started for cooking. Kids cleaned their teeth with twigs. A man went back and forth with a blue garbage bin full of water on his head. His steps were measured and heavy, his burden immense.

I joined the rest of the team for a devotional time in Graeme's room. At seven we had breakfast upstairs, when even Don Scott put a dab of Vegemite on his roll. 'I've had it twice now', the Canadian said, 'first and last time'.

We were at full sweat by the end of breakfast. The temperature was already well into the thirties and would climb to forty plus this day and the next.

We assembled for the air armada and took off like a series of angry gnats. It was about forty minutes to Sena, a large refugee camp.

As we landed, an Antonov flew in behind us. This was a large Russian freighter with a payload of six-and-a-half tonnes. Its presence was powerfully symbolic of the change in world politics: a Russian aircraft, crewed by Russians, carrying US grain organised by World Vision. The plane dumped its load and turned around in less than fifteen minutes. The pilot made the most of a spectacular take off opportunity, lifting his wheels and banking when he was only a few feet off the ground.

Under a tree there were a hundred or more people sitting together. These were the new arrivals. They were coming in for food every day, mostly from villages not too distant.

Malnutrition among them was very high. That meant most of the people were less than seventy-five per cent weight for height. Recovery from less than sixty-five per cent weight for height was considered unlikely by the nurse I spoke to. The new arrivals were registered and classified. Under seventy-five per cent got you a red band. Between seventy-five and eighty-five per cent got you a blue band.

There were four special feeding centres, square huts made from rough hewn poles, grass roofing and earth floors. Each hut represented one of the four phases of recovery from malnutrition. While hunger was obviously a very great problem still in Mozambique, the food *was* arriving – that was why the people were coming. And most were recovering.

In Hut 1 there were many bad cases. It was tragic to watch sick children and their parents' attempts to get food into them. They pushed away the very thing that would save them. The despair in mothers' eyes was pitiful. Gut-wrenching.

One child seemed especially ill. Dr Terry, a World Vision staff doctor, said she was a bad case; she had been receiving food for many weeks but was not improving. 'She has a vaginal infection, and TB', she said. 'I think it is AIDS.' AIDS ran at ten to fifteen per cent of the population in the cities, so it seemed probable that we should see some cases.

We walked down to where the people had set up a huge rambling hut community beside the destroyed railway bridge across the Zambesi. The heat was intense.

Under a water tower, Charles Clayton, from World Vision UK, stopped to see a family. He was bothered by the look of them. They were skinny and listless. He pointed them out to a World Vision nutritionist who began to investigate. Yes, they had tried to get registered, but somehow they weren't successful. The nutritionist thought they went to the wrong place. They had given up and lain down here to die.

Four lives were saved because Charles thought to ask what others of us might have felt was a naive question: 'Why are these people here?'

Jonathan White, our British agriculturalist, took us to see the Ag Paks growing. 'Little Ag Paks are sprouting on the Ag Pak bushes', he said dryly.

What we saw, of course, was maize. As high as an elephant's eye, some of it.

If only we could deliver more of these Paks and get more grain planted. One tonne of Ag Paks resulted in fifty tonnes of food. It took just two agricultural cycles, in theory less than a year, to have families self-sustaining. That required two Ag Paks. In practice we looked at two years, since people didn't always get the complete benefit — either they were unable to plant the full area required, or they didn't plant in time.

But imagine how quickly Mozambican agriculture could recover if we could supply enough Ag Paks! Less than two years and the problem of food security would be history.

An Ag Pak weighed sixteen kilograms. The Antonov carried six-and-a-half tonnes. I calculated that the Antonov could deliver 406 Ag Paks, and the cost of the Paks (at around A$50 each) and flight would be around A$20,000. Two flights per year for two years would fix food security for 400 families. For $80,000.

A door had cracked open in Mozambique. We could continue to pass food packets through the crack, or we could lean on the door with our Ag Pak program and swing it open to let the full light of self-sufficiency shine in.

After a time videoing we traipsed back. Praise God and one of our staff for the soft drinks each plane carried in a large Esky. We gorged ourselves on mineral water, Sprite or Coke. The kids hung around to snatch the precious empty cans. It occurred to me that they would find the contents equally precious. But we were privileged — clearly and undeservedly so.

It was now well into the afternoon and we had intended to be at Sena only for an hour. Videoing always takes longer than anyone estimates, but there were no problems about rearranging the schedule.

We returned to Caia, this time for a proper visit. The town administrator, the local army chief and a dozen other officials lined up for a handshake. Then they took us to yet another tree, in yet another village, where yet another bunch of new arrivals was being processed. Many of these wore clothes made from tree bark, their own clothes having long since worn out. A few were wearing clothes made from the sacks in which the grain was delivered.

'Let's go see the feeding centre', said the administrator. *Good*, I thought, *this will be nearby.* It was two kilometres away. The sun was red hot. The air heated your throat as you breathed. Sweat refused to evaporate in the steamy air.

I only had to carry my camera and myself and I was weary. Women passed me carrying whole sacks of grain on their heads! These people gave new meaning to words like tenacity, endurance, perseverance.

Children by the path said 'Visao Mundial' as we passed. Awareness of World Vision in these communities was very high and our work appreciated.

The feeding centre was in an old school or hospital building in an area once occupied by a Portuguese company. What looked like an abandoned sugar mill stood nearby. Around the area were the blasted and decayed remnants of large, two-storey manor houses. Rooms in the feeding centre were allocated as at Sena to the four phases of malnutrition. The story was depressingly the same.

We left in time to be back in Quelimane by 5.00 p.m. to avoid a late landing charge. That night there was pork on the menu and a different soup, which turned out to be the same bean soup we had the night before. I made the usual joke:

Me: What's the soup tonight, waiter?

Waiter: It's bean soup.

Me: I don't want to know what it's been. I want to know what it is now.

Two of us ate the pork, though Graeme said he always worried about pork. It seemed everything on the menu had caused Graeme to be sick somewhere, sometime! When the next table ordered they were told the pork was finished and all that was left was liver. But lobster and prawns seemed in plentiful supply when the waiter was pressed.

The little game played by the elegant waiters in their white three piece suits brought memories of my last visit flooding back. In those days there was only one thing on the menu, and when it ran out, too bad.

On that previous trip I had travelled with Neil Finn of Crowded House and Penny Mulvey, an ex-Ten journalist. One breakfast our sound technician, Don Connolly, joked about the 'lovely hot shower' he had enjoyed. There was, of course, no hot water in the entire town. Penny, not realising he was joking, asked whether all our showers had been hot or cold. Naturally we lied, leaving her to believe that only her shower had failed to heat up.

Next morning there was a knock on Don's door. It was Penny. 'Have you got hot water?' she asked.

Don, seeing a practical joke staring him in the face, replied, 'Yes, just got out. Had a lovely time.'

'Mine doesn't seem to be working', said Penny. 'I just hate starting the day without a warm shower.'

'Know what you mean', said Don caringly. 'You hop into my bathroom. You can lock the door and be real private.'

So Penny, who had come armed with her shower pack and bath towel, went in and got in the shower. Don said he thought the whole of Quelimane must have heard the howl of dismay as the icy cold water hit her.

She completed her shower and emerged from the bathroom.

'How was it?' asked Don ingenuously.

'Freezing.'

'Oh, what a shame. It must have just run out. It was so lovely and warm earlier.'

Soon we were on the way to have a drink and cashews with the local governor who, according to John Yale, wanted money for his local soccer team. Then to the airport for the flight to Lilongwe, Malawi, in one of our chartered Cessnas.

The immigration person in Quelimane was supposed to be there to check us out of the country, but he didn't turn up. Rather than wait forever, we checked ourselves out. I think we'd paid all our bills in Mozambique.

19 | *After the Fighting's Over ...*

Somalia 1993

Somalia's agony appeared to last a shorter time than Mozambique's, although that may have only been an impression created by lack of media interest after the UN forces left.

Within months of my earlier visit with Bob Hawke, I was back in Somalia with the delegation of World Vision leaders who visited Mozambique in the last chapter.

The Somalia experience focussed some of the issues in emergency relief. There is a way to deliver food aid without it being stolen. There is a way of preserving local community power structures. There is a way to help people in crisis while still keeping an eye on their long term rehabilitation, most of which will rely on their own capability. Agencies have to deliver their own magnificent and impressive capability, while not destroying the capability of the people themselves.

The flight to Lilongwe from Quelimane took about two-and-a-half hours and we had plenty of time to connect with our scheduled Kenyan Airways flight. The process was rather complicated. They wanted to process us through immigration, so we entered Malawi just so we could leave again (and pay the airport tax of US$20).

We queued up for Kenyan Airways while Charles Clayton made droll remarks about how sorry he was that he was the only one with a First Class ticket (the flight having been full by the time he booked). In the end he gave his seat to John Schenk, who had hurt his back.

The flight was 'free seating' and I found myself at the emergency exit door, thankful to God for an extra six inches of leg room. Sitting between me and the window was an Arabic-looking woman and her two children. She had what looked like tattooed feet, but it was explained to me later that this was some kind of henna-based paint that gradually wore off.

On her lap was a baby wearing only a T-shirt. It looked to me as if she just let the kid relieve himself on her own clothes, but I tried not to notice. Maybe she had a towel secreted in the voluminous folds of her many garments.

Every now and then she produced a large breast and stuck it into the mouth of the baby. The first time she did this I actually thought she had produced some kind of leather bottle from her pocket, so easily did she pull it out that it seemed not to be attached to her. *Oh, hello! Errr, excuse me for looking, I thought that you were feeding the child a dead cucumber …*

Feeling embarrassed for no good reason, I concentrated harder on reading my paperback. The boy next to me was about ten years old. He managed to crush five or six biscuits into crumbly powder and litter the seat and floor.

With these interesting companions we flew first to Lusaka in Zambia, then to Nairobi. We got in just before midnight and had to wait while the customs people 'ummed' and 'ahhed' about our video equipment. They also X-rayed our suitcases and wanted to ask questions about mine, which had my portable printer in it. When I said it was a computer printer they said it would have to go into bond. This was plainly ridiculous since they were permitting me and four other people to take much more valuable laptop computers into the country. Just an exercise in petty authority. Our Kenyan colleagues, accustomed to this nonsense, argued their way through.

Off to Somalia next day, but not without drama.

Charles presented himself for the car saying that he had had a rough night with very severe diarrhoea. Everyone had lots of advice for him.

'Take this for your nausea.'
'Take this for the runs.'
'Drink lots of mineral water.'
'Eat some dry bread.'
'A whack on the side of the head is good for that. It'll distract you.'

At the airport he staggered around. Soon he was having a turn which quickly faded. He sat on the ground by a wall and I sat beside him. He was hardly up to talking, although he was making an effort to stay in touch. Finally it became clear to him what seemed pretty clear to the rest of us – that he could not endure a three-hour plane ride to Baidoa.

He agreed to go back to the hotel with Leo Ballard, Africa Relief director, who had turned up to send some supplies with us. As they started to walk off towards Leo's car, Charles stopped by Aba Mpesha, our local director, to say good bye. The next thing I saw was Charles sliding down and Aba having a job holding him.

I leapt up and managed to get my arm under Charles' head and shoulder and lower him gently to the ground. People crowded round. Someone produced what looked like a pillow slip and made a useful breeze with it.

A young man with a close-clipped beard knelt down and took Charles' pulse and started yabbering away in Italian. He seemed to know what he was doing and I guessed he was a nurse or a doctor. He was asking questions.

'Margaret', I called out, remembering that she had told me she spoke a little Italian. She tried to translate what the fellow was saying.

Meanwhile, as the nausea built, Charles was breathing fast as if he was having a fit. Eventually he started to calm down and recover. He opened his eyes and began to come round. In five minutes or so he could stand with help, and by then the ambulance had come. We helped him in and Leo followed in his car. By the time the ambulance pulled up at the first aid station Charles was OK. Leo took him back to the hotel.

Charles was so weakened by the walk up to his room that he fell on his bed fully clothed and slept for five hours.

I concluded he was dehydrated. The same thing had happened to me in the past. It was an experience in Lebanon that brought home to me the value of the Oral Rehydration Therapy that prevented one becoming weakened through dehydration.

Charles' case showed the dangers of this condition. It was easy to see how it could kill children or adults already weakened by malnutrition. Charles recovered in the end because he was healthy. Kids in Hut 1 could not. They died within hours of a major diarrhoea attack.

Meanwhile, Dan the cameraman and I had gone up in the smaller of two twin-engine planes. It was a Piper Aztec with engines that did not seem to work together. As a result the plane described a gentle corkscrew all the way to Baidoa. Dan and I were almost green when we landed and very much in need of a walk and some deep breathing. Three hours and forty-five minutes of pukey flying.

World Vision's Bernard Vicary, from Melbourne, was waiting on the air strip as we approached. We circled for twenty minutes while they got a Hercules off the strip. As we came down, we saw the huge US army encampment nearby. The end of the strip was chewed up where the big transport planes had broken through the hot asphalt.

Our team was well served by some equipment that World Vision Australia provided. Everyone had a two-way radio, and satellite phones connected us to the rest of the world, even if at US$10 a minute. Bernard called up a vehicle and it soon arrived.

We had been delayed by the visit of ten American congressmen. The US army had over-reacted in a big way. They closed the airport for the whole visit (that's why we were circling) and shut down the entire town. Even aid agency people were prevented from visiting their feeding programs. This was hardly impressive, but it turned out to be one of the few blemishes on how the Yanks were handling their role. For the most part they were very effective. Not aggressive – polite but firm.

Soon we were at 'The Bridge' feeding centre, which was beside a bridge over a stream in the centre of town. Dan was shooting and we were getting the guided tour. Bernard was having fun with the kids and showing me round. The story was the same as in Mozambique – malnutrition in evidence, but now controlled. There was danger from measles and other infectious diseases.

Around 4.30 we finished videoing. Bruce Menser, the man in charge of World Vision's team in Baidoa, asked if we would like to walk back to the base, something one could not do before the marines came. We all agreed.

As we walked through the crowded and noisy streets, a small girl was knocked over by a *Medecins sans Frontières* vehicle. Fortunately she seemed to only suffer gravel rash and a fright. A European woman in the car got out and looked her over, while Dan got the video camera on his shoulder and buried himself in the crowd too.

We were just recovering our equilibrium from this when there was a loud gunshot nearby. I froze, checking for bullet holes. Everyone around us went quiet. Bernard commented later that it was now so rare to hear a gun shot that everyone was surprised. From around a car came a man wearing an AK-47 and a sheepish look. We suspected he had let it go off accidentally.

The World Vision base was an ex-hotel, rather like an improved version of the Commando Hotel where we had stayed on the Steve Vizard Ethiopia shoot two years before. It had been self-importantly named the International Hotel and was built around a small courtyard.

The rooms had no facilities save the beds and furniture we had brought in. Along the street frontage the rooms had been turned into offices; the living quarters were to the side and rear. On one side were three rooms with a proper flush toilet, a cold shower and a sink with two taps (cold and cold). The water was nicely refreshing at 5.00 in the evening when the edge was off the heat of the day.

Two tables were brought out into the courtyard and we ate *al fresco* under the stars. We were unsettled by a huge helicopter going over – it sounded like it was right on top of us but it was invisible. These machines were painted matt black so nothing reflected off them. You looked up to where the noise was coming from and saw nothing. The only way you could tell where they were was if they blocked out the stars. Spookey.

Next morning we had breakfast and I agreed to leave my Vegemite for Bernard. Susan was still there from the team I'd met in Mogadishu some months earlier, and Todd Stoltzfus was due to arrive back from R&R on the plane we would be leaving on. Mohamed Abdi, the Somali in charge of local staff, was also there. He reminded me that he had studied agriculture in Gatton, Queensland, and pressed me (and everyone else) for a chance to come to my country. Apart from that there was Aidu, an agriculturalist from Mozambique; Mario, an agriculturalist from India; Cindy and Paul, two nurses from Canada; Bjorn, a Swede who was born in Africa and was acting as base organiser; and Bruce, in charge from the Sudan program.

In addition World Vision had about twenty local Somali employees whom we met the next day for afternoon tea. All the men had

Mohamed in their names somewhere.

When we went out we took two vehicles. World Vision had not purchased any ourselves because of the risk of theft; instead we hired local vehicles and drivers. This also added to the local economy. This day we had two Toyota utilities. The back of the second one had seats along the side, and I sat up there, in the open air, with Jacob Akol and Dan.

We went down the road towards Bur Hakaba to visit the Rowlo feeding centre situated behind CARE's headquarters. Here we were greeted with great joy by the local people because we were picking up their sheik to take him back to visit his now deserted village, also called Rowlo. Everyone wanted to come with us, but the sheik and his two brothers and two sisters (or it might have been one wife and one sister, or two wives) climbed into the back of our ute.

The sheik was over the moon. He shook everyone's hand vigorously. He was going home.

Before we left Baidoa the marines stopped us at a checkpoint. They asked if we had any weapons. The other car was carrying an automatic rifle which they disarmed and took away to check if it was registered. It was, and they returned it and sent us on our way.

We saw road works being accomplished by the huge bulldozers that had been flown in. They were massive machines. Everything about this army was big. Even the jeeps looked like scaled down trucks.

At first the shoulders of the road, which was fast and smooth bitumen, had been cleared back about twenty metres, but soon we were into uncleared territory. Tall thorn bushes grew close to the road, making forward vision more difficult and providing good hiding places for ambushers. It was obvious why road clearing was a priority.

Finally we came to Rowlo. The sheik took Graeme Irvine by the hand and enthusiastically showed him around.

The community had left to walk to Baidoa ten months before. The sheik said they were a faithful Muslim community and believed in peace. There were no weapons in the village. Other less religious communities had begun to act as bandits and had looted their sorghum stores. Eventually the banditry and the poor harvests led to the decision to head for Baidoa. Remarkably, the sheik managed to keep them together.

'Out of a total community of 3,000 people', reported the sheik, '400 died in the fighting with the other communities. One thousand three hundred died of hunger. Only about 1,000 of us remain.'

Bernard reported that fifty-seven per cent of the people from Rowlo died within the first two weeks of their arrival in Baidoa. But by then World Vision's feeding program had begun to have the desired effect.

It was time to eat dust again. We rejoined the bitumen and drove down to a miniature Uluru. This was Bur Hakaba.

Before arriving at the rock we stopped briefly at Dacar (pronounced *Da-hah*), where the local sheik showed us around the feeding centre. The familiar pattern of malnutrition but good recovery rates was repeated. Of course, it was not right to say the problem was over merely because we were controlling most of the hunger-related deaths. Every feeding centre had its critical cases whom a decent cold, TB or measles would kill.

It was hot again and the sheik served us sweet Arab-style tea. There were speeches which fortunately I slept through. Graeme said he almost fell asleep too, but he couldn't afford to because he was the one expected to respond. It was very relaxing travelling with the president.

At Bur Hakaba we had placed the feeding centre in a building originally erected to house British troops. It had the familiar rooms full of cases in descending order of desperation. I did a piece to camera showing that 'the money does get there'. Here, sixty kilometres from Baidoa, in one of the most difficult places World Vision had ever worked, the Unimix was being made and put in the mouths of the suffering.

Typical of our vision, the team was not content simply to feed those who came to the centre. Their goal was the restoration of the hungry, wherever they were. So Susan had organised a team of 'house visitors' who went house to house looking for bad cases and bringing them in. They were finding some every day.

I took a photo of a house visitor with her bag labelled *World Vision House Visitor*. Susan told me this woman had learned just that morning that her husband, missing for three months, had in fact been killed by the soldiers of Siad Barre. She had come to work and done her duty just the same.

Outside Bernard was teaching a group of young boys to say 'G'day' and 'Carn the Blues'. I asked if the kids were good singers and Bernard said, 'Let's get the girls to sing'. I was expecting children, but he actually meant the female staff. Five of them formed a choir around one show-stopping lead singer. Earlier I had pointed her out to Graeme for the way she *danced* between the Unimix bowl and her charges. Now she led the group in the singing of three songs.

The first was about World Vision, although it came out sounding rather like 'World Division'. The second was about Bernard, and the third about Susan. Diana Ross and the Supremes could not have done better!

We climbed back into the cars and sped off home. On the way something pinged off my cap and fell into my lap. It looked like a bee except it was about as big as my thumb! I yelped, whacked it onto the floor of the ute and stomped on it, much to everyone's amusement. Jacob assured me that they didn't bite, or if they did, you wouldn't notice because you'd be dead. I think he was joking.

When we got back to base, Charles was there with a remarkable story about flying to Mombasa then persuading some US marines to fly him up to Baidoa in their Hercules airlift. He told me how grateful he was to me for simply being there. I assured him that if we stayed with World Vision long enough and did more trips like this, he would undoubtedly get the chance to reciprocate.

We held a communion service, led by Graeme, to begin the next day. Then Margaret, Bernard and I waited around the base while everyone else went off to Xarte Qanle (pronounced *Heart de Carnlee*) to see a World Vision food distribution.

Food distribution was a tricky business. It looked easy but it wasn't. World Vision had a lot of experience built up over many years, often by doing it wrong and seeing the results. Some other agencies were just earning their lessons in Somalia.

Russ Kerr, World Vision's vice president for Relief, had earlier described one distribution he had witnessed. A truck simply pulled up to a walled compound and dumped bags off the back, leaving distribution to the locals and control to the French soldiers who were with them. Naturally there was a riot. People were crushed and trampled. The soldiers gave up in disgust. Russ felt that weaker people were probably killed, and certainly the ones most in need of food did not get it.

I had begun to call this the 'dump-and-run approach'.

A few agencies maintained they were only in the food delivery business, not the food distribution business. Distribution, they argued, was someone else's responsibility. But such a position was plainly irresponsible unless they knew there was a proper distribution system in place once they had delivered their part of the process.

The difference with a World Vision food distribution was the work we did in advance. We spoke to the local chiefs and set up a committee to take responsibility for the distribution. They listed the people who were to receive food and a system for recording receipt. When the trucks came, people were organised into orderly lines and the distribution went quickly, efficiently and safely. The whole process was monitored, so that we could guarantee the food got to the right people.

If things got out of hand, we stopped distributing food immediately, put everything back on the trucks and went away. Negotiations would begin again to correct the problems and distribution would recommence.

A few weeks after our visit things did get out of hand at a food distribution in Dacar. A television crew happened to be present and reported on what they called 'the food riot'.

What they were actually seeing was World Vision's operation working to good effect. Some people tried to break out of the queues – hungry people can be desperate, even if they know there is enough food for all. When this happened, and while the soldiers were trying to control the crowd, the distribution was stopped, the trucks reloaded and the supplies taken away for another day. At most, a bag or two of food was 'lost'.

Distribution began again the next day, without the benefit of television.

It found it impossible to understand how any person or agency with a genuine concern for the people of Somalia would not want to ensure that there was something enduring left after the food had been dumped. Whether we played a part in that longer term strategy or not, I knew we had to operate in a way that supported such a strategy. This meant, for example, extending distribution into rural areas to prevent people from coming into the epidemic-ridden towns.

This particular morning the army was to provide an escort for our group, and it turned out that the advance guard of Australian soldiers, thirty-five of them, was part of the escort. I kicked myself that I didn't go. Nevertheless, after a quick phone call, Margaret, Bernard and I arranged to meet Major Dick Stanhope, the advance man for the Aussies. He was supportive and talked about the better ways the Australians were going to treat the aid agencies.

The subsequent visit by the Australian soldiers was a high point in international involvement in Somalia. From all reports they did us proud.

We returned to base and I waited outside our front gate for the others to get back, watching the passing parade of Baidoa. A tall man in a ragged coat, a single article of clothing like a shirt hanging to his ankles, wandered about aimlessly hand in hand with a small child. Large carcasses hung in the open, dusty air in a kiosk-style shop across the road. A woman used her sandal to chase away a group of men for making cheeky remarks. She was selling sweets from a metal tray in her lap which she banged with a spoon to attract attention.

Half the vehicles that passed by were wearing agency stickers and flags: CARE, GOAL, Concern, MSF, Red Cross and World Vision.

Our colleagues eventually returned and we set off to see the feeding at the Rowlo feeding centre. Again the sheik met us.

The contrast between the potentially pleasant village scene where we had taken him the day before and this hellhole could not have been more stark. Not that the Rowlo feeding centre was any worse than the rest – it was simply the same. Too many people crowded together into too little space. Too many in the feeding centre in bad condition. Too many skeletal kids walking around slowly and heavily. Too many sitting on the ground, eyes dropping and heads lolling. Too many coughs. Too many with measles.

Here it goes again, I thought, suddenly weary. There would be deaths there that week. At least no-one would die of starvation. Something else would kill them.

I went out and sat under a tree. A carton lay on the ground. It had been flattened out to form a piece of roofing for a hut but had slid off. The carton had printing on it: 'Gift of Australia. Protein Energy Emergency Product. Arnott's Australia'. High Energy Biscuits. The aid did get through.

Russ Kerr was sitting there too and saw my melancholy look. 'You can visit too many of these feeding centres', he said.

I knew what he meant.

20 | *Australia's Occupied Territories*

April 1993

From 14 to 23 April 1993 I undertook a journey with James Brierley, Ray Minniecon and Kevin May of our Aboriginal Program Office. This book would have no meaning without this final journey.

It took me fifteen years of travelling among the poor and oppressed overseas to finally realise that the world was the same at home.

On this trip I discovered that I had been on a spiritual and intellectual journey of which my physical journeys had been an important part. But more than that, I discovered that I had a lot to learn about my own nation and its history of injustice. More important, I had to discover my own need for humility and forgiveness. I had to discover the need to deal with the beam in my own eyes as I saw specks in the eyes of others.

Redfern

We walked around Redfern. We visited a women's resource centre, a child development centre and a day care facility. We had looked in at the Aboriginal Housing Company, which bought property and rented it cheaply to Aboriginal families. We saw an employment training program which also ran a camping program for street kids, the Aboriginal Medical Centre and the Aboriginal Community Health Program office.

The dominant impression was of wonderful people, saintly

people. With only one exception they were Aborigines, full of compassion, gentleness, and no-nonsense inner strength.

There was Pastor Dick Blair. He had been in Redfern for thirty-three years. When Tony Mundine started to box, Dick had been his trainer.

'First you were a boxer, now you're fighting for the Lord. Which is easier?' I asked.

'Boxing. You've only got one opponent.'

We were sitting in a street corner coffee shop near Redfern Station, enjoying a hearty lunch of roast beef and potatoes. It was run by an Aboriginal Cooperative supported through the 'work-for-the-dole' scheme.

'The biggest problem here is that everyone thinks they're called for it', said Dick. 'It's become a war between the Christians! If we can't create unity in the Body of Christ, forget it. The world won't give us unity.'

The conversation ranged over a wide area. Dick was not impressed with some of the plans he had heard about development. 'TNT want to build a high-tech city next door. "As a benefit to this area", they say. Who are they kidding? It'll wipe out the Aboriginal community.' It sounded like a score of so-called 'development' schemes I had encountered overseas.

'We only ask that we be given a chance to face our problems and challenges ourselves. There's a wall of oppression out there still.'

Sitting next to me was Carole. She was a probation worker. One of her cases was a man who was living at Central Station. 'I got to plug him in somewhere', she said, a hint of desperation in her voice.

'Things are changing at the Probation Department', she explained. 'They are developing policies for dealing with Aboriginal people.'

'You mean, despite the fact that so many Aboriginal people go through the system, they've had no special policies and procedures designed for Aboriginal people?' I asked.

'Quite right.'

Upstairs at the Housing Co-op, we met Mick Mundine. 'We're involved with everything', he said. This was a common theme. Aboriginal people seemed to see the inter-relationships between everything. They thought more holistically than most non-Aboriginals. This was a gift Australia need badly. I had identified it among the poor with whom World Vision worked overseas, and now I found it existed also in Redfern.

Mick was optimistic. 'There's more unity in Redfern now, since the seven major organisations [Aboriginal welfare support and advocacy groups] got together to organise last year's Aboriginal National Week', he said. 'I'm a bit disappointed with the Christians, though. We need more Christian input here. We need to get more love floating around here. But there's a light at the end of the tunnel. No two ways about it.'

Travelling with me were Ray and Sharon Minniecon. Ray worked for World Vision Australia concentrating on Aboriginal leadership issues and Sharon was a community health worker in Redfern. She was opening doors for us.

They told us about an Italian coffee shop in Redfern which refused them service. The owner claimed he was closed when they went in after a church meeting. They went elsewhere and later walked past to find him still serving white customers.

Sharon said that in some shops the assistants came rushing to hover around an Aboriginal person when he or she came in to browse. These same shops did not do this to non-Aboriginals. Afro-Americans had told me the same thing happened in the United States.

'Of course', Ray conceded generously, 'I suppose some Aboriginal people *have* shoplifted'.

'Yes', I replied, 'but it doesn't excuse putting the blame on everyone. In Palestine this is called collective punishment. It's not permitted under international law.'

Around at the Community Health Workers' office the mood was more bleak.

'If something doesn't happen they can just bring in the "bereavement vans", because we'll all be dead', said Val, one of the social workers. 'It's no good just having people like us picking people up off the ground. People have got to have some strength in themselves before they get better.'

Townsville

We began at Aboriginal Radio, an FM station, with the slogan *It's deadly* (Ray assured me this was the local lingo, for 'excellent'). The manager was also the breakfast announcer and he ran a disorganised, frenetic and friendly show.

I was there with Ray and with James Brierley, the manager of World Vision's Aboriginal Program Office. The station manager took all three of us into the studio to be interviewed, but Ray and James talked more than I did.

At nine we went around to the ABC station to be interviewed by the morning announcer, Steve Austin. This was the usual non-Aboriginal approach, with Steve interested in wider world issues but quite willing to hear me say that Australia did not have an Aboriginal problem so much as a non-Aboriginal problem.

I had said the same thing at the first station, and Ray said that this would have gone down really well with an Aboriginal audience. I guessed they knew it already, but it mattered to hear a whitefella say it.

The morning was spent at the Stuart Gaol. LaFai, a big, friendly man who hailed originally from Tuvalu, was our guide. He was the whole Prisoners' Aid Society, trying single-handedly to support prisoner and help prison authorities understand the special needs of Aboriginal and Islander inmates.

The jail was, of course, the last step among the steps of human degradation that faced many Aboriginal and Islander people – especially those who lived in the townships where alcoholism and violence were endemic. Life in these communities was already alienating, but when people were finally sent to Stuart Gaol, their alienation and disorientation was close to total.

LaFai tried, among other things, to keep a sense of connectedness with family and community life. It was an uphill battle.

The day we arrived was the day after the Queensland Minister for Corrective Services had announced that the wall around the main security section of the gaol would be replaced with a chain fence and razor wire to give the prison a more open feel. LaFai told us that the whole gaol had undergone a transformation since the Kennedy Commission inquiry.

The inquiry had come after riots there the previous year. Many officers had been sacked and a new administration, more committed to rehabilitation, installed.

'What used to happen was that any prisoner who spoke up was shanghaied to Rockhampton', LaFai explained. 'We would find out about it and work to get them back. We complained to the Human Rights Commission and things would happen. Now management is very afraid of the Human Rights Commission', he said.

I really warmed to LaFai. His compassion for the prisoners was clear, and his love and service for them unconditional. James, thinking of the kind of religious zealot whose main aim is to get converts, said, 'You don't exactly ram the gospel down their throats'.

'No, I don't', LaFai agreed, 'but there are plenty of opportunities to say, "Look you've tried a lot of other things. Have you ever thought of giving your life to Jesus? You could talk to a priest if you don't want to talk to me about that." Lots of them are very interested.'

LaFai pointed out one young man. 'He's in for rape and murder. After he raped the woman he took a broom handle and rammed it right up through her and it killed her. He was on drugs and alcohol at the time.'

The young man came over and talked to LaFai about some matter concerning his family. He seemed slow in talking and putting his thoughts together. 'These days the doctors have him permanently tranquillised', LaFai explained. 'I've been trying to get them to reduce the dose, because it's so terrible to see him like this, but they're afraid that he'll go wild. He gave his life to God', he added, surprising me. I was still processing the gruesome image of the murder he had committed.

'There's a lot of work to do here yet', Lafai said. 'The spiritual side of life is *so* important for Aboriginals. No-one in the prison authorities really understands this.'

We met Paul, in gaol for some violent crime that might see him paroled in the next few years. He was the president of the elected group that spoke for prisoners. He took us to show us his paintings – outstanding Aboriginal art that would have fetched thousands of dollars in Melbourne.

'I got $500 for that one', he said proudly.

I reckoned he was ripped off, but merely suggested that it would have been worth much more down south.

We also looked at the maximum security section of the prison, which was very modern but profoundly oppressive. Its sheer solidity and sophisticated security systems gave one an overwhelming feeling of being locked in. The cells were well-equipped with TV, a library, reasonable beds and en-suites, but no number of 'creature comforts' could compensate for the fact that a person was locked away from society without freedom of movement. I imagined this would be spirit-crushing for a person from the bush.

I didn't wonder that rural Aboriginals, at least, became suicidal in such surroundings. I might myself.

We left LaFai and drove out to Shalom College, where we were met by Alan Randall, a dynamic, free-talking principal of a new multicultural school run by the Uniting Aboriginal and Islander Congress.

The project comprised a community built around a school. The idea was to involve extended families in community life, with grandparents assisting in the primary school. Alan shared some of his ideas and I warmed to his multicultural approach (not just Aboriginal, and definitely not just white Australian).

We saw the classrooms (it was school holidays so there were no kids) and noted Aboriginal and Islander culture being affirmed along with Spanish, Italian and others. The faculty was multicultural. At that stage the school only catered for Grades 1–3, but over the next few years they planned to become a complete primary and secondary institution.

It was a grand vision and could contribute a lot to the education of all Australians if it achieved its goals. There was something right in this, I thought; something about the *stone that was rejected* playing a central role. Indeed, this may be what God was saying to the Christian Church about the role he wanted for the Aboriginal Church. Could we hear such a message?

We had lunch at the Yalga-Binbi Training Institute, which ran courses on community development for Aborigines and Islanders and was on the same campus as Shalom College.

Shane Blackman, the General Secretary of the Uniting Aboriginal and Islander Congress, a huge man with a big job, arrived after lunch while Alan was still in full song. 'He's full of it', said Shane, 'and it's not bad stuff'.

Yet we could not help but feel that such a powerful non-Aboriginal presence was potentially difficult. Could non-Aborigines rise to the challenge of empowering Aboriginal people? That was the question. So much had been done *for* Aboriginal people that they had become dependent.

I was reminded of Frances O'Gorman's analysis of the way agencies mature. First they *do for* the poor. Then they see this has problems of dependency and paternalism, so they then *do with* the poor. Then they *be with* the poor, and finally they learn to *be for* the poor.

Shane, commenting on the vision for the school, said, 'From an Aboriginal perspective, what we need is a winner.'

Next morning we had a breakfast to which Ray had invited eight local Christian leaders. They were people who would not regularly meet across denominations and areas of interest. World Vision was one of the few groups that could facilitate this sort of thing.

I sat beside a dynamic woman, Grace Smallwood, who spoke scathingly about the health system for Aborigines. Her main topic was the lack of any real awareness of Aboriginal culture and how to modify medical delivery for this. She talked about a hospital in which the occupational therapists were teaching the old women to crochet, knit and watch *Days of Our Lives* when what the old ladies wanted was to sit in the yard with their dogs.

She spoke of ATSIC (Aboriginal and Torres Strait Islander Commission) as if it were a disaster. It was far from the last time we were to hear criticism of the lack of cross-cultural sensitivity of ATSIC on our visit.

Cairns

We had no plans to see any work in Cairns, merely to meet up with Bishop Tony Hall-Matthews who was to be our guide and pilot for our Cape York visit.

We discovered him with a virus that had afflicted his middle ear, and consequently his balance. None of us, least of all him, wanted to try flying when he could not even stand up.

We discussed the alternatives and decided to continue with the planned itinerary with a different aeroplane and pilot, staying overnight in Cairns and embarking the next morning. We got rooms at the Treetops Motel, run jointly by Missionary Aviation Fellowship and the Summer Institute of Linguistics, just north of Cairns overlooking dense tropical rain forest.

Ray and I took a cab into town to get money from our respective banks and to talk to a reporter from the *Cairns Post*.

Cairns had changed a bit since I had last been there in my days as an announcer with 4CA, twenty-three years before. In 1970 there had been a pub on every corner; mercifully few of them remained.

There were some new high-rise buildings and a Hilton Hotel dominating the Pier area. Souvenir shops, cafes and photo shops abounded.

In the evening we went to the Kunjal Cabaret Restaurant. They had a great Aboriginal and Islander dance program. It was thrilling to see Aboriginal culture being presented by young Aboriginal performers in such a positive and proud way.

Twenty years ago this might have seemed ridiculous, such was white prejudice against the worth of Aboriginal culture.

The didgeridoo player was outstanding, and the humour of the people came through strongly and warmly.

Kowanyama

The flight across to the western coast of Cape York Peninsula took almost two hours. We flew with Bill Wilson, a twenty-four year old Cairns man in a twin-engine Piper Seneca.

Kowanyama was very quiet. A thousand people lived here, but most were off fishing.

The Anglican Church was the only one in town and was presently without a priest. We were met by Bob Clifford, who ran the church's Op Shop.

Bob was an eccentric character, but then lots of white people out here probably were. Typical of so many, he remained disconnected from local society. Not that it was an easy society with which to connect; World Vision had supported a couple who attempted to work there as change agents but gave up after three years, finding it impossible to get into the society, even though they had acted with great sensitivity. 'Perhaps too much', suggested James.

Kowanyama had the typically tragic pattern of alcohol abuse and violence.

Two truckloads of grog came into town each week. The canteen, which was owned and run by the community itself, stopped selling beer in slabs and cans, and now only dispensed it from the tap into jugs. Some people brought along their large wheelie-bins and filled them up two jugs at a time.

'Can you imagine drinking beer out of a garbage bin?' asked Bob.

Bob had thought there wasn't much tradition left in the community until a local leader had died not long before. He mentioned her by name, against Aboriginal tradition. 'The reaction showed me there is a lot of tradition still here, but once the older people go, it'll be lost. For two weeks after her death it was very quiet.'

Bishop Hall-Matthews had said that the people in Kowanyama talked about three epochs in the town's history. They called these epochs Church Time, Government Time and Community Time, representing three eras of responsibility.

Enormous resources came into the community these days. Ray reckoned on $200 a week in dole payments per person alone. The government provided free housing. Secondary school children were paid to encourage them to go to school. James said he had heard that eighty per cent of the income went on alcohol and that eighty per cent of the daily calorie intake for adults was from grog.

We walked around and Bob seemed to have no intention of introducing us to any of the families. So Ray went up to the oldest man in each household and said, 'I'm Ray. I'm from Sydney.' James and I followed behind.

The people were friendly. Some were inebriated.

One man sat in his back yard beside a tick-infested dog. Each ear must have been the home for sixty or more of the fat insects. The man said, 'The place was better off before the white man brought that stuff', indicating a can of Victoria Bitter on the ground. Later Ray suggested it wasn't that simple.

'You can't blame the alcohol, or the white man' he said. 'These are factors, sure. But it's not that alone. This place was dry until the community took over. The community decided to have a canteen. The community can decide not to, if it wants to. The real question is what is stopping them from getting these issues under control?

'Leadership is a key. I'm pleased to see so many older people still around here. But maybe they need an elders' council. Democracy imposed on a society with no democratic tradition results in what we see here. We still need the elders.'

We asked Bob if the local people could run the shop. 'No way', he said. 'The pressure on them from the rest of the community would be too great. It wouldn't let them run it responsibly. It'd be broke in two weeks.'

We discussed the size of crocodiles in Magnificent Creek, which ran behind the church house. There was little water and no sign of crocs, but we didn't go down to take a closer look.

We flew on to Weipa, about an hour north, arriving soon after five.

Napranum

Neil, who worked with the Comalco-backed Weipa Aboriginal Society, met us in Weipa and took us down to Napranum, otherwise known as Weipa South.

Here we met a delightful group of mostly elderly Aboriginal women just as they concluded their service in the Uniting Church. They were Joyce Changer, Ina Hall, her daughter, Mary-Anne Coconut, Zoe Boxer, Gertrude Motton and Jean George.

With the help of Neil, who worked as an 'outside change agent' seeking to empower them rather than simply run programs for them, these ladies had formed the Kluthuthu Aboriginal Takeaway Store Committee and opened a shop. They had chosen the name *Kluthuthu* because it means *white dove*, the symbol of peace and the Holy Spirit.

'It's an all-woman committee?' I inquired.

'Yes, in this place it's women here, women there, women everywhere,' said Ina.

'What do the men do?' asked Ray.

Three answers came from three different corners.

'They're idle.'

'They're shy.'

'They're working.'

As we chatted we discovered that they had done the 40 Hour Famine. 'But we only lasted from 6.00 a.m. to 5.00 p.m.' admitted Ina. Joyce told us that her grandfather came to Australia from Vanuatu, brought out by white settlers as a labourer. 'Many teenage boys were brought here like that', she said. 'The Aborigines were too frightened to work for the white settlers, so they had to look elsewhere.'

We asked them to tell us some stories. 'There's the one about the turtle', Ina began.

'Two sisters were digging yams while their two brothers went out fishing. The sisters made a big fire to cook the yams and covered over the ashes. "Don't touch the fire", they told the boys. The sisters came back with some yams and the boys came back with some fish. They put the yams in the earth oven. "Remember, don't touch the fire", they said to the boys.

'But the boys were hungry. They took some yams. Then they

went to find the cyclone plant [a red berry tree used in a ceremony to turn away cyclones]. 'The boys started to eat the berries and turned into turtles.

'The two sisters came along just in time to see them changing. They started to cry, but the boys went into the salt water and swam away.'

Ina paused then laughed. 'I told that story to some children in Atherton and they thought I was talking about Ninjas!'

We walked over to the Kluthuthu store. It was a revelation – not perfect, perhaps, but with so much promise.

It had a takeaway side and a general store side. The year before it had a turnover of nearly half a million dollars, made $60,000 operating profit and contributed $2,000 a month to the church, as well as employing local people and providing a service to the community.

Mary-Anne Coconut pointed at the snake design on the shop front. 'As Moses lifted up the bronze snake in the desert, so we are lifting up the Lord in Napranum', she said.

Thinking of Kowanyama, James asked, 'What if family members come and put pressure on the people behind the counter to give them credit, to share?'

'We just point to the notice board.' It said *No Credit*.

This put the lie to the idea that properly motivated people could not control traditional pressures in the interests of the community and progress. Joyce explained, 'We wanted to help the people to manage their money. If you want to help, you have to be stern sometimes.'

Kluthuthu showed what power Aboriginal people did have to take control of their circumstances when people believed in them enough to let them have the power to take charge. Naturally they needed support and advice, but that was different from decision-making control.

This project had been going for three years and Neil was around for the first two as encourager and enabler. 'But I never ran the store', he assured us, 'they always ran it. I just helped with training and some accounting.'

By way of contrast was the Comalco Training Centre. It was supposed to be run by the Weipa Aboriginal Society (WAS), but this society was not autonomous.

'Too many white advisers', commented Neil, who worked there

himself, 'although some good people among them, I have to say. But they just don't have the right approach very often. They're from Comalco, so they're guided by commercial decisions. That's not the way the Aboriginal people necessarily think. For example, three fellas were employed to run a wood chipper. It's a viable business; lots of demand. The fellas wanted to take it over and run it themselves, but the mines people didn't think that was a good idea. So the boys just walked away from it.'

A key empowering opportunity, to give away control, was missed.

'They've also got a viable screen making business going here, but it's disempowering', Neil continued. 'The people don't run it, they're just trained and employed in it. The work is boring and mind-numbing.'

Imagine if they had been given the responsibility to own it and run it themselves.

Comalco seemed not to have understood the way the Aborigines saw things. Indeed, the idea of putting themselves into the Aborigines' shoes seemed to have hardly been contemplated.

Dr Richard Howitt had evaluated WAS. His report made interesting reading:[1]

> ... the local geography is part of the social fabric – the people and the land are very closely linked. Viewed from Napranum, from an Aboriginal world view, *Comalco is dependent on those people whose traditional lands are being used.* ... it is not so much the people who have become dependent on welfare and other support. Rather, it is Comalco's dependence on their traditional land which has taken away important social and cultural reference points. ... In the process of creating opportunities through the mining development, Comalco has precluded options more directly rooted in Aboriginal tradition.
>
> Yet it is exactly this reciprocal relationship that Comalco has *not* recognised before. Comalco's funding of WAS has largely been seen by the Comalco side as an altruistic contribution to good neighbours ... Viewed from Napranum, the obligation to support WAS is not seen as optional. Viewed from Napranum, this obligation is a function of Comalco's use of the country.

---

[1] From Dr Richard Howitt, 'Weipa Aborigines Society Review: Interim Report to Full WAS Executive', School of Earth Sciences, Macquarie University, December 1992, p. 3. Emphasis is author's.

Dr Howitt argued that not only should Comalco hand over WAS to the Napranum community, but, in so doing, it should recognise and respect them as the traditional landowners. (This was not, his paper points out, an argument about royalties or compensation. That was not a matter between Napranum and Comalco, but between Napranum and the Queensland government.)

We toured WAS, noting the phenomenal resources. Big screen TVs, a dozen networked Macintosh computers, colour photocopier, OHPs, photocopying white-boards. Everything for a dream training centre.

The resources were there, 'But nobody has *really* asked the community. They've made a show of it, but nobody's *really* done it,' said Neil. 'And when it doesn't work, "it's the black fellas fault", of course.'

Thursday Island

And so onward and upward.

Here off the tip of Cape York we were among Ray's family, or so it seemed. His brother-in-law worked for Sunstate Airline and organised us onto the bus and ferry across from Horn Island (where the air strip was) to the smaller Thursday Island. Later we also met Roy's niece.

Others on the boat pointed out Tuesday, Wednesday and Friday Islands too. 'Is there a Monday Island?' I asked obviously. 'I'm not sure', they replied, as if they had never heard such a question before.

Grace Ware arrived with Ray to show us around the island. She was an impressive lady – Chair of the Torres Strait Health Council and a member of the National Women's Consultative Council and the equivalent state body. (I had been *so* impressed by the quality of leadership on this trip. If we could have only set these people free from the constraints of cross-cultural incompetence!)

Among the things Grace discussed was the dam on Badu Island, which sounded like a *Four Corners* or *Sixty Minutes* story to me. It cost *billions* and it didn't hold water, she said. The soil simply let the water drain away!

Grace showed us her work in progress to try to convince ATSIC that the water problem on Badu (and other islands too) could be solved more cheaply by harvesting the rainwater off rooves of houses and storing it in tanks. She had graphs and calculations based on known rainfalls. A lot less costly than dams.

In discussion with another person I was told there was no indigenous Torres Strait Island building company. Mainland companies and workers came and built everything. 'These Australian-style houses are very nice, of course, but they are technological nightmares. If something goes wrong, you can't fix it.'

This was not the only example of the application of inappropriate standards. 'The dole is based on a wrong idea of equity and fairness. People on Steven's Island get the same dole as people who live in a high-rise in Sydney. But the people on Steven's can grow or fish all their own food. And they don't need complex shelters. But people say you cannot set different standards. Well, that's stupid.'

The next morning we held a breakfast for local leaders at a pleasant three-star motel named Jardines. The wind was already strong from the south-east as James and I walked the 200 metres to the venue. I was told the wind blew like this from March to September. Then it swung around to the north-west, bringing days of glassy seas and occasionally heavy rain.

Grace thought she had rounded up thirty people, but only about twelve came. James was mystified about the low number.

Usually one reason for non-attendance at such functions is division within the Body of Christ. Someone says they will come, but then hears that another Christian leader is attending with whom he or she does not wish to identify. I recalled in Hong Kong being told that I should not attempt to put Protestants and Catholics on the same platform. They would both decline the invitation.

Later I wondered if there might be another reason for the low turnout: the name of the venue, Jardines.

> Mrs Jean Jimmy, in recounting the history of her people [in Mapoon], talked of the cattlemen Lachlan Kennedy and Frank Jardine, who were the first whites to settle the area. According to Jean Jimmy, 'they were killing people all the way up. At Dingle Dingle Creek they killed most of the tribe.'
>
> Frank, Don, Harry Toeboy and many other Mapoon elders tell the tales of murder and massacre that were faithfully recounted to them by their parents. At Seven River, for example, white settlers hid in trees and shot any Aborigine they could see. The accounts describe how Jardine killed black children by knocking their heads against trees, and how he and Kennedy together exterminated hundreds of Aborigines.[2]

If I were an Aborigine or Torres Strait Islander, you can bet I would be reluctant to have anything to do with any organisation that commemorated the name of a man who had murdered my ancestors.

In the end, the numbers were fine. More than a dozen would have been cumbersome. Ray asked a few to make comments, in keeping with World Vision's approach around the world: begin by listening to the local people.

The contributions came thick and fast. 'Thank you for giving the opportunity for the community to speak.'

'Youth are looking for leaders that will give guidance. But leaders need to come down.'

'Islanders own nothing.'

'There's no place that is ours. No community centre. ATSIC builds housing for people, but ATSIC owns the house.'

'A single organisation in Brisbane has more money from ATSIC than the whole Torres Strait. We get nothing. We have organisations wringing their hands for money.'

'If you're fair dinkum, you'll let us take charge of our affairs.'

Alan Moseby, a member of the Reconciliation Council, talked about ideas for development of the back of the island (about fifteen minutes' walk from the front). He envisaged an international class resort run by local people, featuring a cultural village. 'You'll pinch my ideas!' he said with a wink.

The Goss Labor government seemed to have had little positive impact on the Islanders. Things that the Nationals had previously agreed to had been stopped. Nothing had been substituted.

'We thought it would be better, but so far it's worse', Grace said.

Competition for land between government departments had pushed the price of land out of the reach of ordinary people. This was a common problem in many places in the world (in Hong Kong, for instance, where multinationals and international banks set the standard).

We were asked whether World Vision could help with administration and management training in the communities. The new TAFE, an impressive facility on the back of the island, would be made available to us.

---

[2] Paul Wilson, *Black Death, White Hands,* Allen & Unwin, 1982, p. 37.

'The people who come here to "help" us – their motives are wrong', some commented. 'They come to Thursday Island to feather their own nests.'

'There are lots of workshops up here, but nothing happens', someone else agreed.

This, I felt, was because the fundamental justice issues were not being addressed. Until they were dealt with, people who came and 'helped' would be on the wrong foot from day one.

After breakfast we went into town. It was one street long. I bought some T-shirts and postcards while James put some film in for one hour processing.

After this we drove around to the back of the island to visit the high school.

A niece of Ray, Anai Ghee, was the Community Education Officer. She was an almost-qualified teacher, the nearest thing the school had to an indigenous teacher. All the rest of the faculty were white mainlanders. Some of the teacher's aides and a few of the administrative staff were Islanders.

'The teachers come from the south without any cultural studies training', she told us. 'They just don't get into the local culture at all. They're cliquey. There's a lot of racism on the staff. Kids here don't come up to the national standards, but the problem is the teachers don't know how to put things into Islander cultural terms.'

The problem was not that these kids were less bright than mainland kids (that should have been axiomatic). Teachers should have been asking, *What will it take to have equivalent educational standards to the mainland?* They didn't ask this question because they didn't have cross-cultural awareness. Or they were not motivated to commit themselves to relevant curriculum development because they saw a stint on Thursday Island as an opportunity to 'pay the price' for later appointments at better postings.

I took all this in, aware of the difficulty of becoming an expert in one day. As usual, what I heard was sincere and genuinely communicated. But, again as usual, I wanted to stay and get the wider story. I didn't doubt that all this was true, but experience had told me that there were usually other 'truths' as well.

At the school we looked over a museum in which an attempt was being made to preserve the national memory. Already many of the carving skills had been lost. Anai was trying to encourage the old people with some of these skills to teach the young people.

Ray organised a ferry and bus to the airport, with some difficulty. It took well over an hour to get there from Thursday Island. Then the plane had to be refuelled. We took off around 2.30 p.m. and were back in Cairns soon after five.

Typical of the double standards in Australian society is the attitude to violence. One rather regularly hears judges saying that rape and other forms of violence are not taken seriously in Aboriginal communities. Such sentiments resonate with misconceptions I have heard about death in third world communities. 'They're used to their kids dying,' I would hear someone say. I knew it to be an awful lie.

One Aboriginal commentator has suggested there are now three kinds of violence in Aboriginal society: alcoholic violence, traditional violence, and bullshit traditional violence. I laughed when I first heard it, but there is an underlying truth that is far from funny. Bullshit traditional violence describes when bashings and abuse are justified by claims that Aboriginal society is inherently violent. Of course, it *was*. But then so was European society. Both had routines of flogging, approved institutional murder and unjust imprisonment. One of my forebears was sentenced to deportation to Australia for stealing a few spoons and a couple of bottles of wine. In European societies, violence existed, but it was controlled by institutions and laws. In Aboriginal societies, it was similarly controlled.

The great difference now is alcohol. As Merle Thomas, the coordinator of the Night Patrol program at Alice Springs, says wryly, 'After you've consumed several litres of Coolabah, anything is traditional.'[3]

But who's really violent? I wondered.

Those who suggested that traditional Aboriginal society was violent, and that this somehow justified or excused rape, murder and wife bashing, should have contemplated mainstream Australian society. It was riddled with violence.

As I typed these thoughts into my diary on Thursday Island, the television channel from the mainland was showing *Terminator 2*. Perhaps an uninformed Thursday Islander would logically come to

---

[3] 'The Agony Within', *The Australian*, Monday, 15 March 1993, p. 17.

the conclusion that mainland Australia was traditionally violent and that this excused the high rate of assaults in Australian capital cities.

Cairns

Tuesday in Cairns turned out to be a rest day.

I had a long chat with Margie Cook in our media department in Melbourne about a news release angled on the idea that I had just visited *Australia's Occupied Territories*. The problems in Kowanyama might have been different to the problems in Gaza, but the underlying causes of dispossession, destruction of homes, marginalisation of a culture, dismantling of a social system and devastation of identity – these were the same among blacks in Soweto, Palestinians in the West Bank and Aboriginal and Islander people in Australia.

We could not point the finger at white South Africans and Israelis without recognising our own history.

This history, may, of course, help us to identify other oppressors. Since we ourselves have been oppressors, it may be not too hard to recognise it in others. It takes one to know one.

James and Ray came for me about 11.00 a.m. and we drove to the airport to put Ray on a plane back to Sydney. Then we went down to the Pier, which had been built on an area which used to be just mud flats. It was now a huge shopping centre.

There we had lunch with Bob Burgess, an old radio buddy and now PR manager for the local Red Cross Blood Bank. He was also a Cairns Council Alderman, now in his second term.

Bob mentioned that an alternative watch-house had been built in Cairns for Aboriginal people that was more culturally appropriate – more like a hostel, apparently. The Goss government had decided not to fund it any more. As a result, any Aborigine found drunk on the Esplanade would go to gaol as before. Brilliant.

We went to catch the plane for Darwin.

Darwin

Kevin May, who worked with World Vision on projects in Western Australia and the Northern Territory, met us at the airport having spent the day before at Kununurra, over 400 kilometres to the south-west, fishing and croc-spotting. We booked into the airport motel, had dinner in the restaurant, worked on the newsline story that Margie had faxed through, and were done around midnight.

The next morning was spent at Nungalinya College. The commitment to holistic Christian training there was impressive.

We joined the staff and some students for devotions, led by Dhalandga, the Assistant Principal. Dhalandga's original name was Rranang Garrawunra, but everyone called him Dhalandga because this was the name of a person who had passed away and whose name, out of great respect, Rranang had adopted.

Sharing this time with Aboriginal brothers and sisters was having an effect on my concepts of human beauty. Some of their faces had such character and expression. Dhalandga had strong features. Shiny skin the colour of night. A forehead that formed an awning over deep eyes. A broad nose. High cheek bones. He was strong, manly and intense.

We looked over the Nungalinya Craft Shop. Part of the College's approach to holistic thinking was the development and marketing of craft.

World Vision was supporting a program of Bi-Cultural Studies for Women. We visited the class. About ten women were working on sewing skills this day. The course also included theology, community organising, craft, literacy, numeracy and some other things.

The program coordinator said that once the women got to fifty years of age they had enormous ability. They had survived alcoholic husbands and huge families. They were great organisers – they could do forty things at once. They had very flexible minds. They were great at coping.

They had enormous potential for leadership.

More than 100 students had been through the program in ten years. These women were now back in their communities organising, coordinating groups, doing craft, running micro-enterprises and so on. Once a year they wanted to bring these old students together. The event would be called *Romdälmilyak* – 'strong woman'.

This year they had ten students but could teach fifty if they had the money. Why didn't they have the money? Good question.

Les Brockway, the Principal, explained that ATSIC used to fund the college to the extent of $73,000. Now it got nothing. The reason was ironic. They wanted to get their courses accredited as TAFE courses, but once they did, ATSIC said the courses were the responsibility of the Education Department. The Education

Department passed the buck to the Northern Territory government. And so far the Territory government had not come up with the money.

Three years had gone by!

From Nungalinya we went to FORWAARD, an aboriginal alcohol rehabilitation program. They gave us a magnificent lunch of which we were totally unworthy, having only helped them in a little way by paying some airfares to a conference in North America. I had never read the 'Twelve Steps' of Alcoholics Anonymous before, and was surprised to see how Christian they were.

I did an interview here for local ABC-TV. The reporter put together a very nice piece for the 7.00 p.m. news that gave publicity to FORWAARD, Nungalinya College and World Vision and stressed the responsibility of non-Aboriginal Australia to get our attitudes straight.

Next we went around to the Uniting Church and the Aboriginal Resource Centre, headed by Djiniyini Gondarra. Some of his team, including Wali Fejo and Richard Trudgeon joined us for a conversation.

We talked a bit about the blind spot that I had grown up with in relation to my understanding of white Australia as oppressors. I had observed the way that dominating cultures fabricated fictions about conquered peoples, but hadn't realised until quite recently that we white Australians, myself included, were just the same. We had also invented and perpetuated myths about Aboriginal society.

When Mark Liebler accused me of hypocrisy for attacking the Israelis but not commenting with equal vigour on my own people's treatment of Aborigines, there was more truth in the accusation than I thought. At the time I had been offended by the irrelevance of the comment, and I had also thought it unfair. It was still irrelevant, a rhetorical diversion attempting to alter the terms of the argument; but, irrelevant or not, rhetorical device or not, I now realised it was, in its own right, a fair comment.

Richard asked, 'Do you understand the reasons for this myth-making?'

I didn't.

He referred me to Paolo Friere, who had analysed this process whereby a dominant culture creates myths about a conquered culture. We discussed some of the myths that white Australia had devised, such as the myths of *terra nullius* (that the land was devoid of people when we came), that Aborigines have smaller brains (in fact they have bigger brains than white people – not that it matters), that they are traditionally violent, that they smell and so on.

I reflected on my thoughts about *beauty* earlier in the day. I had come to believe, and to believe sincerely, that Aboriginal people were *not* beautiful. It was difficult for me to shake this belief. I thought it was an absolute truth.

All this would be bad enough even if we kept these myths to ourselves. But what dominating societies did was to transfer the myths onto the conquered people, so that many of them also came to believe the lies about themselves. This was what created the social destruction that led to real violence, alcoholism and so on. It also created a huge generation gap between older people, who tried to preserve the old culture, and young people who believed the myths.

It was a very destructive process.

Another Day in Darwin

We started out at 7.15 a.m. to be shown where the *long grass* mob lived. Our guide was Jone (John) Lotu, a Fijian whose parents had been missionaries in Arnhem Land, so he knew the Aboriginal people and some language.

These people were called the *long grass* mob because that's where they lived. When they were asked to give their address by the Employment Office or Social Services, they said 'long grass'.

They were the drifters who camped out at night near ablution blocks at various sites around town.

We began at Lee Point, well out of town by the sea. We arrived around 7.30 and unfortunately the people there were still asleep. We woke them.

They stirred sleepily and Jone talked to them.

The people were lying on ground sheets under the stars. In Darwin in April this was by no means uncomfortable. For water they walked a few hundred metres to a tap, and the sea was nearby. They could walk along the foreshore into Darwin itself or hitch a ride from someone staying at a caravan park down the road.

We visited another site near the casino, and a few more along the shores of Fannie Bay, then a spot near Lim's Hotel. No-one was at any of these locations and Jone said he was not really surprised, as the grass had been mown down and there was now too much development going on. Local people complained and so the police moved the drifters on.

Alice Springs

The view coming into Alice is beautiful and so uniquely Australian. We flew over the MacDonnell Ranges, two long folds in the earth's surface against which the town is built. The airport is on the other side. The Todd River runs through the ranges at one point and that's how you get into town.

We checked into our motel and without dropping our bags were on our way to CAAPU – the Central Australian Aboriginal Alcohol Programs Unit.

Here Eric Shirt from Canada – an *aboriginal* Canadian – was working with Australian Aborigines to transfer his successful ideas for alcohol rehabilitation. It seemed to be a very good program and operating with some success.

Like everyone we met, they had complaints about funding. Money seemed to be in short supply, and getting it was bureaucratic and frustrating. Doug Walker, a non-drinking alcoholic,[4] was coordinator of the unit.

'ATSIC's a bloody nightmare', he said. 'They have twenty-eight million for the Black Deaths in Custody, and $250 million for a national Aboriginal health strategy. When you get down to programs like ours, there's nothing.'

'I've heard this a lot lately', I commented.

'Where does it all go?' Doug asked mystified.

Eric and Doug wanted to train Aboriginal counsellors, but the funding for this was hard to find. Once again we heard a story of buck-passing between departments and locations. From Canberra to Darwin to Alice Springs and back. From November until April, no result. And the course they were applying to fund started in two weeks' time.

So much for empowerment.

---

[4] Once an alcoholic, always an alcoholic. Some alcoholics, by dint of their own efforts, and sometimes through treatment as well, conquer their addiction. One is tempted to describe them as *reformed* or *recovered*. But both adjectives tell only part of the story, as each day is a battle to remain alcohol-free.

Next day we stopped by the Tangentyere Nursery, base of the Tangentyere Land Care Program. The nursery provided free shade and fruit trees and other plants to rural communities in an area about the size of Victoria.

Here was another program that had suffered funding cuts from ATSIC in recent years. It was hard to fathom.

World Vision funded the appointment of an Aboriginal manager, David McNamara, and although it was Friday (apparently everyone's day off), and none of the Aboriginal people were there, the two white staff talked to us about the program.

They were especially complimentary about David and his participatory management style. He had really empowered the people, they said. 'Everyone loves to come to work!'

In town we stopped by to see an anti-grog march get under way, protesting a council decision to grant additional licences for liquor outlets. Then it was onto our respective planes for the flight home – James to Sydney, Kevin to Perth and me to Melbourne, via Adelaide.

Post-script

On the plane I tried to make sense of all I had seen and heard. As I reflected I wrote:

'I am surprised how really tired and drained I felt the last few days. I could not blame the heat, nor, despite James' apologies, the pace of the itinerary. Nothing about the program was too difficult, nor too much pressure.

'I suspect the reason for my tiredness was the emotional and intellectual challenge of the paradigm shift going on in my own soul. Catharsis takes energy.

'Everyone says that the first time you visit the field, your life changes. I say it. It's true. My life was changed by my first foreign encounter. In India. In 1977.

'What I have discovered is that the first time you visit Aboriginal Australia, your life changes too.

'Maybe this is not true for everyone. But for a sixth generation non-Aboriginal Australian the need to squarely face the truth about your own history is life-changing.

'I wonder what the Lord will do with this experience in my own life? I wait eagerly for that further revelation.'

21 | *Final Thoughts*

The 'trip to Australia' described in the last chapter fulfilled a long held desire.

Soon after Geoff Renner assumed executive responsibility for Aboriginal Programs at World Vision Australia in the late 1980s, he gave an address to staff. He drew from many sources, including the book *Blood on the Wattle: Massacres and Maltreatment of Australian Aborigines Since 1788*.[1] His presentation revealed to me, for the first time in my life, information about the genocide committed by my forebears (or their compatriots) against Australia's original inhabitants.

I was shocked. I felt betrayed — by an education system and mass media which had a monumental blind spot.[2]

I discovered that historical revisionism was not merely a feature of totalitarian regimes in distant and bizarre places, but a feature of Australian society.

I had grown up believing myself to be a moderate, liberal, well informed white Australian. I deplored the media's emphasis on the negative images of indigenous Australians. Yet I could not understand how Aborigines could let themselves down with violence, alcoholism and a failure to grasp the many opportunities that white society seemed to offer them.

---

[1] Bruce Elder, *Blood on the Wattle: Massacres and Maltreatment of Australian Aborigines Since 1788*, Child & Associates, 1988.

[2] I found out that younger people did not share my ignorance to so great an extent. It seems that information about the massacre of Aborigines has gradually become more accessible in recent years.

I had a blind spot myself and I didn't realise it.

As I worked with World Vision over the years I discovered some things about the poor, but it took me a little longer to apply these lessons to my own country.

First, I discovered the common humanity I had with all humankind. Whether they were Vietnamese boat people, Chinese office workers in Hong Kong, Maasai farmers in Kenya, angry South Africans in Soweto or carefree Californians in the United States, I discovered more things that bound us together as children of God than differentiated us as cultural beings. I still did not feel the same about my own indigenous countrymen and women.

Of course, I had met some extremely *human* Aborigines – Senator Neville Bonner and others who worked with World Vision. But looking back (and I cringe to admit it) I subconsciously saw such people as exceptions.

That is until I read Sally Morgan's book *My Place*.[3]

The revelation of this book lay in the sheer humanity of its characters. They were not only real people. They were a lot like me. I readily embraced this revelation since it was absolutely consistent with my experience overseas. Now I could see, more profoundly, Aboriginal Australians as real brothers and sisters. I felt repentance and the need for forgiveness.

Second, as I worked at World Vision, I discovered that there was, in dozens of marginalised communities around the world, a pattern of institutionalised injustice and oppression. This pattern created dysfunction within the oppressed people themselves.

I saw this first in Uganda in the late 1970s when Idi Amin was driven out. Ugandan society had been so abused by Amin's murderous violence that revenge and killing had become a way of life. Later, in the Occupied Territories, I saw how the violence of the Palestinian people had emerged after their violent uprooting in 1948, and later in 1967.

In South Africa, I found a dispossessed and oppressed people reacting with violence themselves. I will never forget the almost palpable feeling of violence in a Soweto *shebeen* as I discussed life in the black communities.

---

[3] Fremantle Arts Centre Press, Fremantle, 1987.

In country after country, I discovered a common pattern:

1. An oppressor emerged.

2. The oppressor took away the people's homes, sometimes destroying them, often relocating the people.

3. The oppressed people lost most of their possessions.

4. They were crowded together into refugee camps or reserves.

5. By one means or another, often with apparently reasonable excuses, families were split up.

6. They were policed by military style forces, or government officials. Often a 'Ministry' for their affairs was created. This devised rules to control their lives. Only limited self-government was permitted, and often none. Where it existed it was highly controlled by the oppressors.

7. Myths were created about the oppressed people. They were labelled as dangerous and deviant (terrorists, barbaric, savage, lacking culture, lazy).

8. Very often the myth was created that the oppressed people had no true society before the oppressor stepping in (in Australia this myth was called *terra nullius*).

9. Some years on, the oppressed society became increasingly violent. Most of the violence was internal. Crime rates, especially crimes such as murder and assault, were twenty to fifty times greater than in mainstream society. This tended to confirm the myth that the oppressed people were lesser beings.

10. Often 'radical' groups emerged and attacked the mainstream society. This confirmed the myth that the oppressed society was dangerous.

11. The dominant society appeared to put money into services to 'help' the dysfunctional community, but much of this money appeared to do little good. Stories were common that the money was wasted.

12. Drug abuse (usually alcohol) was commonplace. This confirmed the myth that the people were lazy or incapable of self-control.

Of course, I also discovered many people within these oppressed communities preaching peace, reconciliation and love. They totally contradicted the myths and stereotypes around them. From them I realised that the true humanity of these societies must have been grossly distorted by some external force. Deep down, these people were very beautiful.

I came to understand that there was an intimate connection between the original oppression and the current state of these societies. To state it clearly, the original oppression had *created* the violence and dysfunctional aspects under which the oppressed communities laboured.

Although I discovered this in a dozen or more places outside Australia, it was only later that I came to see it applied to my own country and its indigenous people.

The arrival of the white settlers after 1788 was, for the Aborigines, an act of violence. It created their death and displacement. They became the dispossessed, refugees within their own land. Their homes, their cultures, their beliefs, their organisational structures were destroyed and replaced by anomie and alienation. And the result, in Australia just as it had been all around the world, was a dysfunctional, violent society.

What I learned from my journey through Aboriginal Australia was that the real challenge for our country lies not with Aborigines, but with whites. I discovered the enormous capability of Aboriginal people to begin to get it right. But they would not – indeed they *could* not – until non-Aboriginal society faced the original cause of their plight and then *behaved* differently in the light of that awareness.

We had to stop blaming the victims – really stop. We had to realise we did not have an *Aboriginal* problem in Australia, any more than the South Africans had a *black* problem or the Israelis had a *Palestinian* problem. What we had in Australia was a *non-Aboriginal* problem.

We had created modern Aboriginal society in the image of our own oppression. It was therefore our responsibility to take whatever affirmative action was needed to change that reality.

What would this require? Since we caused the problem, I supposed we had better begin by looking at ourselves. We needed to change.

First, we needed to discover the true humanity of Aboriginal Australia. This would require encounter – not merely the opportunity to meet an Aboriginal Australian (something too few white Australians have ever done) but also the opportunity to discover and value Aboriginal heritage. As Australians, it ought to be our heritage too.

This meant we needed an education system that honoured Aboriginal Australia, that taught its culture, that affirmed its contribution to national identity (an identity which did not just begin in 1770). We also needed a media that honoured Aboriginal Australia with positive images rather than the conscious and unconscious racism that pervaded much of it. This would help us, for example, to the difficult realisation that unconscious racism (as in sport) is still racism.

Second, we needed to support Aboriginal recovery. There was a lot of money around, yet too many really excellent Aboriginal programs were starved for funds. Not only that, but there was so little support for workers in Aboriginal communities (and especially for Aboriginal workers) that burnout and disillusionment were the biggest problems.

My trip came at a time when world attention was being directed to such questions. Nineteen eighty-three was International Year of Indigenous People, and on 13 January *The Koori Mail* reported Prime Minister Paul Keating's speech at Redfern, NSW, launching Australia's celebration of the Year. It was titled 'Time to reflect, understand, be sorry, and look ahead'. It was an important statement.

Mr Keating said:

> More I think than most Australians recognise, the plight of Aboriginal Australians affects us all ... We simply cannot sweep injustice aside. Even if our own conscience allowed us to, I am sure, that in due course, the world and the people of our region would not ...
>
> We non-Aboriginal Australians should perhaps remind ourselves that Australia once reached out for us. Didn't Australia provide opportunity and care for the dispossessed Irish? The poor of Britain? The refugees from war and famine and persecution in the countries of Europe and Asia?
>
> ... the starting point might be to recognise that the problem starts with us non-Aboriginal Australians. It begins, I think with that act of

recognition. Recognition that it was we who did the dispossessing. We took the traditional lands and smashed the traditional way of life. We brought the diseases. The alcohol. We committed the murders. We took the children from their mothers. We practised discrimination and exclusion. It was our ignorance and our prejudice. And our failure to imagine these things being done to us ...

Imagine if ours was the oldest culture in the world and we were told that it was worthless. Imagine if we had resisted this settlement, suffered and died in the defence of our land, and then were told in history books that we had given up without a fight. Imagine if non-Aboriginal Australians had served their country in peace and war, then were ignored in history books. Imagine if our feats on sporting fields had inspired admiration and patriotism and yet did nothing to diminish prejudice. Imagine if our spiritual life was denied and ridiculed. Imagine if we had suffered the injustice and then were blamed for it.

It seems to me that if we can imagine the injustice, we can imagine the opposite.

Finally, a word about my family history. For two weeks I tried to touch a culture that is tens of thousands of years old. My own family tradition also extends back that far, only I can't trace it much beyond two hundred years.

Richard Hunt was born in Winchester, England, on 29 March 1797. He came to Australia on a complimentary passage, along with his brother, convicted of the same crime, in 1817. He was, as they say, chosen for the journey by the best judges in England.

Richard Hunt was a victim. He was a member of the lowest class. Upper class British society had created myths about Richard's class and doubtless Richard believed these myths himself. The people of his class were held to be naturally criminal, small brained, ugly and beyond redemption.

Richard Hunt served his time in Sydney. He married a free-born woman, Lydia Barber, and had six children including, George Thomas Hunt, my great-great-grandfather. They lived in Parramatta, NSW. When Lydia died, Richard married Sarah Ellison and moved to Gundagai, where he worked at his trade as a saddler. They had five children. Richard was the Superintendent of the Gundagai Wesleyan Sunday School.

In 1852 a flood drowned Richard, Sarah and all their children, along with many others. The town of Gundagai was destroyed and rebuilt further up the hill on its present site.

Meanwhile, my great-great-grandfather, George Thomas Hunt, became respectable in Parramatta, assisting to found Leigh Memorial Methodist Church. Among George's children was John Charles Hunt, who became wealthy as an orchardist with properties in Parramatta and Dural. John Charles was my great-grandfather. He became a politician and was the local member for Parramatta.

Within two generations in my family, the myths that so many upper class British people believed about the lower classes were proven to be simply that – myths. Since then Australian white society had developed from its criminal roots into one of the most law-abiding, safe and prosperous societies on earth.

How should I be judged if I cannot see that what was possible for the Hunt family is possible for all people, if only they have the chance to live in freedom and justice?

He was in his eighties. Conversations with him were always opportunities for him to offer his firm views on a wide variety of subjects. He was dogmatic, but his opinions were typical of many of his generation. If he was racist he was not consciously or intentionally so. Like so many Australians he had learned his racism unconsciously – the same way I had.

'What are we going to do about these Abos?' he asked. I greatly disliked the label *Abos*; it had become an alarm bell for prejudice. Few of my generation used it, preferring *Aborigine* or *Aboriginal* (although technically the latter was often misused as a noun). Younger people often referred to indigenous Australians as *Kooris* or *Murris*.

'What do you mean *do*?' I asked.

'This whole Mabo thing. I reckon they want too much.'

'Well, I don't know …'

'You can't turn the clock back 200 years. What's been done has been done.'

'I agree. But I don't think anyone has asked for the clock to be turned back 200 years. I hear Aborigines asking for us to live and act responsibly with the knowledge of the oppression that has been there in our history', I suggested.

'When I was in Cairns I knew this Abo at Yarrabah' he responded. 'Best Abo I ever knew. A real white man, you know what I mean?' Regrettably, I did know what he meant. I toyed with the idea of attacking the concept of calling a black man a 'real white man' as if it were a compliment. Why do we value black culture and identity so little that we cannot honour a person by calling him a real black man? I bit my tongue and let it pass.

'This fellow said something once', he continued. 'He said that before white man came the Abos were nomadic and living off the land. But that was all gone now. They couldn't go back to that. But they couldn't become white men either. They couldn't go back, and they couldn't go forward.'

'He was a very wise man', I said.

'Some of these modern Abos aren't Abos at all, are they?'

'How do you mean?'

'Well, you look at 'em. If they have one great-grandma who was an Abo they reckon they're Abos. They hang onto any shred of it.'

'But so do we white people.'

'No, we don't.'

'Well, I think we do. Judy (my wife) reckons she's a bit of a Scot because way back three or four generations her people came from Scotland. And I hang onto the fact that my great-great-great-grandfather was an English convict.'

'It's not the same.'

'I think it's similar enough.'

He changed tack. 'We tried to do something for the Abos you know. I knew the matron at the Cairns Base Hospital. She was keen to get some Abo girls into nursing. One girl who had done really well in class at Yarrabah was keen to try and she was accepted. She lasted less than six months. She was doing all right and then she just left and went walkabout. Hopeless.'

'I reckon you have to answer the question asked by the "real white man" from Yarrabah', I said.

'What's that?' he asked.

'Until we realise that we are dealing with a people who have lost their sense of identity and community self-worth, we are going to continue to see these symptoms. You can't give education to a person who lacks self-esteem and expect them to stick with it. You can't build a house for a person without a sense of worthwhile identity and expect them to care for it. You can't tell someone to get their act together while at the same time you deny their right to affirm their Aboriginal heritage because ninety per cent of their genes came from white people. What we have to do is to answer your mate from Yarrabah's question: How can we restore Aboriginal identity and value and self-worth?'

The old man only stopped for a second. 'What about those Broncos? Don't you reckon that football team has got swelled heads?'